LIVING PSYCHOANALYSIS

Living Psychoanalysis: From theory to experience brings clinical psychoanalysis and its theoretical foundations to life. Representing a decade of work from one of today's leading psychoanalysts, it offers vivid examples from the consulting room and new developments in analytic theory, such as the concepts of *avant-coup* and the internal analytic setting. Michael Parsons also explores connections between psychoanalysis and both art and literature, showing how psychoanalytic insights can enrich our lives far beyond the clinical situation.

Living Psychoanalysis: From theory to experience asks:

What does it mean to be fully and creatively alive?

How do concepts of sexuality, narcissism, the Oedipus complex and countertransference continue to evolve today?

Do analysts listen to patients in the same way that artists look at the world?

What is the theoretical basis of Independent clinical technique?

How do different approaches to training help, or hinder, the development of an analytic identity?

Living Psychoanalysis: From theory to experience will be a valuable resource for all those wishing to extend their vision of psychoanalysis and to understand more about the links between culture and the mind.

Michael Parsons is a Training Analyst of the British Psychoanalytical Society and a member of the French Psychoanalytic Association. With more than thirty years of experience in his field, he teaches and lectures all over the world. He is the author of *The Dove that Returns, The Dove that Vanishes: Paradox and Creativity in Psychoanalysis* (Routledge, 2000).

THE NEW LIBRARY OF PSYCHOANALYSIS
General Editor: Alessandra Lemma

The New Library of Psychoanalysis was launched in 1987 in association with the Institute of Psychoanalysis, London. It took over from the International Psychoanalytical Library which published many of the early translations of the works of Freud and the writings of most of the leading British and Continental psychoanalysts.

The purpose of the New Library of Psychoanalysis is to facilitate a greater and more widespread appreciation of psychoanalysis and to provide a forum for increasing mutual understanding between psychoanalysts and those working in other disciplines such as the social sciences, medicine, philosophy, history, linguistics, literature and the arts. It aims to represent different trends both in British psychoanalysis and in psychoanalysis generally. The New Library of Psychoanalysis is well placed to make available to the English-speaking world psychoanalytic writings from other European countries and to increase the interchange of ideas between British and American psychoanalysts. Through the *Teaching Series*, the New Library of Psychoanalysis now also publishes books that provide comprehensive, yet accessible, overviews of selected subject areas aimed at those studying psychoanalysis and related fields such as the social sciences, philosophy, literature and the arts.

The Institute, together with the British Psychoanalytical Society, runs a low-fee psychoanalytic clinic, organizes lectures and scientific events concerned with psychoanalysis and publishes the *International Journal of Psychoanalysis*. It runs a training course in psychoanalysis which leads to membership of the International Psychoanalytical Association – the body which preserves internationally agreed standards of training, of professional entry, and of professional ethics and practice for psychoanalysis as initiated and developed by Sigmund Freud. Distinguished members of the Institute have included Michael Balint, Wilfred Bion, Ronald Fairbairn, Anna Freud, Ernest Jones, Melanie Klein, John Rickman and Donald Winnicott.

Previous general editors have included David Tuckett, who played a very active role in the establishment of the New Library. He was followed as general editor by Elizabeth Bott Spillius, who was in turn followed by Susan Budd and then by Dana Birksted-Breen.

Current members of the Advisory Board include Liz Allison, Giovanna di Ceglie, Rosemary Davies and Richard Rusbridger.

Previous Members of the Advisory Board include Christopher Bollas, Ronald Britton, Catalina Bronstein, Donald Campbell, Sara Flanders, Stephen grosz, John Keene, Eglé Laufer, Alessandra Lemma, Juliet Mitchell, Michael Parsons, Rosine Jozef Perelberg, Mary Target and David Taylor.

ALSO IN THIS SERIES

Psychoanalysis on the Move: The Work of Joseph Sandler Edited by Peter Fonagy, Arnold M. Cooper and Robert S. Wallerstein

The Dead Mother: The Work of André Green Edited by Gregorio Kohon

The Fabric of Affect in the Psychoanalytic Discourse André Green

The Bi-Personal Field: Experiences of Child Analysis Antonino Ferro

The Dove that Returns, the Dove that Vanishes: Paradox and Creativity in Psychoanalysis Michael Parsons

Ordinary People, Extra-ordinary Protections: A Post Kleinian Approach to the Treatment of Primitive Mental States Judith Mitrani

The Violence of Interpretation: From Pictogram to Statement Piera Aulagnier

The Importance of Fathers: A Psychoanalytic Re-Evaluation Judith Trowell and Alicia Etchegoyen

Dreams That Turn Over a Page: Paradoxical Dreams in Psychoanalysis Jean-Michel Quinodoz

The Couch and the Silver Screen: Psychoanalytic Reflections on European Cinema Andrea Sabbadini

In Pursuit of Psychic Change: The Betty Joseph Workshop Edited by Edith Hargreaves and Arturo Varchevker

The Quiet Revolution in American Psychoanalysis: Selected Papers of Arnold M. Cooper Arnold M. Cooper, Edited and Introduced by Elizabeth L. Auchincloss

Seeds of Illness and Seeds of Recovery: The genesis of suffering and the role of psychoanalysis Antonino Ferro

The Work of Psychic Figurability: Mental States Without Representation César Botella and Sára Botella

Key Ideas for a Contemporary Psychoanalysis: Misrecognition and Recognition of the Unconscious André Green

The Telescoping of Generations: Listening to the Narcissistic Links Between Generations Haydée Faimberg

Glacial Times: A Journey through the World of Madness Salomon Resnik

This Art of Psychoanalysis: Dreaming Undreamt Dreams and Interrupted Cries Thomas H. Ogden

Psychoanalysis and Religion in the 21ˢᵗ Century: Competitors or Collaborators? David M. Black

Recovery of the Lost Good Object Eric Brenman

The Many Voices of Psychoanalysis Roger Kennedy

Feeling the Words: Neuropsychoanalytic Understanding of Memory and the Unconscious Mauro Mancia

Constructions and the Analytic Field: History, Scenes and Destiny Domenico Chianese

Projected Shadows: Psychoanalytic Reflections on the Representation of Loss in European Cinema Edited by Andrea Sabbadini

Encounters with Melanie Klein: Selected Papers of Elizabeth Spillius Elizabeth Spillius

Yesterday, Today and Tomorrow Hanna Segal

TITLES IN THE NEW LIBRARY OF PSYCHOANALYSIS
TEACHING SERIES

Initiating Psychoanalysis: Perspectives Bernard Reith, Sven Lagerlöf, Penelope Crick, Mette Møller and Elisabeth Skale
Infant Observation Frances Salo
Reading Anna Freud Nick Midgley

TITLES IN THE NEW LIBRARY OF PSYCHOANALYSIS
'BEYOND THE COUCH' SERIES

Under the Skin: A Psychoanalytic Study of Body Modification Alessandra Lemma
Engaging with Climate Change: Psychoanalytic and Interdisciplinary Perspectives Edited by Sally Weintrobe
Research on the Couch: Single Case Studies, Subjectivity, and Psychoanalytic Knowledge R.D. Hinshelwood
Psychoanalysis in the Technoculture Era Edited by Alessandra Lemma and Luigi Caparrotta
Moving Images: Psychoanalytic Reflections on Film Andrea Sabbadini

THE NEW LIBRARY OF PSYCHOANALYSIS

LIVING PSYCHOANALYSIS

From theory to experience

Michael Parsons

Routledge
Taylor & Francis Group

LONDON AND NEW YORK

First published 2014
by Routledge
27 Church Road, Hove, East Sussex BN3 2FA

and by Routledge
711 Third Avenue, New York, NY 10017

Routledge is an imprint of the Taylor & Francis Group, an informa business

A catalogue record for this book is available from the British Library

Library of Congress Cataloging in Publication Data
Parsons, Michael, 1941–
Living psychoanalysis : from theory to experience / Michael Parsons.
pages cm –– (The new library of psychoanalysis)
1. Psychoanalysis. I. Title.
BF173.P287 2014
150.19'5––dc23
2013044456

ISBN: 978-0-415-62646-0 (hbk)
ISBN: 978-0-415-62647-7 (pbk)
ISBN: 978-1-315-77818-1 (ebk)

Typeset in Bembo
by Saxon Graphics Ltd, Derby

For Mela

*with deep love
and gratitude*

CONTENTS

FIGURES

ACKNOWLEDGEMENTS

More people than I can mention, and no doubt more than I am consciously aware of, have contributed to the making of this book.

Its clinical examples reveal how much, in the first place, I owe to my patients. The thirty years I have spent behind the couch and face-to-face, while people trusted me with what they did not know about themselves, have been an extraordinary privilege.

Alongside the British Psychoanalytical Society, always a good home base, I have found a second home, and a warm welcome, in the French Psychoanalytic Association. Discussion in a new kind of atmosphere and with new colleagues has been fascinating, and contributed to Chapters 6 and 13 in particular. I am especially grateful to Laurence Kahn for her encouragement, as President of the Association, when I applied for membership. Regarding Chapter 13, I am also grateful for discussion about the question of psychoanalytic identity with colleagues of the Psychoanalytic Society for Research and Training (SPRF), in Paris.

Most of the chapters stem from lectures or papers that I was invited to present, and I am indebted to all those who, in offering me these opportunities, set my thinking going. I am also grateful for the discussions on these occasions, which were often stimulating and produced ideas that have found their way into these pages. Elizabeth Wolf invited me to write a paper (Parsons, 2009) which, being a discussion of other papers, does not have a place in this book, but the thinking that went into it contributed to Chapters 12 and 13.

I am grateful to the analytic candidates I have taught; for the fun we have had together, and for the liveliness and fresh ideas our interactions have generated.[1] I hope the seminars mentioned in Chapters 4 and 13 may give some notion of this.

There are many colleagues from whom I have learned as we have shared our thoughts and bounced ideas off one another. The continuity of regular meetings with Rosemary Davies, Roger Kennedy and Jonathan Sklar has been especially important.

I am grateful to Alessandra Lemma, Editor of the New Library of Psychoanalysis, and Kate Hawes, Publisher at Routledge, for their enthusiasm for the book; to Kirsten Buchanan, Senior Editorial Assistant at Routledge; to

Rob Brown, Production Director at Saxon Graphics, and to Gale Winskill, for her very helpful copy-editing.

Special thanks to my friend Aris Georgiou for his generosity with the photographs used in the cover design.

Most of all, my thanks, more than I know how to express, go to my wife Melanie Hart. She has sustained and encouraged me, and without her loving support the book would not exist. She helped me beyond measure to clarify what I was trying to say and how to say it, and readers owe her a lot.

The origins of the individual chapters are as follows:

Chapters 1 and 2 are based on the Annual Freud Lectures given in Melbourne, on 25th May, 2009, at a conference entitled *Vermeer, Orpheus and the Blues*. A shorter paper called '*Après-coup and avant-coup*: death and the primal scene' was presented at the European Psychoanalytic Federation conference in Brussels, on 4th April, 2009. These chapters have not been published previously.

Chapter 3 was written as I was putting the book together. It was originally an Appendix to Chapters 1 and 2, extending their discussion of memory, but it grew into a chapter in its own right.

Chapter 4 derives from a paper presented to the Paris Psychoanalytic Society on 24th March, 2007, and published in French ('*Als estrangers tan pao que valgon*', in *Inquiétante Etrangeté*, Danon-Boileau, L. (Ed.) Paris: PUF, 2009: 75–88). It was revised at the invitation of Elizabeth Allison, to form part of the online catalogue of the exhibition *Psychoanalysis: the unconscious in everyday life* at the Science Museum, London, October 2010–April 2011. This much extended version of the catalogue essay has not been published before.

Chapter 5 is revised from a paper presented in London on 10th October, 1998, at the British Psychoanalytical Society's English-Speaking Weekend Conference, and published in the *International Journal of Psychoanalysis* (2000), 81: 37–51.

Chapter 6 is based on a paper given to the Hellenic Psychoanalytic Society in Athens, on 23rd March, 2002. This revised version was presented at a conference of the French Psychoanalytic Association, on 11th December, 2010, and has been published in French ('*La désidentification oedipienne: au nom du fils, au nom de la fille*', *Annuel de l'APF*, 2012: 53–67, Paris: PUF).

Chapter 7 is based on a paper published in French in a Festschrift for André Green ('*L'Ajax de Sophocle: une étude du narcissisme et de l'intérêt porté à l'autre*', in *Penser les Limites: Ecrits en l'honneur d'André Green*, Botella, C. (Ed.), Paris: Delachaux et Niestlé, 2002: 375–81).

Neither Chapter 6 nor Chapter 7 has appeared before in English.

Chapter 8 originates from an unpublished talk given at a psychoanalytic workshop in Oslo, on 14th June, 2004, and presented in October 2004, at the 6th Delphi International Psychoanalytic Symposium.

Chapter 9 is based on a paper presented at the New York Freudian Society on 6th October, 2001, and published in the *International Journal of Psychoanalysis* (2006), 87: 1183–98.

Chapter 10 is revised from a paper presented in London, on 14th October, 2006, at the British Psychoanalytical Society's English-Speaking Weekend Conference, and published in the *International Journal of Psychoanalysis* (2007), 88: 1441–56.

Chapter 11 is based on an unpublished paper presented in May 2010, at the Annual Conference of the German Psychoanalytic Society (DPG).

Chapter 12 is a considerably revised version of a paper published in *Psychoanalytic Dialogues* (2009, 19: 221–35), and in *Independent Psychoanalysis Today* (Williams, Keene and Dermen, 2012).

Chapter 13 was written for this book and has not been published before. Section VI (pp. 212–215), about neutrality in training analyses, is based on an article that appeared in German ('*Analytische Neutralität in der Lehranalyse*', in *Entgleisungen in der Psychanalyse: Berufsethische Probleme*, Zwettler-Otte, S. (Ed.), Göttingen, Vandenhoeck und Ruprecht, 2007: 143–9).

Copyright material in Chapters 5, 9 and 10 is republished by permission of John Wiley and Sons.

Copyright material in Chapter 12 is republished by permission of Taylor & Francis (http://www.tandfonline.com).

Lines from 'Fern Hill' by Dylan Thomas, from *The Poems of Dylan Thomas* (copyright 1945 by The Trustees for the Copyrights of Dylan Thomas) are reprinted by permission of David Higham Associates and New Directions Publishing Corporation.

Lines from 'Burnt Norton' and 'East Coker', from *Four Quartets* by T.S. Eliot, are quoted by permission of Faber and Faber, and Houghton, Mifflin, Harcourt (copyright 1936, by Houghton Mifflin Harcourt; copyright renewed 1964, by T.S. Eliot. Copyright 1940 by T.S. Eliot; copyright renewed 1968, by Esme Valerie Eliot. All rights reserved).

Lines from 'Morning Song', from *Ariel: Poems by Sylvia Plath* (copyright 1961, 1962, 1963, 1964, 1966 by Ted Hughes) are quoted by permission of Faber and Faber and Harper Collins.

'The Rain Stick' by Seamus Heaney, from *Opened Ground: Poems 1966–1996* (copyright 1998 by Seamus Heaney), and lines from 'To Yvor Winters, 1955' by Thom Gunn, from *Collected Poems* (copyright 1994 by Thom Gunn) are reprinted by permission of Faber and Faber and Farrar, Strauss and Giroux.

Martin Buber's *The Legend of the Baal-Shem* is quoted by permission of the Ward & Balkin Agency, Amherst, MA, USA.

André Schwarz-Bart's *The Last of the Just* is quoted by permission of *Les Editions du Seuil* (*Le Dernier des Justes* © Editions du Seuil 1959 and 1980) and of Georges Borchardt.

Translations from Rilke in Chapter 2, from Augustine and Dante in Chapter 3, and from Sophocles in Chapter 7 are my own.

Illustrations are reproduced by permission as follows:

Johannes Vermeer, *The Kitchen Maid*: Rijksmuseum, Amsterdam.

Edouard Manet, *Le Déjeuner sur l'Herbe*: © RMN-Grand Palais (Musée d'Orsay)/Hervé Lewandowski.

Anthony Caro, *Déjeuner sur l'Herbe II*: © Barford Sculptures Ltd.

Marcantonio Raimondi, *The Judgement of Paris*: engraving after a drawing by Raphael: © The Trustees of the British Museum.

Titian, *The Flaying of Marsyas*: Archbishopric of Olomouc, Czech Republic.

Francis Bacon, *Head VI*: Arts Council Collection, Southbank Centre, London. © The Estate of Francis Bacon. All rights reserved DACS 2012.

Vincent van Gogh, *Shepherd with a Flock of Sheep (After the Storm)*: Museo Soumaya, Carlos Slim Foundation, Mexico City.

Claude Monet, *The Studio Boat (Le Bateau-atelier)*: Image © 2013 The Barnes Foundation.

John Constable, *Sketch for 'Hadleigh Castle'*: © Tate Gallery, London, 2013.

Perugino, *Madonna and Child with Four Saints* and Raphael, *Madonna of the Meadow*: Kunsthistorisches Museum, Vienna.

Notes

1 'Candidate' is the term generally used, as it is in this book, for someone who is training to become a psychoanalyst.

All journeys have secret destinations of which the traveller is unaware.

Martin Buber, *The Legend of the Baal-Shem*, (1956: 36)

INTRODUCTION

This book is based on articles, lectures and seminars belonging to the last dozen years. Only four of the thirteen chapters have appeared before in English, and those have been significantly revised from their original publication. Collecting together work from just over a decade has been like casting a net off the stern of a moving boat. What sort of catch would I haul aboard? I was not at all sure, but I wanted to see what was in the net, and what relation the different species might bear to one another.

There turns out to be a dynamic running through the book, between specifically psychoanalytic thinking and existential matters of life and death. The relation between psychoanalysis and what lies beyond its own specialised confines has always been important to me, and it is not by chance that the likes of Vermeer and Raphael, Augustine and John Locke, cognitive scientists investigating memory, Sophocles, Rilke and Seamus Heaney turn up in these pages. Freud remarked that if one were founding a college of psychoanalysis the curriculum would need to include such subjects as 'the history of civilisation, mythology, the psychology of religion and the science of literature. Unless he is well at home in these subjects, an analyst can make nothing of a large amount of his material' (Freud, 1926a: 246). This is not just a pragmatic question of needing to know what patients are talking about. It is to do with the place of psychoanalysis in relation to other fields of knowledge and modes of understanding. Science, art, literature, religion, philosophy and psychoanalysis are all aspects of mankind's attempt to understand itself, and give meaning to existence. In a paper not included in this volume (Parsons, 2005) I have pictured Freud's encounter with Michelangelo when, during his visit to Rome in 1901, he went to see the *Moses*. He could not help recognising, I suggest, that across the centuries he was in the presence of a colleague, a fellow investigator of the human condition. What baffled him, though, was to know how their respective contributions could possibly connect up with each other (see Chapter 1, p.12 and Chapter 8, pp.117ff). The same frustration shows itself in Freud's attitude to Dostoevsky (p.118) and in his lifelong love–hate relationship with philosophy (Parsons, 2000: 78–80). This sense of perplexity reveals a feeling in Freud that, as well as psychoanalysis casting light on other disciplines, there should also be, somehow or other, a more intrinsic partnership between his work and that of, say, Michelangelo, Dostoevsky and his own philosophy teacher Brentano. One of the unspoken themes of this book is an exploration of the ways in which artists, writers, philosophers and psychoanalysts do belong in the same company.

The chapters are independent of each other, except for the first three, which need to be read in sequence. But there are links between them, and connections through the book as a whole. There is a double movement in the structure of the book. It opens with the elemental question of what it means to be fully and creatively alive. There follow discussions of broad psychoanalytic concepts; of how analysts listen in general to patients; of specific aspects of clinical technique; of the theory behind a particular clinical approach; and lastly, of the details of psychoanalytic training. This progressive narrowing of the focus is set against a movement in the opposite direction. The book begins, one could also say, with a specifically psychoanalytic investigation of what 'aliveness' means. From there the perspective opens, so that in Chapter 8, for example, the analyst's listening is seen to exemplify a way of relating to the world that extends far beyond psychoanalysis. In the final chapter, the aim of psychoanalytic training turns out to be to help prospective analysts become fully and creatively alive as analysts, in order to help their patients be more alive as human beings.

This double movement is an expression of the dynamic mentioned above: between psychoanalytic thinking and life-and-death questions of existence. There is plenty of theory in these chapters. My chief hope, though, is that reading through them will offer an experience of this dynamic, whose form varies from chapter to chapter but which is always there, and that the reader finishing the book will be different from the one that began it.

Part I

BETWEEN DEATH AND THE PRIMAL SCENE

'It's a poor sort of memory that only works backwards,'
the Queen remarked.

Lewis Carroll, *Through the Looking-Glass,*
and What Alice Found There (1871: Chapter 5)

1

KEEPING DEATH ALIVE

What does it mean to be fully and creatively alive? The question is at the heart of this book. It is the focus of this chapter and the next, and it resonates through all the rest.

Have psychoanalysts anything to say about this? Are there specifically psychoanalytic ideas about what constitutes being alive in the full sense of the word? The answer given by this book is strongly in the affirmative. Psychoanalysis has a lot to offer on the subject, and two analysts who make a good starting point are Donald Winnicott and Thomas Ogden.

Winnicott's work has been called 'a kind of biography of the sense of aliveness as it unfolds in infancy and throughout a lifetime' (Eigen, 1996: xxi). As regards infancy, Winnicott said that work with borderline patients took him 'to the early human condition, and here I mean to the early life of the individual rather than to the mental mechanisms of earliest infancy' (Winnicott, 1965: 235). At the other end of life, Winnicott's prayer, 'May I be alive when I die!'—reported by his wife Clare (Winnicott, C., 1989: 4)—confirms the continual importance to him of true aliveness.

In his book *Playing and Reality,* Winnicott makes a fundamental distinction between two ways of living. The first is based on a relationship to reality that he calls 'creative apperception' (Winnicott, 1971a: 65). 'Apperception' is an unfamiliar word but an important concept. It means perceiving something *and setting it in relation to past experience.* This is how we create our personal repertoires of meaning. Unconscious linking allows new perceptions to take on idiosyncratic significance, structuring an alive and dynamic internal world. Psychological health or illness depends on the extent to which this happens: on how far we are able, or find ourselves unable, to live creatively in this manner. And it does go this way round. It is not that our quality of living depends on the level of psychological health we have achieved. It is rather that our psychological health, or lack of it, is a manifestation of the quality of aliveness we have achieved.

Claiming that a central aspect of psychoanalysis is to develop the capacity for being alive is more radical than it might seem. Psychoanalysis began as a treatment for neurotic symptoms, then came to encompass character disturbance, perverse and borderline conditions and psychotic states. All these affect the quality of people's lives. The assumption might be that analysis improves the quality of patients' living by the way it deals with such disorders. Change in how patients experience their lives would then be seen as a consequence—a desirable one, but still essentially a by-product—of the primary psychoanalytic work of addressing the mental mechanisms of pathology. The shift implied by Winnicott, which I am developing and extending, is to take how people experience their living as a central focus of psychoanalysis, and to give primary status to the question of how a person's aliveness is impaired. Neurotic and character disturbances can be viewed, not as pathological entities requiring specific treatment, but as markers of the way that people are not managing to be as fully alive as they could be.

Ogden also regards a capacity for aliveness as fundamental to a person's well-being.

> I believe that every form of psychopathology represents a specific type of limitation of the individual's capacity to be fully alive as a human being. The goal of analysis from this point of view is larger than that of the resolution of unconscious intrapsychic conflict, the diminution of symptomatology, the enhancement of reflective subjectivity and self-understanding, and the increase of sense of personal agency. Although one's sense of being alive is intimately intertwined with each of the above-mentioned capacities, I believe that the experience of aliveness is a quality that is superordinate to these capacities and must be considered as an aspect of the analytic experience *in its own terms*.
>
> (Ogden, 1995: 696)

Ogden lays stress on aliveness as something to be actively experienced. Bion's concepts of beta-elements, alpha-elements and alpha-function have become a familiar part of the psychoanalytic vocabulary. But they were developed for a specific reason. Bion needed them in order to conceptualise the difference between experiencing something and, on the other hand, having it merely happen to one. In the latter case, one may feel pain 'but will not suffer it and so cannot be said to discover it ... The patient who will not suffer pain fails to "suffer" pleasure' (Bion, 1970: 9). Bion and Ogden are addressing, in highly condensed fashion, two different things at the same time: the experience of living one's life with conscious awareness of its significance; and the need for an unconscious internal organisation that allows that to happen. The quality of our living is determined by how far the latter allows us to discover the former.

The second way of living described by Winnicott results from the lack of such an internal organisation. He calls this 'living by compliance', and it comprises a very different relationship to reality from creative apperception. Compliance is essentially a failure of independence. 'The world and its details [are] recognised, but only as something to be fitted in with or demanding adaptation' (Winnicott, 1971a: 65). The contrast Winnicott draws between these ways of being is stark. He calls them 'alternatives of living creatively or uncreatively'. Creative apperception, he says, 'makes the individual feel that life is worth living'. Compliance 'carries with it a sense of futility' and is 'a sick basis for life' (Winnicott, 1971a: 65). Sometimes, of course, adapting to the world around us is necessary and valuable as a matter of choice. But the capacity to exercise this inward freedom of choice cannot be taken for granted. It needs the right sort of experience to have been available for a child; one which the child has been able to make use of for the development of its independent psychic structure.

In his paper 'The theory of the parent–infant relationship' Winnicott (1965 [1960]: 37–55) sets out to clarify how this sort of early experience evolves. He sees it as a series of stages to which, taken together, he gave the name of 'holding'. The infant progresses from 'absolute dependence' through 'relative dependence' to a last stage, which one might expect to be the attainment of independence and its consolidation. Instead, however, Winnicott calls it 'towards independence'. The unfinished quality of the movement which this indicates reveals that dependence is not denied. To depend, for the evolution of internal psychic structure, on a reliable developmental framework is not what Winnicott means by compliance. On the contrary, being able to depend on such a framework is the precursor of an identity that will be capable of independence. If such a framework is absent, however, or cannot be internalised by the child, there is an unconscious, anxiety-driven deadening of psychic evolution, giving rise to a compliant dependence on the opinions and attitudes of others as the basis for life.

The three stages which comprise 'holding' are followed in Winnicott's scheme by 'mother and infant living together' and finally 'father, mother and infant, all three living together' (Winnicott, 1965 [1960]: 43). 'Living' is a charged word. Ogden has made a particular study of the evocative, multilayered ways in which Winnicott uses language. 'The life of the writing', he says of Winnicott's work, 'is critical to, and inseparable from, the life of the ideas' (Ogden, 2001: 206). There is a chapter in *Playing and Reality* (Winnicott, 1971a: 104–110) called 'The place where we live'. This might be taken to mean the mental space which we inhabit, like the house, or the street, where we live. But true aliveness was a lifelong concern of Winnicott's, and his linguistic subtlety allows us to read this also as 'The place where we LIVE'; meaning the place in which, when we manage to be in it, we become fully alive.

If a family (whatever its make-up) has been 'living together' in the sense of being fully alive together, the child's internal movement towards independence will be that much easier. The eventual shift from 'father, mother and infant living together', to the child being able to live separately, is a developmental transformation. The late adolescent or young adult moving away from under the parents' roof has to make an internal move as well, and the most important

5

function of the change of address may be to get this inward leaving home under way.

A further sort of 'inwardly leaving home' faces everyone throughout life. We all have ways of being that we take for granted, which operate as a kind of psychic home base. Creative living means not complying automatically with these. The German title of Freud's (1919b) paper known in English as 'The Uncanny' is '*Das Unheimliche*', a word that evokes a sense of alien strangeness with a distinctly frightening quality. Deriving from the root '*heim-*', meaning 'home', it connotes all that with which we are not 'at home'. Creative living implies being open to our own particular '*Unheimliche*'.

This has a special importance in psychoanalytic therapy. There is a risk that the demands of the clinical situation may evoke in analysts and therapists a kind of internal compliance. Analysts have different styles and personalities. They have an analytic superego internalised from their trainers; invisible assumptions about the analytic relationship which go back to their own analyses; and preconceptions about what kind of work they do best. If these are never challenged an analyst may continue silently complying with them, hardly even conscious that they are there. The result will be analysis which is unobjectionable in a routine sort of way, but uncreative. For analysts to avoid this entails a degree of suspicion towards ways of analysing with which they are too much at ease. They need to not be compliant with what they are at home with in themselves.

The analytic process can be viewed from different kinds of vantage points (Parsons, 2000: 192ff; see also Chapter 11, p.200). Analysts may see it as something on which to capitalise, so as to extract understanding from it and convey that to the patient. This vantage point produces interpretations aiming to convey relatively specific insights, in the hope that the patient will comprehend them and benefit from them in the manner intended by the analyst. The analytic process may also be seen as unfolding by its own momentum and finding its own direction. The analyst's main concern in this case is not to get in the way of what is happening. When interpretations emanate from this different vantage point, the analyst's hope is for them to take on a life of their own in the patient's mind, undergoing all sorts of surprising transformations. Analysts should, in principle, be able to shift freely back and forth along a dimension between these vantage points, sensitive both to where the patient is at the moment, and to the long-term needs of the analysis. Analysts vary, however, in whereabouts they work most comfortably on this dimension. Different analysts will feel more at home at different points on it. The difficult necessity is to pay deliberate attention to the parts of it where they do not feel at home: to where it may feel *unheimlich*.

Here is an example of the need to be on guard against a kind of clinical automatism. A patient in analysis reported two dreams from the previous night. In the first *she is in a city. It is all dark and seems dangerous. There are explosions going off. Or they might be fireworks.* In the second dream, *there is a car, which seems to be in a tent. In the car are a mother and daughter who are friends of the patient's. Some gas is getting into the tent. Suddenly there is a big explosion, the car is blown up, the mother and daughter are killed. Then the patient is in a train, and the daughter who was in the car is also there, apparently alive. The patient thinks the daughter must be a hallucination, but then thinks 'Even if she is, it's still nice to see her again'.* The dream ended there, and the patient said she was frustrated at her dreams still being dominated by her destructiveness, just as they were at the beginning of her analysis.

Turning explosions into fireworks and bringing the daughter killed in the explosion back to life could be seen as showing a wish by the patient to deny her destructiveness. On the other hand, the fireworks and the daughter's restoration might be clues to a creative, life-enhancing aspect of the patient which she is 'in-tent' on denying, by going on seeing herself as destructive.

Whether the analyst takes up the patient's destructiveness or her attempts to be more alive will depend on other indications, and the overall state of the analysis. It will also be more generally influenced by the analyst's clinical style, theoretical preconceptions and individual personality. All analysts have their predispositions which incline them to particular modes of understanding and interpretation. The clinical need, however, is to offer whatever intervention may be most helpful to a patient: silence, specific interpretations, open-ended interpretations; of the transference, in the transference, extra-transference, and so on. It may be assumed that analysts arrive at their theoretical and clinical orientations by an evaluation, influenced of course by their own analysis and by important teachers, of the relative scientific merits of the viewpoints they encounter. What is not much discussed is how analysts adopt the positions that they do because certain analytic standpoints suit their character structure better than others. For analysts to remain inwardly available across a range of possibilities involves keeping themselves open specifically in directions contrary to their theoretical preconceptions and personal inclinations. To analyse well on one's psychic home ground is not such a problem. For consistent good results one has to play well away from home too.

There are different kinds of strangeness. Some things are outside our familiar range of experience but, when they happen, are still encompassable by our usual ways of thinking. Unexpected as they are, we can still be at home with them. What is *unheimlich*, however, destabilises our habitual ways of making sense of the world, producing a particular quality of anxiety as it does so. It calls into question the framework of understanding within which we feel safe. This is the *Unheimliche* to which we must be open if we are to be fully alive, both personally and as therapists.

The difference is illustrated by the following clinical examples.

A man who had gained considerably from analytic therapy in the past sought further analysis because he still did not really feel his life had meaning. After coming five times a week for about a year, he said the gains from his previous treatment had been genuine, but they were also like the cloud of ink that a squid releases to obscure itself from an attacker. He thought he used his improvements to conceal a deeper refusal to allow some central part of himself to be touched. This seems a useful insight, and his being able to say it appears to indicate a developing trust in the analytic relationship. On the other hand, how much was the apparent progress that this implies yet another cloud of ink hiding his determination not to let his analyst get close to him? Behind this straightforward caution about a concealed negative transference, I had a different and more unnerving sensation. The image implied that we were both underwater. For this man to imagine himself, and invite me to imagine him, as a squid, had something obscurely repellent about it, and the darkness of the ink diffusing in the water as it came towards me felt malign and dangerous. Far from being just a helpful metaphor, the patient's words in fact conveyed to me something uncannily horrible.

It was important for me not to take refuge in the correct and useful understanding he had voiced about utilising his improvement defensively. I needed to accept, and not distance myself from, the experience of being overtaken, deep underwater, by a black miasma. This patient was not English and sometimes, when looking for the expression that he wanted, he would first use a word in his own language. He did so on this occasion, before working his way round to the English word 'squid'. Attempting to hold on to the uncanny horror I had felt, I was interested to try and find, in a dictionary of his language, the word he had first used. It turned out to mean not simply 'squid', but a giant, monster squid; and the word had a secondary meaning of a person with insatiable demands who never lets go of their prey. It seemed that my uncanny sense of foreboding was well-founded.

Compare this with another patient: a woman who said that what she longed for most of all would be to coat me from head to foot in her shit, and for me to find this the most desirable thing I could imagine. The similarities are clear, in that both patients want to push something noxious out of themselves and envelop me in it. The bizarreness of the second example, however, does not feel to me uncanny. The desire this woman expresses, and that she wants me to have as well, is certainly strange, and it would be easy to find it alien; but it is recognisable. I can situate it in the landscape of perversion. In this sense I can, however reluctantly, be at home with it. With the first patient, on the other hand, there is a peculiar dislocation between the benign offer of self-understanding, and the grotesque terror going on beneath it in the depths of the ocean. Suddenly engulfed in a cloud of ink, with a dangerous monster close at hand, I have no bearings and no idea what may happen next. The stripping away of my familiar frames of reference leaves me uncannily exposed.

The need for analysts and therapists to expose themselves to the *Unheimliche* in the clinical situation is a specific instance of a broader necessity. Human beings in general, if we are to maintain and develop our aliveness in whatever aspect of life, need to resist a compliance that seeks, externally or internally, to avoid any strangeness that will take us beyond the limits of our psychic comfort zone. Resisting this compliance, and staying open to what we find *unheimlich*, depends on our allowing the sum of past experience to infuse what is encountered in the present with unexpected, unpredictable meaning. This is the work of creative apperception, and it depends, in turn, on a particular use of memory.

In Freud's paper 'Remembering, repeating and working through', he regards repetition as a way of avoiding memory. The analyst 'celebrates it as a triumph for the treatment if he can bring it about that something which the patient wishes to discharge in action is disposed of through the work of remembering' (Freud, 1914a: 153). Freud puts memory and action into such strong opposition that it is easy to forget that remembering is itself an activity. 'The work of remembering' is an important phrase. The idea that memory can involve work slips in and out of focus in the paper, because Freud considers different sorts of remembering without keeping distinctions between them clear. At first, he mentions both 'the work of interpretation' and 'the expenditure of work which the patient had to make in being obliged to overcome his criticism of his free associations' (1914a: 147). Then Freud describes an evolution of analytic technique such that when 'the doctor uncovers the resistances which are unknown to the patient … the patient often relates the forgotten situations and connections without any difficulty'. The doctor's work of interpreting is still there, but the work required of the patient in remembering seems to have disappeared. Freud summarises: 'The aim of these different techniques has, of course, remained the same. Descriptively speaking, it is to fill in the gaps in memory; dynamically speaking, it is to overcome resistances due to repression' (1914a: 147f). 'To fill in the gaps': Freud often implies that derepression and lifting childhood amnesia simply involve removing obstacles to awareness, so as to bring into view what is already there but invisible. But is remembering a passive event, which simply happens to the patient as a result of the analyst's successful interpretation of resistance, or is it an activity involving psychic work by the patient? If the latter, what is the nature of this work of remembering? Freud's paper implies these questions, but does not spell them out or answer them.

Imagine a commemorative plaque on a new building, covered until the opening ceremony. When the covering is removed, the inscription that was behind it all the time is exposed. If memory consists simply of reproducing accurately in the mind something unchanged from when it disappeared from awareness, then the analyst overcoming resistances is like the mayor who pulls aside the curtain. He reveals what was always there but could not be seen. Like the passive spectators at the ceremony, the patient does not have to 'work' to remember. What comes into view undergoes no change from its covered up, repressed state to its visible, remembered state. Memory of this sort could be called 'recollection'. The word 'remember', however, can also mean to 're-member' an experience; that is, to articulate it in a fresh way. This indicates a more imaginatively active process, in which the past is not simply reflected in the present mind of the rememberer as in a mirror, but where, instead, the rememberer actively creates the present-time experience called memory, in relation to the experience of the past.

Therapeutically, this makes sense. Freud's tendency to let go of the 'work' of remembering, so that remembering becomes simply what happens when resistances are removed, does not explain where the therapeutic benefit lies. It is all very well filling in the gaps, but that just leaves one knowing more about what happened. Dynamic change depends on what one *does* psychically with what is freshly remembered. One of the characters in William Faulkner's *Requiem for a Nun* declares 'The past is never dead. It's not even past' (Faulkner, 1953: 85).[1] In the context of the play this is an admonition about the impossibility of hoping ever to escape the past. What matters in ordinary life, however, as in the consulting room, is to see that although the past remains present and alive, this does not represent a sentence of imprisonment within it, but an opportunity. It is the very thing that makes fresh growth possible. Patients in analysis remember, repeat and work through the experience of their past in all sorts of permutations and combinations of these three processes. One thing is consistent, however: working through involves a particular use of memory which allows past and present to come into a new relation with each other. This is the 'work of remembering'.

Although Freud does not spell out what this involves, one aspect of it, as I mentioned above, is the 'work' of creative apperception. This largely unconscious process brings past experience to bear on the present, in such a way that what is experienced in the present is enriched with unexpected layers of fresh meaning that it would otherwise lack.

There is also, however, a second aspect of the work of remembering which operates the other way round in time, to illuminate past experience in the light of the present. At a certain moment in 'Remembering, repeating and working through' we trip rather startlingly over Winnicott's roots. Freud says we render the repetition compulsion harmless, and even useful, by:

> ... admit[ting] it into the transference as a playground in which it is allowed to expand in almost complete freedom ... The transference thus creates an intermediate region between illness and real life through which the transition from one to the other is made.
>
> (Freud, 1914a: 154)

For Winnicott, playing, in an intermediate, transitional, area of experience, is essential to creative living (Winnicott, 1971a: 50). Freud describes the transference in identical terms, as an 'intermediate region' of 'transition', which functions as a 'playground'. Reading Freud's essay through Winnicottian eyes, we may understand it to imply that transference is the essential avenue to creative living offered by the analytic setting. No surprise, we might think: the centrality of the transference is universally agreed. But analysis of the transference does not work through creative apperception. The link between transference analysis and creative living operates in the reverse direction. Transference (at least as it is most often understood) could be said to be a misplaced, uncreative apperception. It brings the past to bear in an erroneous way which distorts the experience of a present-time relationship.[2] The play of analysis resolves this by re-membering the past in a fresh way so as to undo the distortion. This is the second aspect of the work of remembering: to refashion what is held in memory, so as to give new meaning to the past in the light of a person's present-day experience. This process and creative apperception together constitute the work of remembering. To be fully and creatively alive involves a conscious and unconscious freedom of imaginative movement in both directions, up and down the developmental experience of a life.

Who we are is always dependent on who we have been. If we are not merely to be, however, but to go on becoming, we have also to be independent of who we have been. In David Grossman's novel *See under: Love* it is said of someone: 'He thought about his life, a life which had never been his. Not really his. Because force of habit had always deprived him of it' (Grossman, 1990: 94). To resist compliance externally, and be independent of the expectations of the world around, is hard enough. More problematic still is to be independent of our own habitual expectations and assumptions about ourselves. If we simply comply with what our past says about us we cannot continue developing the potential of who we might become. So the freedom of imaginative movement is not only between past and present. It needs to extend into the future as well. The future, though, is not homely and familiar. It is hidden, unknowable, full of secrets. Not just for therapists, therefore, but for anybody working in whatever way to fulfil the potential of their being, there is a need to open themselves, against the force of habit, to what is *unheimlich*.

This contradicts Freud. He appreciated the uncanny when consciously deployed as an artistic device in a work of literature. Personal experience of the uncanny, though, was another matter. For Freud this was always reducible to the same simple explanations.

> Anyone who has completely and finally rid himself of animistic beliefs will be insensible to this type of the uncanny ... The whole thing is purely an affair of 'reality-testing', a question of the material reality of the phenomena.
>
> (Freud, 1919b: 248)

> An uncanny experience occurs either when infantile complexes which have been repressed are once more revived by some impression, or when primitive beliefs which have been surmounted seem once more to be confirmed.
>
> (Ibid: 249)

Freud recognised, as with the 'oceanic feeling' (Freud, 1930: 64f), that personal experience of the uncanny did not play much part in his own life. 'The writer of the present contribution, indeed, must himself plead guilty to a special obtuseness in the matter … It is long since he has experienced or heard of anything which has given him an uncanny impression' (1919b: 220). Perhaps not so very long. Consider his encounter, five years earlier, with the 'inscrutable' (Freud's word) *Moses* of Michelangelo.

> No piece of statuary has ever made a stronger impression on me than this. How often have I mounted the steep steps from the unlovely Corso Cavour to the lonely piazza where the deserted church stands, and have essayed to support the angry scorn of the hero's glance! Sometimes I have crept cautiously out of the half-gloom of the interior as though I myself belonged to the mob upon whom his eye is turned— the mob which can hold fast no conviction, which has neither faith nor patience, and which rejoices when it has regained its illusory idols.
>
> (Freud, 1914b: 213)

Freud is sending himself up; but he is doing so as a way of dealing with a real experience. He does seem to have been more at home commenting on the uncanny than encountering it (but see Chapter 4, p.59).

Freud's devaluing of personal experience of the *Unheimliche* is undermined, however, by his own exploration of the word '*heimlich*'. From meaning 'that which belongs within the home', and so must be kept private from strangers, it comes to mean something which, having to be kept secret and not revealed, becomes fearsome and mysterious. Freud's discussion, and the dictionary references that he cites (1919b: 220–6), show that '*heimlich*' and '*unheimlich*', although presenting themselves as opposites, meet round the back, so to speak, where they merge together. If the *Unheimliche* is liable to become the *Heimliche*, Freud's project of exorcising it through making oneself at home with reality-testing becomes less certain.[3]

My encounter with the uncanny, when my patient pictured himself as a giant squid that could engulf me in black ink, was valuable as well as disturbing. It helped me see more about what might be going on in the submarine depths of the analysis. Accounts in the analytic literature suggest likewise that a certain kind of disruption of normal psychic stability and orientation may make something of value perceptible that is otherwise kept out of view. Two examples follow which indicate what can be latent in an uncanny experience, and may come to light when the uncanny is accepted.

A paper by Michel de M'Uzan (1978) is a meditation on what it means to entertain the thought 'If I were dead … ' There is an uncanny quality to the idea of being dead yet still aware of one's existence, 'experiencing oneself as one's own ghost', as De M'Uzan describes it. He considers whether the thought could be a resurgence of castration anxiety: the revival of a repressed infantile complex as Freud claimed. But for De M'Uzan that does not do justice to the intricate layerings of the 'if I were dead' experience. It may lead, he says, to a depersonalised state where one sees another person as one's double, and then feels dependent on an identification with them for one's own continued existence. Does this exemplify Freud's second explanation for uncanny experience, seeming to confirm after all an outdated primitive idea like that of the *doppelgänger*? But again, De M'Uzan sees a value in the uncanny experience which belies such a reductive explanation. He illustrates this with a patient's dream in which she encountered her double, but grown very old and apparently not far from death. This suggests to De M'Uzan the idea of a 'work of dying'. He writes of the 'augmented passion', an intensification of experience, perhaps including a sense of heightened creativity, that someone approaching death may discover in themselves. De M'Uzan believes that at this final point in a person's life there is a specific piece of psychic work to be done, in integrating this intensified state of feeling into their overall sense of the person that they are. The idea recalls Winnicott's prayer to be alive when he died. De M'Uzan's article implies that the uncanniness of 'experiencing oneself as one's own ghost' arises from attempting prematurely this 'work of dying', as he conceives it, whilst still in the middle of living.

A parallel to what De M'Uzan means by the 'work of dying' may be found in the closing stages of an analysis. The relentless approach of the termination date in the diary can give the sessions an intensity that belongs especially to this situation. There is a steadily shrinking amount of time left to do whatever work is still to be done, and a heightened sense of urgency about doing it. The dying days of an analysis are like no other part of it. The work that is so particular to them, however, still needs to be integrated into the sum of the patient's analytic experience. This analytic 'work of terminating' seems closely parallel to De M'Uzan's 'work of dying'.

Another clinical encounter with the uncanny is notably described by César and Sára Botella (2005: 71ff) in their book *The Work of Psychic Figurability*, discussed further in Chapter 8 (pp.122ff). A patient described a dream in which *he and the analyst were together and the analyst was going to have a shower. He did not follow the analyst into the shower.* The next day, the patient talked of thinking he had seen the analyst walking in the street wearing sunglasses. He got agitated about whether he had really seen the analyst or not; and the sunglasses became, as he spoke, more like the dark glasses worn by blind people. The analyst felt overcome by a feeling of derealisation. He lost touch with his recollection of the pleasant stroll that he had indeed taken, and had a nightmarish sensation of being overcome first by blindness, and then by a rigidity which seemed to be that of a corpse. The patient went on about whether he had in fact seen the analyst, and said 'I am looking for you in the image and I cannot find you any more'. Hearing himself disappear like this from the patient's memory made the analyst fall further into a state of nightmarish depersonalisation. The patient spoke of an elderly Jewish couple who had been deported during the war. The husband had now died and his wife, said the patient, obviously did not want to follow him. Just as the patient, thought the analyst, had not wanted to follow him into the shower … into death! The shower took on the meaning of a gas chamber. The thread running through the session, from the corpse-like rigidity, through the negative hallucination of the analyst vanished from the 'image', to the shower that was not to be entered, revealed itself to be the idea of death.

I commented earlier on how informative was my uncanny experience with the patient who likened himself to a squid. The Botellas write similarly about the episode they are describing:

> ... there occurred in the analyst a work of figurability in the form of a nightmare. Are there not grounds for thinking ... that there is a correspondence between the void of the analyst's disappearance from the analysand's 'image' and the fullness of the means of figuration employed by the analyst's nightmare? Further, that the analyst's nightmare is the counterpart, the complement, the positive of the analysand's negative hallucination? And moreover that the analyst's psyche served as a 'darkroom' revealing what could only be inscribed negatively in the analysand?
>
> (Botella and Botella, 2005: 73f)

To make use of the experience in this way depends on the analyst's being able to bear the nightmare. Everybody feels to some degree the desire to escape from the uncanny. At arm's length, as an aesthetically satisfying literary device, it can be appreciated. But close encounters with it always involve an element of fear. In Freud's discussion of Michelangelo's *Moses* he explicitly refuses meaning to what cannot be represented (see Chapter 8, p.117). The uncanny takes us into areas of our minds where what Freud (1900: 339ff) called 'considerations of representability' no longer obtain. Here we encounter what we have no way of representing to ourselves, and it is terrifying to feel at the mercy of something that has no form.

Both these examples revolve around the idea of death, which is central also to my uncanny horror at the monster squid. Death is the paradigm instance of that which cannot be represented. If independence means having the internal freedom to leave home for foreign parts, we want to know that there goes on being a home that will welcome us back, and we need to be capable ourselves of turning back home. But death is 'the undiscovered country from whose borne no traveller returns' (Shakespeare: *Hamlet*, III, i, 78–9). It is an 'event horizon', the boundary in space around a black hole beyond which descent into it is irreversible. Death can be described and investigated as a biological fact. Speculations and fantasies about what it is like can be represented. However, to represent the experience itself one would have to die, but not have died. This is the territory of De M'Uzan's paper. Freud remarks:

> There is scarcely any other matter upon which our thoughts and feelings have changed so little since the very earliest times, and in

which discarded forms have been so completely preserved under a thin disguise, as our relation to death.

(Freud, 1919b: 241f)

The reason for this is that death is always and for ever unrepresentable. We have in principle no way of giving it form. It is not that one day we may be able to reduce it to something we can feel at home with after all. Amongst all the phenomena of life, death is something with which we can never hope to be on home ground. Its *unheimlich* quality is absolute.

I have said that being fully and creatively alive means trying to keep oneself open to what is *unheimlich*, and also that imaginative movement up and down the developmental pathways of one's life needs to extend into the future. Since death is ultimately *unheimlich*, this implies that being creatively alive means staying imaginatively open to death; not just as a fact that we know about, but as something we shall inevitably experience. Allowing, or inviting, death to enter our experience when it is still, we hope, far off may seem a dark idea. I am putting it forward, though, as a necessary condition for the brightness of creative energy in a life.[4] Death, like independence, is what we are always moving 'towards'. The next chapter will explore this further, arriving finally at the idea that we need to be able to 'dream our dying'. In mediaeval times it was common to see the inscription '*memento mori*', usually translated as 'remember you will die'. But '*mori*' is the infinitive of the verb, not the future tense, and a closer translation would be 'remember there is death'. This might be dismissed as gruesome mediaeval morbidity. On the other hand, it may be, as I have said, a psychologically accurate reminder of what is necessary for being fully alive. Dylan Thomas' poem 'Fern Hill' is an extraordinary celebration of the aliveness generated in a young man by the recognition of his mortality. Its closing lines are a modern *memento mori*:

> Oh as I was young and easy in the mercy of his means,
> Time held me green and dying
> Though I sang in my chains like the sea.

(Thomas, 1952: 161)

Notes

1   Thanks to Rosemary Davies for this reference.
2   I am using 'transference' here in the conventional sense of a psychic process which distorts the perception of reality because experiences in the present, such as an analytic relationship, are mistakenly assimilated to experiences belonging to the past. Transference can also be seen as a necessary element in a person's exploration of reality, essential for developing a structured understanding of the external world, and for developing internal psychic structure as well.

> Transference is the 'dynamism' by which the instinctual life of man, the id, becomes ego and by which reality becomes integrated and maturity is achieved. Without such transference—of the intensity of the unconscious, of the infantile

ways of experiencing life that have no language and little organisation, but the indestructibility and power of the origins of life—to the preconscious and to present-day life and contemporary objects—without such transference, or to the extent to which such transference miscarries, human life becomes sterile and an empty shell.

(Loewald, 1980 [1960]: 250)

I think this understanding of transference is extremely important. Nevertheless, at this point I am using the concept in its more standard sense that implies a distortion in perceiving reality.

3　There seems to have been a change in usage since Freud's time. Etymologically, '*heimlich*' and '*unheimlich*' share the root '*heim-*', meaning 'home', and the negative prefix '*un-*' makes '*unheimlich*' the linguistic opposite of '*heimlich*'. In today's language, however, their meanings are not related. While '*unheimlich*' means 'uncanny', '*heimlich*' means 'secret' or 'secretive'. Semantically, they are not opposites, and contemporary German speakers would not necessarily make a connection between '*heimlich*' and 'home'. In Freud's time it was different. He quotes (1919b: 222–6, 253–6) from two standard German dictionaries (Sanders, 1860; Grimm, 1877), to show that alongside 'secret' or 'concealed', '*heimlich*' had other strands of meaning. It meant 'intimate', 'familiar', and connoted the security of home. From this, the meaning extended to signify what belongs within the home and so must be kept private from strangers; and, by further extension, something which, because it must not be revealed, becomes mysterious and frightening. These polysemous connotations of '*heimlich*' have been lost. Today, the words used to signify 'comfortably familiar' or 'homely' would probably be '*heimelig*' or '*häuslich*', and neither of these develops its meaning in the direction of 'mysterious' or 'dangerous'. Freud's discussion of '*heimlich*' in the terms of his day, prior to this impoverishment, concludes with a telling quotation from Grimm (1877: 878).

The notion of something hidden and dangerous is still further developed so that '*heimlich*' comes to have the meaning usually ascribed to '*unheimlich*'. Thus: 'At times I feel like a man who walks in the night and believes in ghosts; every corner is *heimlich* and full of terrors for him' (Klinger, *Theater*, 3: 298)

(Freud, 1919b: 226)

I am grateful to Professor David Yeandle, Professor Martin Swales and Dr Sylvia Zwettler-Otte for their helpful linguistic advice.

4　For a similar perspective on something that appears extremely dark, see Marion Milner's account of Christ's crucifixion as being not a blood sacrifice with magical powers of redemption, but 'the culminating poetic dramatisation of an inner process of immense importance to humanity, a process which was not an escape from reality, but the only condition under which the inner reality could be fully perceived' (Milner, 1986: 139).

2

WHY DID ORPHEUS LOOK BACK?
Après-coup, avant-coup

Winnicott's touchstone of being fully and creatively alive, the process he called creative apperception, is only half the story. Creative apperception gives meaning to present-time experience by relating it to all that has made up a person's life so far. But the past must also be able to take on fresh meaning. Creative apperception will only truly 'make the individual feel that life is worth living' (Winnicott, 1971a: 65; see p.5) if the present is related to a past that is reconstituted afresh in the present moment. What matters is not just how someone experiences their past but how they continue to re-experience it. As was discussed in Chapter 1, this is not passive recollection which simply readmits to consciousness what once disappeared from it, but the active operation of memory as an imaginative re-membering of the past. This makes possible an interchange between past and present—in either direction—that can rearticulate both to their mutual enrichment.

The process of giving fresh meaning to the past in the light of subsequent and present-day experience was described by Freud as '*Nachträglichkeit*': '*The traumas of childhood operate in a deferred fashion as though they were fresh experiences; but they do so unconsciously*' (Freud, 1896a: 167fn, Freud's italics). The *Standard Edition* (1950–1974) of Freud's works translated '*Nachträglichkeit*' as 'deferred action', but this proved unmanageable, and the concept has become more familiarly and usefully known by the French term '*après-coup*'. What I described in Chapter 1 as the second aspect of the 'work of remembering' (p.10) turns out, in fact, to be no more nor less than *après-coup*. Two other French words are also relevant for their distinction between different kinds of memory. '*Souvenir*', corresponding to the English 'recollection', denotes a memory, once present, that disappeared from consciousness and has now come back again. The more complex '*remémoration*' refers to the work of memory which refashions the relation between past and present. When it reconstitutes the past in a new way, *remémoration* is the process on which *après-coup* depends. When it draws on the past to deepen the meaning of present experience, it supports the work of creative apperception.

Freud's statement of the function of remembering has been quoted already (p.9): 'Descriptively speaking, it is to fill in the gaps in memory; dynamically speaking, it is to overcome resistances due to repression' (Freud, 1914a: 147). Rosine Perelberg (2006) has extended the distinction between descriptive and dynamic to the concept of *après-coup*. Suppose that, last week, I felt lacking in energy, without enthusiasm for things I normally enjoy, and could not understand why. Today, my analyst interprets that I may not have realised how angry I am at the way a certain person has been treating me. Now I realise, with a new understanding in the present, that the meaning of my apathy last week is that I was depressed; and that my depression resulted from repressing, and turning inward, the aggressive feelings of which today's session has made me conscious. This retrospective understanding of my lethargy is an example of descriptive *après-coup*.

Compare this with Freud's paradigm example of *Nachträglichkeit* in his account of the Wolf Man (Freud, 1918). Aged eighteen months the Wolf Man sees his parents having intercourse. When he is almost four, his precocious six-year-old sister seduces him into sexual games with her and he becomes disturbed, with violent temper tantrums and obsessional symptoms. Freud called his patient the 'Wolf Man' because of a significant dream in which wolves appeared sitting in a tree (Freud, 1918: 29ff). Analysis of this dream revealed that the Wolf Man's childhood disturbance arose because, at the age of four, he related retrospectively what he had seen his parents doing two and a half years earlier to the sexual feelings he was now experiencing with his sister. This describes how his understanding operates by *après-coup*, but it is more than just descriptive. It demonstrates the essential role of *après-coup* in structuring the forward movement of psychic development. Perelberg claims that this dynamic operation of *après-coup* underlies the whole of Freud's metapsychology. She quotes (2006: 1203) from a paper by Thomä and Cheshire:

> Freud approaches his concept [*après-coup*] from two different standpoints in time: sometimes he looks backwards from the point of view of the therapist reconstructing a phenomenal-developmental sequence of events and experiences, and sometimes he is looking forward as if through the eyes of the original traumatic event which is setting off a series of potentially pathogenic developments, and some of whose effects are going to be 'carried over' into the future.
>
> (Thomä and Cheshire, 1991: 421)

Perelberg's point is that this does not apply only to traumatic events and pathogenic developments. It underlies normal psychic development as well. Dynamic *après-coup* operates, consciously and unconsciously, as an ever-present influence in a person's continually developing experience of his or her life as a whole.

Thomä and Cheshire highlight the interaction between a backward gaze from present to past, and a forward gaze from past to present. The backward gaze, by which the past is reinterpreted in the light of present experience, is the gaze of *après-coup*. The forward gaze from past to present, which sets present-time experience in the context of all that has happened previously, is what Winnicott describes as creative apperception. The previous chapter showed that this freedom of imaginative movement needs to extend into the future as well, and there is a corresponding pair, of forward and backward gazes, where the future is concerned. The future cannot be reinterpreted like the past, but one may be either more, or less, psychically available for experiencing it. Working to fulfil the potential of one's being involves opening oneself to the unknownness of the future and, in particular, to the *unheimlich* possibility of experience that makes demands beyond the range of one's present repertoires. This requires an imaginative gaze forward *from* the present and a backward gaze *to* the present, from the unrealised and unknown future. Like *après-coup* and creative apperception, these are essential aspects of being creatively alive. The present is enriched by a continual unconscious reconfiguring of one's availability to the future. This enlivening of the present enlarges, in turn, the potential of one's future life. It seems right to give this capacity the name of dynamic *avant-coup*.

The terms 'creative apperception', '*après-coup*', '*remémoration*' and '*avant-coup*' can be confusing. Their similarities and distinctions are complicated, and to have their meanings summarised may help the reader navigate between them.

All these terms refer to processes in our minds which happen, of course, in the present. These present-time mental events involve different kinds of interaction between our past and present, and present and future experience.

> **Creative apperception** allows an experience in the present to take on layers of meaning, because we relate it to a whole variety of past experiences. The past influences how we experience, and give meaning to, the present.

> *Après-coup* gives new layers of meaning to past experiences, because an experience in the present prompts us to re-evaluate and reinterpret them. The present influences how we (re)experience, and give meaning to, the past.

Creative apperception and *après-coup* both operate mostly at an unconscious level. They interact in a kind of spiral. The past which enriches present experience by creative apperception is a past which is constantly being enriched *from* the present by *après-coup*. The present which enriches past experience by *après-coup* is a present which is constantly being enriched *from* the past by creative apperception.

> **Remémoration** is the activity of memory which allows us to remember past experience in such a way that:
> 1   past experience is susceptible of being interpreted afresh (making possible the process of *après-coup*).
> 2   past experience is able to bring fresh meaning into the present (making possible the process of creative apperception).

Avant-coup, as I have described it, is more than the 'future' counterpart of *après-coup*. It also includes a 'future' counterpart of creative apperception. It covers movement between present and future in both directions, so that:

1   future experience takes on a richer potential because its range of possibility can be constantly imagined afresh from the present. This is the 'future' counterpart of *après-coup*.

2   present experience acquires a greater range of possibility by being reimagined from the standpoint of a future that has not yet taken form. This is the 'future' counterpart of creative apperception.

'A person lives his life at a crossroads: at the point where a past that has affected him and a future that lies open meet in the present' (Wollheim, 1984: 31). The idea is familiar enough; but I am saying something more. The present moment is created by the unconscious encounter between *après-coup* and *avant-coup*. It is not a matter of 'Here I am in the present, which lets me look back into the past and ahead into the future'. It is rather—and I emphasise that this is at an unconscious level—'Here is what I have made so far of all that has happened to me; and here is however I might be able to deal with what comes my way. The relation between these tells me where I am at this point in my life'.[1] I was struck to find in an essay by Barack Obama the following statement: 'Abraham Lincoln ... also reminded me of a larger, fundamental element of American life—the enduring belief that we can constantly remake ourselves to fit our larger dreams' (2005). This is not only good political rhetoric. It expresses very exactly the encounter between dynamic *après-coup* ('we can constantly remake ourselves') and *avant-coup* ('our larger dreams'). And it suggests the aliveness in the present which this encounter can generate.

The present punctuates an expanse which extends as far back as the operation of *après-coup*, and as far forward as the operation of *avant-coup*, can reach. There are natural boundaries to this expanse. Its extension into the future is limited by death, which is inescapable yet forever unrepresentable. This makes death—not the concept but the experience—absolutely and irreducibly *unheimlich* (see pp.14f). The ultimate challenge to our capacity for *avant-coup* is the inexorable unknowability of death. A comparable existential boundary at the beginning of life is the primal scene. This means not just parental intercourse in general, but the specific, unique conjunction that resulted in one's own conception. In his novel *Tristram Shandy*, Laurence Sterne imagined, under the guise of comedy, a man for whom the primal scene was fractured.

> I wish either my father or my mother, or indeed both of them, had minded what they were about when they begot me ... 'Pray my dear', quoth my mother, 'have you not forgot to wind up the clock?' 'Good G—!' cried my father. 'Did ever woman, since the creation of the world, interrupt a man with such a silly question?'
>
> (Sterne, 1759–1767: Volume 1, Chapter 1)

Sylvia Plath, on the other hand, celebrates the sexuality that conceived her daughter.

> Love set you going like a fat gold watch.
> The midwife slapped your footsoles, and your bald cry
> Took its place among the elements.
>
> (Plath, 1965: 'Morning Song')

Sterne and Plath both knew, in their different ways, that time is set going by the primal scene. For analysands, and others seeking to develop their sense of who they are, the process of *après-coup* needs to extend as far as the origin of their existence. Just as death is irreducibly *unheimlich*, this also is something undeniable, yet impossible to bring within the compass of experience. The work of re-membering always extends beyond what can be merely recollected.

To give significance to the sexuality that brought one into existence, and to the death that will take one out of it, is a lifelong psychic work. Being fully alive means making use of *après-coup* and *avant-coup* together, in such a way that both origin and extinction can resonate with meaning in one's life today.

On the one hand, the present is a moment in the passage of time. Aliveness depends on inhabiting it with as much freedom of movement as possible between it and both past and future. But the present moment is also timeless. The same movement up and down a lifetime makes the present a point of encounter between *remémoration* of the past and imaginative openness to the *Unheimliche* of the future. This meeting point contains all of a person's past and possible future experience. T.S. Eliot wrote in 'Burnt Norton':

> Time present and time past
> Are both perhaps present in time future
> And time future contained in time past.
> If all time is eternally present
> All time is unredeemable.
>
> (Eliot, 1969a [1935]: 171)

To inhabit the crossing point between *après-coup* and *avant-coup* is to live at the intersection of time and timelessness. Winnicott found a title for one of his books in lines from the next of Eliot's *Four Quartets*, 'East Coker', which describe this intersection again, but without such pessimism.

> Home is where one starts from. As we grow older
> The world becomes stranger, the pattern more complicated
> Of dead and living. Not the intense moment
> Isolated, with no before and after,
> But a lifetime burning in every moment …
>
> (Eliot, 1969b [1940]: 182)

Perhaps to be eternally present makes a lifetime redeemable after all. A psychoanalyst must certainly hope so.[2]

Outside this continual psychic work of aliveness is a larger timelessness. The natural boundaries of the primal scene and death, Eros and Thanatos, represent our passage, like Bede's sparrow flying through the banqueting hall, from non-existence into existence and out again. In Marion Milner's words (1957: 159), 'the astounding experience of how it feels to be alive' involves living where life's temporality encounters the timelessness of 'a lifetime burning in every moment', surrounded by the different timelessness of non-being.

Here is an old woman talking about a patchwork quilt that she made.

> It took me more than twenty years, nearly twenty-five, I reckon, in the evenings after supper when the children were all put to bed. My whole life is in that quilt. It scares me sometimes when I look at it. All my joys and all my sorrows are stitched into those little pieces. When I was proud of the boys and when I was downright provoked and angry with them. When the girls annoyed me or when they gave me a warm feeling around my heart. And John too. He was stitched into that quilt and all the thirty years we were married. Sometimes I loved him and sometimes I sat there hating him as I pieced the patches together. So they are all in that quilt, my hopes and fears, my joys and sorrows, my loves and hates. I tremble sometimes when I remember what that quilt knows about me.
>
> (Ickis, 1959: 270)

And here is a woman at the bedside of her desperately ill daughter. In December 1991, Paula, the twenty-seven-year-old daughter of the novelist Isabel Allende, sustained brain damage from a chronic illness, and fell into a coma. She did not regain consciousness and, a year later, she died. During that year, Allende sat with her daughter, writing for her, in case she should recover, a memoir of their family's history and of her own and Paula's lives.

> Carmen, my agent, comes from time to time with sympathies from my editors or news about my books, but I don't know what she's talking about. Nothing exists but you, Paula, and this space without time in which we are both trapped.
>
> In the long silent hours I am trampled by memories, all happening in one instant, as if my entire life were a single, unfathomable image. The child and girl I was, the woman I am, the old woman I shall be, are all water in the same rushing torrent. My memory is like a Mexican mural in which all times are simultaneous.
>
> (Allende, 1995: 23)

Intersections between life's temporality and a lifetime timeless in the present moment.

22

For psychoanalysts the first association with the idea of timelessness is likely to be the timelessness of the unconscious; and the most direct, immediate contact with the unconscious is in the experience of dreaming. Some patients do not dream or, more accurately, unconsciously do not allow themselves to remember dreams. Dreams may not come to mind during sessions, or may be remembered during holiday periods only. What is being avoided in such cases? The experience of dreaming lies outside the temporality of everyday life. Dreams are a plumb line into the unconscious. In dreaming, the temporal structures of everyday life are usurped by unstructured timelessness. Telling a dream in the analytic setting, therefore, is more than simple narration. It is to expose one's dreaming; and this is to place oneself where time and timelessness intersect.

The linear structure of existence within time makes it, at least in principle, predictable. There is a kind of mathematical puzzle which presents a series of numbers and asks what number would come next. We are invited to believe, whether or not we can detect the sequence, that each number does have a relation to the one before it. The temporality of existence invites faith that at least some aspects of life are predictable. In conditions of timelessness this disappears. There is no before or after. An event cannot be either cause or consequence of another event. There is no predicting or controlling what may happen. No wonder some patients avoid the intersection of time and timelessness that is involved in telling a dream. Or else the telling of it may become an exercise in working out what the dream means, thus safely reducing the timelessness of the dream experience to the linearity of an explanation. If telling a dream does not involve a reliving of the dream experience, the dream becomes just a *souvenir*. This is not wrong. If it happens it belongs to the analysis, and the analyst's task is to help the patient think about why it should need to happen. If a patient is able, on the other hand, to tell the dream as a *remémoration*, analysing the dream can become a new, shared *remémoration* on the part of patient and analyst together.

A man in analysis five times a week dreamed of *a building. It occupied an island in the middle of a lake, which was connected to the shore by a narrow strip of land like a causeway. It was a single-storey building, shaped like a geometrical figure with several sides all the same length. Its walls seemed like slabs of stone or metal, leaning inwards to a low roof which sloped slightly upwards from each wall to a point in the centre. The building was regular and symmetrical in shape, with a hard, angular feel to it. There did not seem to be any door, but as well as seeing it from the outside, the dreamer was inside it. It seemed much larger inside than one would expect and it was full of strange, ultra-modern machinery.* Nothing happened in the dream. It consisted simply of these two images: the building on its island; and the impression of its interior.

The patient's associations went in three directions. Firstly, the construction of the building, with its walls sloping slightly inwards and its flattish roof, made him remember how, when he was little, his mother tried to teach him to build houses of playing cards. He liked doing it with her, but he was never very good

23

at it, and was unhappy when, as soon as he got two or three storeys up, his house always fell down. Secondly, the geometrical shape of the building reminded him of primary school, where he was an intelligent but rather lonely child. When he was left out of other children's games he would console himself by studying, and sometimes the abstract beauty of geometrical theorems gave him the sense of another world he could escape into. This linked to the third set of associations. The place that was unexpectedly large on the inside, and full of futuristic machinery, recalled Dr Who's *Tardis*, and this patient had very much liked watching the TV series about the Time Lord with apparently magical powers, who could travel between universes.

One could take a classical view of this dream. Associations show a little boy who wants to make something with his mother, and who is disappointed at failing because he cannot get his construction as tall as he wants. This seems to exemplify well Freud's formulation of dreams as the concealed expression of a childhood sexual wish. Freud had difficulty, however, with the idea that dreams could be creative. The unconscious might be ingenious in the forms that the dream-work took, but he resisted the idea that dreams could themselves generate fresh meaning (Freud, 1900: 506n., 579n.; 1916–17: 182). In this dream, however, the work of *remémoration* seems to do exactly that. This man's memories of his lack of success at building card houses, and of sitting alone with a geometry book while other children play, come together in the design of the building. This connection generates the theme of abstraction as a refuge from failure at playing, giving more meaning to these memories than either carries alone. The Tardis-like qualities of the building connect this theme to the dreamer's identification with the character of Dr ... Who? The conjunction of these three elements, in the card-house geometry of the science-fiction building, further relates this theme of failed play and the escape from it into abstraction, to the patient's difficulties in knowing who he is. This is the work of *remémoration*, which begins with the unconscious processes that create the dream and is continued in the analytic session.

The analysis was some years old when this dream occurred, and the patient's difficulty in being playful and spontaneous, his awkwardness in relationships and his tendency to retreat into abstract thinking were well recognised. The fresh and striking insight offered by the dream was that these tendencies, and particularly the way in which they were connected, were expressions of a structure in the patient's mind. This made it possible to re-member afresh (*remémorer*) all sorts of episodes in the analysis: when the analyst had felt excluded from the patient's mind; when the patient had seemed mechanically preoccupied with abstract thoughts that went nowhere; and when he was frustrated as he felt locked into something that he could not break out of. Such episodes could be rearticulated in terms of this internal structure he had built for himself: elegant but unyielding; full of machinery which was supposed to be exciting, but did not give the satisfaction that was hoped for; and with no possibility of intercourse between inside and outside. Re-membering their way through such occasions between them gave both analyst and patient a vivid sense of how these were not merely transferential repetitions but contained the cumulative history of the patient's lifelong attempts to reconfigure this pattern. The joint *remémoration* of this history gave new meaning *après-coup* to these episodes; and the *après-coup* was dynamic in that it allowed a developmental restructuring in the patient's mind. The pattern of failed play leading to isolation, abstraction and omnipotent identification, represented by the building in the dream, could gradually be modified so that this man became more alive to the world around him, and to his own inner world. Also, by a process now of dynamic *avant-coup*, he was more curious and thoughtful about his future, and more potentially available, in richer and more flexible ways, for whatever experience it might bring him.

This approach involves more than exposing the latent content of a dream. A dream is not simply a cryptogram to be deciphered. It is an experience lived where time and timelessness intersect. If being fully and creatively alive means living at such a crossing point, then telling one's analyst a dream becomes a bid for aliveness.

Bion extended the idea of what 'dreaming' means (rather as Freud extended the idea of sexuality) in a way that is helpful for understanding the link between dreaming and aliveness. 'Alpha-function' is Bion's name for a certain kind of internal work that is required if emotional experience is to be used for thinking: that is, to produce thoughts as opposed to mere happenings in the mind. A person without alpha-function may hallucinate or try to evacuate unmanageable mental events, but cannot think. Bion realised that this same process—of making unconscious connections between elements of experience so as to create meaningful psychic structures—occurred also during sleep. In the waking state, alpha-function creates thoughts. In sleep, the meaningful psychic structures created are dreams. Someone who lacks alpha-function may have psychic experiences while asleep but they will not amount to dreams. Recognising that the same process operates in the same way both in sleep and the waking state, Bion could have expressed this by saying that we think while we are asleep. Instead he said, more interestingly, that we dream while we are awake (Bion, 1962: 6f, 15–17). Ogden writes that for Bion dreaming involves 'unconscious psychological work achieved through the linking of elements of experience … in the creation of dream-thought. This work of making unconscious linkages … allows one unconsciously and consciously to think about and make psychological use of experience' (Ogden, 2003: 19). This belongs as much to waking as to sleep; and Bion indeed saw dream-work, in the sense of linking elements of experience together by alpha-function, as being not merely possible during waking life, but an essential part of it. The unconscious linkages that creative apperception and *après-coup* make between present and past, are an example. They are sponsored by *remémoration* and formed by the process that Bion calls dreaming. This is what lets them bring fresh texture and complexity to the experience of life. The aliveness depends upon the dreaming.

The implications of this extend beyond the therapeutic situation. Dreaming, like the present moment, is a crossing point of time and timelessness. If a capacity for dreaming, asleep and awake, is an expression of aliveness, then the crossing point of time and timelessness, both in dreaming and in the experience of the present moment, becomes a base from which to live one's life.

This is captured in astonishing fashion by the Dutch artist Johannes Vermeer, in his painting *The Kitchen Maid* (Figure 2.1). The extraordinary stillness that emanates from this rather small painting seems to fill the room where it hangs in Amsterdam's Rijksmuseum.[3] The maid's body is in perfect equilibrium. Her arms and the tilt of her torso and head balance precisely the weight of the milk jug. The milk is flowing out of the jug, but Vermeer seems to deny the flow. He paints the milk in sharp focus, heightening its definition with a clarity that freezes movement. The emptiness of the wall behind the maid deliberately allows no distraction from this woman's absolute absorption in the moment.[4] Nothing is moving, or seems to need to move. This is the stillness of time suspended.

But what about the milk? Before long, the maid is going to have to tip the jug further or put it down. Her task has a beginning and an end. The family that she serves with such concentrated dreaming grace may be waiting for its breakfast. The flow of time, like the flow of milk, cannot be ignored. The bread in the still life on the table is painted with a perfection of detail that, again, gives it a suspended existence. But this bread is going to be eaten. And the blank wall carries a history. The pockmarks in it are holes where nails that once had objects hanging on them have been pulled out. Go close up to the canvas, and the large hole to the right of the maid's head shows in photographic granular detail that seventeenth-century Dutch plaster could fragment in just the same frustrating manner as today's. This wall has been made use of over time.

The art historian Arthur Wheelock declares that the kitchen maid 'conveys a physical and moral presence unequalled by any other figure in Dutch art' (Wheelock, 1995: 108). A remarkable claim. But what is it about the maid that gives her presence its extraordinary quality? Unconsciously, the viewer registers how Vermeer positions her at the intersection between the timelessness of the suspended moment and its location in a continuing story that has a past and a future. The wall, with its evidence of previous use, is behind the maid, and the bread, destined to be eaten, is in front of her. The spatial arrangement represents visually the insertion of the timeless into history. The central focus of the painting, the jug, bowl and stream of milk—the primal nutrient of psychic life —presents a movement out of one darkness, through brightness, into another darkness. This picture makes imaginable Wordsworth's 'unimaginable touch of time' (Wordsworth, 1822).

An analyst with a particular interest in the relation between the internal past and internal future was Hans Loewald. In his paper, 'Psychoanalysis as an art and the fantasy character of the psychoanalytic situation', he describes how analysis helps patients to re-establish connections:

Figure 2.1 Johannes Vermeer, *The Kitchen Maid.*

… that give renewed meaning to memories and fantasy life and to the patient's actual life in the present. Insofar as the patient's experiences in the analytic situation become part of his mental life, they influence his future life.

(Loewald, 1980 [1975]: 367)

Loewald's paper 'Superego and time' proposes that, as physical structures are related to space, so psychic structures are related to time. He connects the superego with the future and, after listing certain of its functions, writes:

All this we can do with ourselves only insofar as we are ahead of ourselves, looking back at ourselves from a point of reference that is provided by the potentialities we envisage for ourselves or of which we despair. Conscience speaks to us from the viewpoint of an inner future.

(Loewald, 1980 [1962]: 46)

The resonance with *avant-coup* is striking.

Here is an episode from a clinical seminar.[5] A patient was presented whose childhood and adolescence had been very disturbed. He was abandoned in his earliest years by first one parent, then both; was looked after by a muddle of grandparents and neighbours; was reclaimed by one parent and subjected to a bizarre, eccentric lifestyle; then escaped to the other parent, by now a stranger, only to be treated more chaotically still. Certain features of the story were especially disturbing. Eventually he moved away and tried to put his life together, but became psychologically quite ill. Now he had found his way into analysis. I began the subsequent discussion by asking 'What has it been like for us, listening to this?' The seminar group felt overwhelmed by the absence of structure and boundaries, not just in this man's life, but in their own experience of listening to the story. The elements of which this man's nightmare was made up seemed to have no relation to each other. It was a kaleidoscope of random trauma. The unpredictability had been terrifying for him, and for the group it was unnerving to listen, with no idea what kind of shock might be coming next.

We tried as best we could to relate our listening experience to the details of the patient's history, and the seminar had been going on for about forty-five minutes when someone asked, 'How old is he?' This was a remarkable moment. A patient's age is basic information, mentioned in the first sentence of a presentation. If it is not, someone will always make a point of asking. Without it one does not know how to envisage the patient. Yet we had discussed this man for three-quarters of an hour and nobody had mentioned his age. We realised that the absence of temporal structure in the patient's experience had conveyed itself, through the presentation, into the group's listening, so that we were unconsciously caught up in it as well.

The presenter answered that the patient was in his late thirties. This was another jolt. We had all assumed we were hearing about someone at least ten years younger. There was a rush of questions about the history of these unexpected years. How had he lived? And where? For how long? Sexual relationships? Work? It was as though we were shocked by suddenly recognising how we had fallen out of time, and were trying to scramble back into it. I tried to help the group to avoid now using the patient's history as a refuge from the disconcerting timelessness in which we had been caught. I thought we needed to savour the quality of both at the same … time. To keep this interplay alive in the discussion was what mattered. Working to hold myself and the group at this point of intersection called for a particular kind of internal poise. I needed, in Bion's terms, to dream the seminar, so as to help the seminar group dream the patient; just as analysts need to dream their patients, so as to help their patients dream themselves.[6]

This intersection between time and timelessness arose out of a case discussion, but the point of the story is what happened in the seminar group. Now follows an example from the consulting room. It is not special or unusual but, for that very reason, it shows how these themes, though not necessarily manifest, can be found at work beneath the surface of any ordinary analysis.

The patient, a woman aged around sixty, began by commenting that a plant in my front garden seemed to be on its last legs. She then gave a long account of an argument with her husband. This led to a detailed description of a row they had had in a hotel years earlier. Then she talked about a man who knew her marriage was unhappy and wanted to have an affair with her, but she did not think he would give her the kind of relationship she wanted. She tried to explain this to him, but he did not understand. All this took about thirty minutes during which time I said nothing. After some silence, she said she was thinking about me going away. (My summer holiday was to start in two weeks' time.) She went back to talking about her would-be lover. He wanted her to spend time with him, but she did not want to have to put on a performance for him. She was fed up with role-playing.

I said I thought she was telling me that I was not giving her the relationship she wanted from me. I needed to know how to keep growing creatures alive, instead of abandoning them to die.

This is an obvious enough transference interpretation. But I am also doing something else. My oblique allusion to the plant, whose only mention had been half an hour previously, picks up something out of a past which the patient and I now share. Her comment felt significant at the time, and I am interested to see, from where we have got to now, what meaning the work of *après-coup* in the session will have given to it. Patients may get clues, from such an intervention, to a kind of unconscious structuring of experience that works by stitching significance back and forth between apparently diverse elements of it.

The patient caught my reference and said, 'It won't die. It just won't flower properly.'

I said, 'Ah! so it's not just about growing but about flowering.'

She said she thought that at her age she was more of a dying plant than a flowering one.

I said I thought this idea that she was past it was a role she had to play because she was frightened to let me know how much she did want to grow and flower.

Neither she nor I knows, at this stage, what we mean by the idea of her flowering. My move in the direction of *après-coup* seems to have led us into the realm of *avant-coup*. It is also worth noting that this talk of her potential for flowering has in the background the idea of her dying. I do not take it up in this session, but her death is undoubtedly in the room with us.

29

She said the trouble about the break is that at the moment I am the easiest relationship in her life, because I don't seem to mind what she does. But then she wondered: does that mean I don't *care* what she does?

'A big difference', I say.

'Very big', she answers, and says she is tired of people minding what she does all the time.

'And of always accommodating yourself to that', I add. (Living by compliance, that is to say.)

She said she thought everything she did was a performance. It went right down to her roots. There was nothing about her that did not have some kind of performance to it.

I said I thought it certainly went *back* to her roots, at the beginning of her life. Her father had seemed not to care what she did as long as she did not bother him.

She reacted strongly, saying that was absolutely what it had been like.

The role, I said, that she felt he wanted her to play was not to be there.

She told me there was a photograph of her on a beach, aged about nine, looking gawky and awkward. Her eyes didn't look the same as each other and her face was all askew. That was what she really felt like as a child.

I said, quietly but emphatically: '*That's* who you want to feel free to bring here.'

She talked more about other photos from her childhood and eventually said, 'Who I am has always been this awkward, graceless person.'

When she talks about her role-playing 'going down to her roots' it is something she believes about herself as a person. My shifting this to 'going *back* to her roots' makes it a statement about her history instead; and my comment about her father seeming to wish she were not there is a comment, again not elaborated, about her primal scene. It leads to the appearance of the awkward child that she has never been able to rearticulate by re-membering her from a fresh perspective. This failure of dynamic *après-coup* is reflected in her difficulties with *avant-coup* regarding her potential for the rest of her life.

She began the next session by saying she was surprised to discover that the self she offers to the world is, in fact, a bit of stage scenery, with the gawky little nine-year-old peeping out from behind it: a different person, she said, with very different needs. The idea that the nine-year-old could even *have* needs, let alone any thought of what they might be, is already a move towards re-membering her in a new way.

The question with which this book began, of what it means to be fully alive, has turned into a question about how past and future can become a field for the creation of meaning. This material shows the link between a patient's reconfiguring her understanding of her past and the chance of reconfiguring her availability to her future. It also illustrates that this work depends on patient and analyst 'living together' at an intersection in the present moment, between a temporality that extends between death and the primal scene, and the timelessness of a lifetime present in every moment.

Chapter 1 closed with the thought that being fully and creatively alive involves being imaginatively open to the inexorably *unheimlich* experience of one's own death. This might be rephrased now, to say that true aliveness involves the capacity to dream one's dying. Let us imagine a patient, a renowned musician, who tells the following dream. *His wife was bitten by a snake and died.*[7] *He went down into the underworld to try and bring her back. The King of the Underworld demanded that he show what a great musician he was. Enchanted by the patient's beautiful playing, the king agreed that his wife should return to the world of the living, on one condition: she would follow him out of the underworld, but he must not look back at her before they reached the upper world again. They started out, but the closer the patient got to the light, the more desperate he became to make sure his wife really was there behind him. Finally, he could not resist turning round. And there indeed she was, disappearing now helplessly back into the darkness.*

This is a dream about the failure of dreaming. The patient's wife represents an aspect of himself; his creative aliveness. Her death in the dream reveals his awareness that his own death is inevitable. But his desperation to undo the fact of her death shows that he finds this knowledge unbearable. For this man, life requires the negation of death, and to dream the death of his aliveness can be only a nightmare. To reassure himself against such *unheimlich* dread, he insists on a total separation between life and death, and has to invalidate whatever might call into question the absoluteness of this divide. He is offered the possibility of life, provided he can keep his wife, his creative self, alive in the dreaming vision of his imagination. The problem for him is that if his dreaming vision of her coming alive again is valid, his dreaming vision of her in the underworld must also be valid. Since he insists on an absolute disjunction between life and death, he has to check, as a concrete, physical fact, that he really has extracted her from the underworld. This inability to trust his imaginative vision condemns him to watch her, with his external vision, vanishing for ever. His need to protect himself against the awareness of his death makes it impossible for him to dream his aliveness into life.

The darkness of the underworld, home to disembodied spirits, where no events unfold, represents the timeless unconscious into which dreams drop their plumb line. The world above is structured in time. There, lives are lived and one thing leads to another. Orpheus respects only one kind of vision. He denies the intersection of the two worlds. The myth of Persephone, who had to live half the year in Hades and the other half on Earth, acknowledges that the underworld cannot be obliterated. This is an alternation between time and timelessness: they do not, in this myth, intersect. Hades' instruction to Orpheus points in a different direction.[8] He seems to say: 'You can take Eurydice with you, but not if that means killing off your awareness of this place. If you have to turn and check, by looking, that you are physically separating Eurydice from the underworld, she will be imaginatively dead to you. Create her with the inner vision of your imagination, and she will live'.

Like all great myths, the story of Orpheus and Eurydice embodies universal themes and has evoked multiple responses. In making use of it to prompt my own reflections I am following a well-trodden path. Maurice Blanchot's meditation on the myth, for example, takes Orpheus as the iconic figure of the artist. 'When Orpheus goes in search of Eurydice, art is the power that penetrates the dark' (Blanchot, 1982 [1955]: 177). But the true object of the artist's desire is 'the heart of darkness in the dark', and he can only attain this other darkness, which the dark conceals, by keeping his gaze averted. The artist is bound to transgress, however, and look at what he must not look at. For Blanchot it is paradoxically a condition of his artistic creativity that Orpheus should, in this way, sacrifice his art.[9] To Rainer Maria Rilke Orpheus brought liberation. Rilke (1923) records in the *Sonnets to Orpheus* how, after a barren period in his writing, he was released by the figure of Orpheus into fresh creativity.

> Do not put up a gravestone. Only let
> the rose bloom every year for him, for it
> itself is Orpheus. He becomes now this,
> now that, coming and going, continually
> transformed. No need to search for other names.
> Whatever sings is always Orpheus.
>
> (Rilke, 1923: I, 5: 1–6)

Rilke learns from Orpheus that '*Gesang ist Dasein*' (I, 3: 7)—'Song is Being'—and the sequence closes:

> And when you are forgotten by the world,
> tell the silent earth: I flow.
> To the whisper of the water say: I am.
>
> (Rilke, 1923: II, 29: 12–14)[10]

The universal theme contained in the reading of the myth I offer here is that of a developmental challenge. Unconscious psychic structures created in the vicissitudes of childhood may inhibit the development of potential, and this may bring people into therapy in the hope of changing. These structures, though, have become *heimlich*. They are hidden and secret and, in the older meaning of the word (see p.16 n.3), they are a familiar home base from which it may be hard to venture out. If my Orpheus-patient were a real patient, who brought this Orpheus-dream to a session, the fact of his being able to have a dream that represents his failure of dreaming, and his desire to tell the dream, would be, as I put it earlier, a bid for aliveness: a bid to recover his dreaming by inhabiting, not fleeing from, the place where time and timelessness meet.

My task as analyst would be to do likewise, helping him to stay poised at that intersection by listening to his dream from the same crossing point myself.

A patient in middle age, whose mother died of a sudden illness during his childhood, was living his life on the assumption that she was still alive. Most of what he did was based on trying to please her and justify himself in her eyes. He had never truly grieved her loss, because he had not lost her. He was unconsciously afraid that if he did let her become part of his past, not only would he feel terribly bereft, but she also would feel desperate at being abandoned by him. Some three years into his analysis, he had come to understand quite well the structure of his intrapsychic scenario, and it was only too clear how the requirement to be his dead mother's perfect little boy was blighting his life. On the other hand, he seemed to have no desire to give this up. Then one day, he said that on his way to the session, walking in the beautiful sunshine and enjoying its warmth, he had found himself feeling completely relaxed and thinking he did not have a care in the world. At that moment he suddenly became frightened. The same thing had happened the night before: lying in bed, he realised that all his problems seemed to have sorted themselves out. This thought scared him, and he began trying desperately to think of something he needed to worry about. I remarked on his fear of being free of his difficulties, and he said that having no anxieties would be like being made to change profession, like a chef who was suddenly required to work as a carpenter when he knew nothing about wood.

There is a powerful attachment to what is *heimlich*. The work of analysis, and the work of creative aliveness in whatever situation, is to question such structures, momentarily opening doors to the *Unheimliche* of greater freedom. The terror of passing through these doors is the terror of not going on being the self that is familiar: the terror of dying. It takes courage and time to discover that beyond them may lie a fuller kind of living.

This patient is terrified of death. More particularly he is terrified of reaching his death feeling he has done nothing with his life and made no use of it; just as my mythic Orpheus-patient, being unable to dream his death, could not be truly alive. The real patient exemplifies very specifically the internal predicament that I used the imaginary patient to describe. He also is trying to deal with the death of a woman who was central to his life. His problem is that instead of carrying her in his imagination while he looks ahead to where life is to be lived, he cannot stop looking over his shoulder to confirm that she is alive in a reality which is delusional. If only he could accept her death, then he really could keep her alive in his imagination. And who knows? This might give him more chance of dreaming his own death in a way that would allow him to be more imaginatively alive.

It must be said, though, that for this man to register the experiences which reveal the *unheimlich*, frightening quality that internal freedom has for him, and for him to start his session by telling them, is like my imaginary patient being able to have his Orpheus-dream and then to bring it. Out of some inward

Hades he is trying to offer himself the chance of dreaming his way back down the experience of his life, and of finding fresh meanings in it. This might help him also to dream a wider range of potential meaning into his yet unlived life. He would have less need, then, to fear a sense of meaninglessness when, finally, he does cross the event horizon of his death.

Notes

1 Compare the more linguistic formulation of Lacan:

> What is realised in my history is neither the past definite as what was, since it is no more, nor even the perfect as what has been in what I am, but the future anterior in what I will have been, given what I am in the process of becoming.
>
> Lacan (2006 [1953]: 247)

2 Compare these quotations from *Four Quartets* with the following passage from an essay by Eliot:

> The historical sense involves a perception, not only of the pastness of the past, but of its presence ... This historical sense, which is a sense of the timeless as well as of the temporal and of the timeless and of the temporal together, is what makes a writer traditional. And it is at the same time what makes a writer most acutely conscious of his place in time, of his contemporaneity.
>
> (Eliot, 1920: 44)

3 The painting measures 45.5 × 41 cm. It will be displayed differently from 2013, following the Rijksmuseum's refurbishment.

4 X-ray evidence shows that Vermeer obliterated a picture, or map, that he had originally placed on the wall (Wheelock, 1995: 108f).

5 I am grateful to the presenter for permission to mention this case.

6 This kind of 'dreaming' is discussed further in relation to 'reverie' and 'imaginative perception' in Chapter 10 (pp.157f).

7 As in the Garden of Eden, the serpent, mankind's primal enemy, introduces death, and the inexorability of time. (I am indebted to Melanie Hart for this thought.)

8 In Greek mythology Hades was the underworld realm inhabited by the spirits of the dead. 'Hades' was also the name of the god who ruled over it.

9 See Davies (2011) for some illuminating comments on Blanchot's essay.

10 See Hass (1987: xxxviii–xliv) for an insightful discussion of the *Sonnets to Orpheus*.

3

MORE ABOUT MEMORY

This chapter picks up and elaborates a single topic from the previous two chapters: that of memory. Memory was discussed in those chapters sufficiently to support their argument, and to go into greater detail would have unbalanced them. However, there is more to say about memory that is relevant to the issues they raise, and this chapter continues the discussion of the topic on a broader front.

Two distinct views of memory appeared in Chapters 1 and 2. It may be considered as a process of recollection, reproducing accurately a record of experience that has been lodged in the mind, more or less unchanged, since the events in question happened. On the other hand, a person remembering can be seen as creating more actively in the present moment the experience of memory in relation to the past. Among researchers in the field of memory both these views have been held. The former has been referred to as the 'reappearance hypothesis' of memory (Neisser, 1967: 285). According to the latter view, by contrast, our recollections are not mere records of facts: they reflect the manner in which we elaborate our experience. 'Memories are not simply activated pictures in the mind but complex constructions' (Schacter, 1996: 209). This second view of memory is known as the 'constructivist' hypothesis.

The reappearance hypothesis is illustrated dramatically by the work of the neurosurgeon Wilder Penfield in the 1950s. In cases of intractable epilepsy, Penfield would surgically remove the cluster of cells in the brain which was generating the epileptic seizures. He determined the location of this focus by stimulating areas of the brain electrically, while the patient was still conscious. In the course of this work he observed that when particular areas in the temporal lobe were stimulated the patient would relive an experience from the past, crystal clear in the present moment. Restimulation of the same area would reliably bring back a vivid re-experiencing, in just the same form, of the same memory. On the face of it, this seemed strong evidence that a record of experience was laid down as a neural memory trace, which could be reactivated to yield a memory that was an accurate reproduction of the original event (Penfield, 1969; Penfield and Perot, 1963).

This appears to correspond well with Freud's favourite comparison between memory and archaeology (Breuer and Freud, 1893–5: 139; Freud, 1896b: 192, 198; 1901b: 12; 1909: 176; 1937a: 259–60). Freud likens the scraps of memory and fragmentary associations, from which an analyst reconstructs the patient's early life, to the long-buried artefacts and foundations of ruined buildings from which an archaeologist reconstructs a vanished civilisation. The implication is that what is buried in the patient's mind remains there in its original form until the analyst digs it up and reveals it.

Caution is required, however. An artefact has no significance until the archaeologist decides what it is. Even material objects dug out of the ground have to be interpreted. The excavations of Heinrich Schliemann provide a famous example. Schliemann was a German merchant turned archaeologist who was obsessed with the idea of proving that Homer's *Iliad* was literal truth. Excavating in Turkey in the early 1870s, he discovered what is, indeed, now accepted as the site of Troy. His excavations uncovered quantities of impressive gold ornaments and jewellery. What had he found? For Schliemann, this was unquestionably the treasure of Priam and the jewels of Helen. These artefacts were, for him, the corroboration of Homer. For later archaeologists they are evidence relating to technological development and trading connections at a certain period in the history of Anatolia. The objects are the same all along, but to say what they are is necessarily to interpret them.

Freud gives another analogy in his paper 'A Note upon the "Mystic Writing Pad"' (Freud, 1925a). He reminds the reader that he has previously asked why endless new impressions do not clog up the mind's storage capacity (Freud, 1900: 540). Despite an ever-increasing store of memories the mind manages to stay open to new experience. Now Freud has come across a device which illustrates in material terms what he thinks must go on in the mind. The children's toy known as the 'Mystic Writing Pad' is a small block with three components. The surface is a sheet of celluloid, behind which there is a sheet of transparent waxed paper. Immediately behind this, in contact with the paper, is a layer of wax. The sheet of celluloid is fixed, but the paper behind it can be moved. Scoring the celluloid with a stylus depresses the waxed paper onto the wax, and words written or pictures drawn like this remain visible. If the paper beneath the celluloid is moved, however, its contact with the wax behind it is broken and the lines imprinted in the wax no longer show up. Words and pictures disappear and the block is free to be used again. What intrigues Freud especially is that, although what was written or drawn on the block is no longer visible, the marks made by the stylus remain inscribed in the layer of wax underneath the paper. Dismantle the apparatus and there they are, still legible 'in suitable lights' (Freud, 1925a: 230). The analogy with the limitless storage capacity of the mind holds only so far. The wax block will eventually become so covered with inscriptions that new impressions do obliterate old ones. Leaving this quibble aside, however, we can accept Freud's statement that the Mystic Writing Pad provides 'both an ever-ready receptive surface and permanent traces of the notes that have been made upon it' (Freud, 1925a: 228).

The reappearance hypothesis of how memory operates is illustrated very clearly by the Mystic Writing Pad. Freud's enthusiasm for the analogy between it and his model of the mind is evident, and he explores the parallels in detail. The image of a trace which disappears from the surface but is preserved at a deeper level, ready for a suitable light to reveal it as it was originally inscribed, clearly corresponds to his view of mental functioning and the work of analysis.

This view of the mind as a container of memories was shared by another notable writer on the subject. The *Confessions* of Augustine of Hippo, one of the greatest of philosophers and theologians, date from the end of the fourth century AD. In this spiritual autobiography Augustine tries to understand the workings of his inner life. Book 10 is largely given over to considering the nature of memory.

Augustine sees memory as a kind of internal space where the records of what he experiences—sounds, visual images, physical sensations, events of all sorts—are contained. He writes of memory as a 'treasure-house of innumerable images', and of the 'more hidden reservoirs' and 'unnumbered caverns' of his memory (Augustine, *Confessions* 10.8.12, 10.17.26). His most striking image of this sort occurs when he is puzzled about how one can recollect times of sadness, or of happiness, without necessarily feeling sad or happy as one remembers them.[1] He says memory must be 'like the mind's stomach', where food taken in is stored but no longer tasted. Recollection is like what happens when a ruminant animal brings something back up from the stomach to chew it over again. Augustine laughs at his analogy, but still thinks it is a good one (10.14.21).

So far, so like the Mystic Writing Pad, which also contains the record, invisible until brought back into view, of its past impressions.[2] For Augustine, however, memory is far more than a receptacle for past experience. Any kind of understanding is related by him in the end to memory. Moral behaviour and spiritual aspiration, for example, depend on recognising concepts that have already been encountered and laid up in memory (10.20.29). Scientific knowledge and understanding of the liberal arts depend on remembered experience. Some ideas do not draw on sensory perception but arise from the mind's internal thought processes. But even these, says Augustine, we arrive at by organising piecemeal bits of knowledge which do originate from sense experience and are available in memory (10.11.18). Knowledge itself, once acquired, becomes an object of memory.

However completely Augustine tries to explore the nature of memory he never comes to its end (10.17.26). The function of memory expands for him, in fact, to the point where it equates to the mind as a whole. 'It is I who remember, I my own mind' (10.16.25). 'Great is the strength of memory, something unknown and awesome ... a deep and infinite multiplicity; and this is my mind, this is my very self' (10.17.26).

Most people experience themselves, like Augustine, as having a more or less stable sense of their identity linked to a more or less reliable recollection (gaps notwithstanding) of their lives to date. We have, as it appears to us, a store of memories which constitute the record of how we came to be the selves we know. To call up a memory, or be reminded of something, is to retrieve an item stored in this memory bank, or have it brought to our attention, and we keep it in awareness until it is time for it to slip back again into the 'unnumbered caverns'. This account corresponds so clearly to subjective experience that it is easily taken for granted, and the 'reappearance hypothesis' of memory may seem like a statement of the obvious. Endell Tulving, well known for his research on memory in the 1980s, spoke of the 'overpowering influence' of the traditional theory that a memory is simply the activated record of a past event (Schacter, 1996: 71).

According to the constructivist hypothesis, by contrast, our memories are not just factual records of our experience. The relation between our present recollections and what happened in the past is more fluid and complicated. This may feel disconcerting, and even seem to put at risk our sense of who we are. Nevertheless, scientific opinion regarding memory has moved decisively in this direction. In Tulving's time an investigation of views held about memory showed 84% of psychologists believing that memory is an accurate record of experience stored permanently in the mind, which persists, available for recall, in the form in which it was laid down (Loftus and Loftus, 1980). Nowadays, virtually all psychologists would disagree. In 2009, a comparable study asked a sample of the general population, and a group of psychologists, whether memory 'accurately records the events we see and hear so that we can review and inspect them later', and whether 'once you have experienced an event and formed a memory of it, that memory does not change'. The psychologists universally rejected both statements (Simons and Chabris, 2011).

This dramatic shift of view is the result of two factors. The first is the reconsideration of previously accepted results. For example, Wilder Penfield's work, mentioned above, had been received with great enthusiasm. Careful examination of his data, however, revealed that only a very small proportion, in the range of 3–8%, of his patients receiving temporal lobe stimulation reported anything that could be interpreted as a memory. Nor did Penfield establish adequately whether these reports were memories of actual events, fantasies or hallucinations (Loftus and Loftus, 1980; Schacter, 1996: 77f). The second factor has been a series of investigations which demonstrate that remembering does not consist simply of retrieving a record of past experience. Several of these are described usefully and accessibly by Daniel Schacter (1996: 18ff, 39ff), a leading researcher on the topic of memory.

It is worth saying a word about what sort of memory has been the subject of these investigations. Augustine showed how closely the sense of self is bound up with the faculty of memory. The identities we form are rooted in the experience of our lives, and if we are able to remember something it is because it has been part of that experience. In this respect all memory is autobiographical by definition. There is a difference, however, between the everyday memories that come to us of particular episodes in our lives, and the deliberate use of memory to recapture our life story. The former are known as 'episodic' memories. Reflecting on our lives as a whole involves using memory in other ways besides this, and the term 'autobiographical memory' generally denotes the full range of memory usage that is brought into play when we think in specifically autobiographical fashion. Episodic memories form only part of the complex autobiographical memory system. They lend themselves, however, to controlled investigation and experiment, and for this reason they are the memories that the research just mentioned has tended to study.

Such memories are classed into 'field' and 'observer' categories, depending on whether the person remembering sees themselves as a figure in the scene or not. In a field memory it is as though they are looking out through their own eyes, recalling what was in their visual field at the time. The rememberer does not appear in the scene. In an observer memory, on the other hand, the person remembering sees the whole scene, including themselves, and can observe the part they were playing in it. One research study called for people to remember personal events from their lives. Some were asked to do so while focusing on the feelings attached to the episode remembered, while others were asked to focus on its factual content. The subjects focusing on their feelings reported more field memories, while the group focusing on the objective situation reported more observer memories (Nigro and Neisser, 1983). This implies that significant aspects of the way an event is remembered may be constructed at the time of recall, depending on how the rememberer's mind is working at that moment. In another study participants were asked to recall episodes from their lives, noting whether these yielded field or observer memories. They were also asked how emotionally intense both the original experience, and its recollection in the present, had been. Some of those who had produced field memories were then asked to recall the same episodes again, but switching viewpoints, so that this time they remembered them in the observer mode. This group reported that the original experience now felt less intense and that its recollection also produced less emotion (Robinson and Swanson, 1993). This indicates that the emotional value given to past events may be governed by circumstances in the present surrounding the recall of the memory. In another experiment (Tulving, 1985: 7f), people were shown a list of words, and were then asked to recall as many of them as they could. For each item recalled, the subjects were asked to indicate 'whether they actually "remembered" its occurrence on the list, or whether they simply "knew" on some other basis that the item was a member of the study list'. Subjects who recalled an item spontaneously were more likely to say that they remembered it specifically, whereas subjects who were given extra hints to trigger their memory were more likely to say that they just knew somehow that the word had been on the list. Schacter (1996: 25) comments on this result that 'once again, the recollective experience of the rememberer depends on the way in which a memory is retrieved'.

Research also suggests that a memory is not lodged in the mind as a complete, unitary experience. Neuropsychological studies using brain-imaging techniques show that no single location in the brain contains the complete record of a particular past experience (Damasio, 1989; Damasio and Damasio, 1994). Incoming data are represented in more or less fragmentary form, and it is out of these bits and pieces of recorded experience that memories as we know them subjectively are constructed. 'The retrieved memory is a temporary constellation of activity in several distinct brain regions—a construction with many contributors' (Schacter, 1996: 66).

How the piecemeal elements of experience are encoded in the first place depends not only on their objective form, but also, to a great degree, on what is going on in our minds at the time, and on the ways of encoding experience that have become habitual to us. (The question of how individuals develop their particular strategies for encoding experience is one that psychoanalysts, from their own perspective, are constantly concerned with.) Again when it comes to retrieval, the manner in which these stored elements are elaborated to form a memory may be influenced considerably by what stimulates the recollection. For example, subjects were shown photographs of people while hearing them speak in either a pleasant or unpleasant fashion. Later they reviewed the photographs, and tried to remember whether the person in question had spoken pleasantly or unpleasantly. There was, in fact, no correlation between facial expression and tone of voice; but when the face had a smile people were more likely to remember the voice as being pleasant, while the opposite was true if the face had an unfriendly expression (Schacter, 1996: 70f). A memory, it appears, is a product of the original experience together with the present-time situation in which it is remembered.

The studies mentioned so far have dealt with the recall of particular events happening at a certain time and place. Extending beyond these 'episodic' memories, as was noted earlier, is a larger, more complex, system of 'autobiographical' memory. Episodic memory is only one component in a hierarchy of types of recollection, which together make up the subjective experience of a person's life story.

This hierarchy of autobiographical memories has three levels (Conway and Rubin, 1993; Conway and Pleydell-Pearce, 2000). Whole segments of a lifetime, perhaps encompassing many years, may be remembered as an entity. 'My adolescence', 'the time I spent at university', 'when I used to live abroad', 'since I have retired': these are examples of 'lifetime periods'. One level down from lifetime periods is the recollection of so-called 'general events'. This is a term used in memory research to denote sets of events that are linked in some way. Maybe they were regular occurrences, such as the matches of my local football team that I remember going to. Or they might cluster round a theme, such as the things I did and places I went to in pursuing some hobby or interest. I do not recall every single football match, but I remember vividly how it mattered to me to go and support my team. I do not recollect every cathedral city I visited, or every book I read about gothic architecture, but I have a general memory of those weekend expeditions and the lectures I went to. Below this 'general events' level of memory comes the memory of specific individual events and the circumstances surrounding them: 'that time I got lost when I was five', 'my first serious date', 'when I played so badly in the final', 'moving into the new house'. This is the level of episodic memory.

Autobiographical memory seems radically personal. When we call up memories of our past it is the private experience of our own lives that we are recollecting. We may naturally assume that this is something we register and retain, in greater or lesser detail, and that when we think autobiographically we are accessing a subjective history of ourselves that we carry within us. Where autobiographical memory is concerned, when we are dealing with our own personal life story, surely then, at least, the reappearance hypothesis must be valid, and we can believe we are revisiting in the present the record that we laid down of events in our past.

However, one category of autobiographical memory is that of episodic memory, and we have seen already that such memories may, to a large extent, be constructed as they are remembered. This may feel bewildering enough, but what if the autobiographical memory system as a whole, despite our subjective conviction of knowing our own history, operates in the same way?

There is an extensive scientific literature, valuably reviewed by Holland and Kensinger (2010), to show that this is in fact the case. Autobiographical memory is not stored in the brain as a historic record of events, but is put together in the act of remembering (see especially Conway, 1996; Conway and Pleydell-Pearce, 2000).

Autobiographical memory has been thought to serve various purposes, but three functions for it in particular are generally recognised: directive, social and self-representative (Bluck et al., 2005). The directive function draws on past experience as a guide for handling situations in the present; for solving current problems and planning future courses of action. A social function is served when autobiographical memories are used for sharing and comparing experiences in a way that helps develop social bonds and relationships. Personal memories of a life are also important in consolidating a coherent sense of identity. This is the self-representative function of autobiographical memory. Bluck and her colleagues emphasise especially its importance for a sense of personal continuity: the capacity to maintain a biographical identity, and a coherent self-concept, across an entire lifespan (Bluck et al., 2005: 110).

Autobiographical memories do not appear in our minds by chance. When we recall what has happened to us in the past, it is because something in the present has induced us to do so. Depending on which of the functions just described, or what mixture of them, an autobiographical memory is being asked to fulfil, we draw on the various possible levels of autobiographical memory to provide the kind of recollection that will meet the need of the moment.

41

Lifetime periods are extended chapters in our lives which serve as large-scale reference points, lending overall structure to how we think about our existence. Groups of 'general event' memories give us more detail about ourselves, while still evoking distinctive aspects of the general flavour of our lives. Episodic memories contain autobiographical knowledge related to single individual events: so-called 'event-specific knowledge'.

The directive function requires autobiographical memories to contain sufficient detail to provide a guide, or 'schema', for thinking and action that can be generalised to fresh situations in the present and future. Memories at the 'general events' level, which evoke patterns of behaviour, are more helpful for this than memory couched in terms of lifetime periods. If patterns of general events do not yield a useful schema, we may have to draw on event-specific knowledge from individual episodic memories (Pillemer, 2003).

The social function brings into play memories from all three levels of the hierarchy. Comparing the experience of lifetime periods, sharing interests and concerns embodied in 'general event' memories, and going into detail about particular happenings in our lives, all combine in myriad ways, depending on what kind of intimate or formal, individual or collective, relationships we are establishing and consolidating.

Where representation of the self is concerned, and especially its continuity, lifetime periods are the most significant ingredient of autobiographical memory. Memories of general events may also be important as an expression of what was occupying us during a certain period, but event-specific knowledge based on a single episode will probably have only a small part to play.

Neuropsychological research has identified an autobiographical memory network located in certain areas of the prefrontal cortex, the posterior cingulate cortex and the medial temporal lobe, especially the hippocampus. Within this overall network, recollection at the different autobiographical levels, of lifetime periods, general events and specific episodes, activates different neuronal systems (Ford, Addis and Giovanello, 2011; Holland and Kensinger, 2010: sec. 2.2). Thus, the particular psychological purpose that prompts us to call up memories from our past makes the brain operate in specific ways to give us the kind of autobiographical memory we need at that precise moment. It has also been shown that 'emotions and emotional goals experienced at the time of autobiographical retrieval can influence the information recalled' (Holland and Kensinger, 2010: 88). This is to say that not only do the quality and intensity of the original experience affect what remembering it is like. That much is not surprising. In addition, the content and emotional quality of a memory are influenced by the context in which it is recalled, and by a person's emotional situation at the time of recall: a finding that is pertinent for the psychoanalytic process. Holland and Kensinger (2010: secs. 3 & 4) review studies showing that both factual details in autobiographical memories, and the emotions remembered as being associated with events in our lives, are reconstructed in the process of remembering.

Tulving's comment, on the 'overpowering influence' of the idea that a memory is the activated record of a past event, has already been noted (p.38). Penfield's work, for example, until it came to be examined in more detail, had aroused an enormously enthusiastic response. It seemed to provide scientific confirmation of subjective, intuitive assumptions about how we record and store our personal histories. Maybe one reason it was so hard even for professionals to give up the traditional view of memory is that our sense of identity is so much bound up with autobiographical memory. The idea that memories of our own lives are not stable—in a way that lets us take them out, look at them and put them back in the drawer again—might seem threatening to our ideas of who we are. Nevertheless, the research referred to above suggests that 'we must leave behind our familiar preconceptions if we are to understand how we convert the fragmentary remains of experience into autobiographical narratives' that become 'tales of who we are' (Schacter, 1996: 71, 73).

In literature, one of the most famous acts of memory is the recollection by Marcel, the narrator in Marcel Proust's novel *In Search of Lost Time* (Proust, 1992 [1913–1927]), of the taste of the madeleine dipped in tea which his aunt Léonie used to give him as a child on Sunday mornings. Jonah Lehrer (2007: 75–95) takes this as the starting point for a comparison between Proust's view of memory, which he developed by intuitive introspection, and recent scientific research on the subject. Lehrer notes, for example, that Marcel's memory of Aunt Léonie giving him the madeleine does not float unbidden into his mind. Something unknown is evoked by the taste of a madeleine Marcel eats while taking tea with his mother, and he then has to make several attempts at recapturing the origin of the mysterious sensation. To begin with these fail, and Marcel realises that the answer must lie not in the objective taste of the tea-soaked madeleine, but in what he is doing with that taste in his mind. This releases the memory of the Sunday mornings with Aunt Léonie, as a narrative reconstructed by Marcel in the present moment. Lehrer mentions apparent inconsistencies in the novel, such as the beauty spot on Albertine's face which appears in different places at different times: now her cheek; now her chin; now her lip. But this should not be seen as carelessness on Proust's part. The instability of memory is what the novel is all about. Lehrer quotes a letter from Proust to Jacques Rivière: 'I am obliged to depict errors without feeling compelled to say that I consider them to be errors' (Lehrer, 2007: 82).

The stories of our lives, so familiar and essential a part of our being, are apparently not based on a persisting inner historical record, but are assembled in the present from what Schacter (above) described as 'fragmentary remains'. This is disconcerting indeed and not, perhaps, the kind of archaeology that Freud had in mind. Researchers whose work has led to this conclusion sometimes feel the need to justify it by explaining its counterintuitive advantages.

Much work has demonstrated that our personal memories contain inaccuracies or imperfections, even for highly arousing and personally significant events. Although it is tempting to view these distortions as problematic, it is informative to consider these findings in light of the functions of autobiographical memory ... For example, remembering our past experiences and behaviors as more positive than they actually were may allow us to maintain a coherent, positive sense of self and to forge positive social relationships. Similarly, the flexibility in the construction of events at retrieval may enable us to direct our future behavior and to regulate our emotions.

(Holland and Kensinger, 2010: 109)

This latter point is also emphasised by Schacter and Addis:

Future events are not exact replicas of past events, and a memory system that simply stored rote records would not be well-suited to simulating future events. A system built according to constructive principles may be a better tool for the job: it can draw on the elements and gist of the past, and extract, recombine and reassemble them into imaginary events that never occurred in that exact form. Such a system will occasionally produce memory errors, but it also provides considerable flexibility.

(Schacter and Addis, 2007)

Interestingly, this recalls a statement by Augustine. He comments that memory deals not only with the past, but with present experience. He can only recognise things for what they are because his memory already contains knowledge of them (*Conf.* 10.15.23). And the work of memory embraces not only the present but extends even into the future.

There [in memory] is everything that I remember, either from experience or having come to believe it. From this same store I weave together the likenesses of things experienced, or believed on the basis of my experience, with what has happened in the past. *And from this I consider even my future actions, outcomes and hopes, contemplating all these as though they were back in the present.*

(Augustine, *Conf.* 10.8.14; author's emphasis)

Augustine's 'weaving together' of memory with a 'contemplation' of his future 'actions, outcomes and hopes' has a more existential flavour than Schacter's and Addis' comments, couched in the pragmatic language of autobiographical memory's 'directive' function. Augustine seems to accept that this perpetual resonance of past, present and future is part of what being human involves. His statement corresponds strikingly to the necessity, stressed in Chapters 1 and 2, for a freedom of imaginative movement up and down the entirety of a life, in both directions. Schacter and Addis, as well as Holland and Kensinger, certainly emphasise, on the basis of their research, that there is no such thing as the uncontaminated record of a past event. A memory is bound to be influenced by the context and circumstances of its recollection. When they refer, however, to 'inaccuracies or imperfections' and 'errors' of memory, this seems to imply that there could be a more accurate, veridical version of the past if only we were able to reach it.

We see again how hard it is to give up the desire for a definitive account of our lives that will be unquestionably authentic and reliable. But the personal history that our memory constructs is not an approximation to some real truth that regrettably eludes us. It is all we have and all we can ever have. Its indeterminate quality is, in fact, the very thing that enables our psychic growth. Psychoanalysts, as well as research psychologists, have had their difficulties in recognising this. Donald Spence's (1982) book *Narrative Truth and Historical Truth* argued that the clinical aim, of recovering memories which gave a true record of a patient's life history, was not merely difficult in practice, but theoretically impossible in the first place. Spence argued that for all sorts of reasons the patient's free association and the analyst's free-floating attention did not, and more importantly could not in principle, produce recollections by a patient whose factual accuracy could be trusted. The fundamental purpose of his book was to make analysts 'sceptical about the role of historical truth in the psychoanalytic process' (Spence, 1982: 28). In his foreword to the book Robert Wallerstein, who was soon to be President of the International Psychoanalytical Association, wrote of its 'extraordinarily disturbing implications for our discipline' (Wallerstein, 1982: 13). Reviewers of the book also found it troubling. One said it questioned 'whether or not psychoanalysis has ever been what it purports to be' (Ahlskog, 1983: 291). Another said that 'in this most subversive book, [Spence] attacks the scientific foundations for psychoanalytic work' (Shengold, 1985: 240). The conflict of views among analysts about the role of memory continued, and even seventeen years later, Peter Fonagy, for example, could say that 'some still appear to believe that the recovery of memory is part of the therapeutic action of the treatment. There is no evidence for this and in my view to cling to this idea is damaging to the field' (Fonagy, 1999: 215).

In Shengold's review of Spence's book, he accepts implicitly, as Spence insists and the research cited above demonstrates, that autobiographical truthfulness is not a matter of arriving at a definitive version of the historical record, but he resists Spence's wholesale dismissal of historical truth. Holland and Kensinger's remark already quoted, shows where such a dismissal can lead: 'remembering our past experiences and behaviors as more positive than they actually were may allow us to maintain a coherent, positive sense of self'. Yes, but at what cost in terms of denial and repression? A 'coherent, positive sense of self' achieved in this way is founded on unconscious internal dishonesty, and will be correspondingly fragile. An authentic identity depends on being true to one's sense of self. If the history on which our sense of self is based has no fixed form, does this mean we are at liberty to invent, or discard, whatever identity we care to? What happens then to the notion of authenticity? This is not to disagree with the research findings, but to recognise that they pose profound ethical questions.[3] Shengold points in this direction at the conclusion of his review.

> Aiming for 'historical' truth while realising we can only approximate it keeps analysts *moral*, tempering the temptation to supply soothing or seductive 'narrative fit'. Reading Spence's book, and taking his critique in moderation, can help keep us from becoming *righteous*—so that we can do our necessary and necessarily deficient exploration with full and humble awareness of our limitations.
>
> (Shengold, 1985: 244)

The autobiographical use of memory is not itself in question. For patients to feel that their life story belongs to them, and that they are connected to their developmental history, is at the heart of psychoanalytic work. The doubt concerns recollection which purports to recover the objective truth of facts as they 'really' happened. The scientific research I have described confirms something which many analysts, whatever the official theory may be, have understood for a long time from their clinical experience. It is not a matter of delineating what kind of once-and-for-all experience in the past has determined who we are. What counts is that we can continually create for ourselves, actively though largely unconsciously, an identity whose flexible plasticity allows growth and development to continue throughout life.

> To be adult means among other things to see one's own life in perspective, both in retrospect and prospect. By accepting some definition as to who he is, usually on the basis of a function in an economy, a place in the sequence of generations, and a status in the structure of society, the adult is able to selectively reconstruct his past in such a way that, step for step, it seems to have planned him, or better, he seems to have planned it. In this sense, psychologically we do choose our parents, our family history, and the history of our kings, heroes and gods. By making them our own, we manoeuver ourselves into the inner position of proprietors, of creators.
>
> (Erikson, 1958: 111f)

Note Erikson's phrase 'both in retrospect and prospect'. Psychoanalysts do, of course, try to help people discover, and confront if necessary, truths about themselves. But they are equally concerned to help people, through the processes of *après-coup* and *avant-coup* discussed in Chapters 1 and 2, not to feel locked by their memories into any single, fixed view of themselves, their past, or their future.

Notes

1   Compare Dante, *Inferno*, Canto 5, 121–123:
     There is no greater pain
     than to remember times of happiness
     in present misery.
2   Like Freud, Augustine knows his metaphor is only a metaphor. He writes of 'an inner place that is not a place' (10.9.16), and asks why he should look for the place in his memory where God abides 'as though there really were places in it' (10.25.36).
3   How analysts assess the capacity of patients to be inwardly honest with themselves is a question beyond the scope of this chapter, but the discussions of countertransference in Chapters 9 and 10 are relevant.

4

IN DEFENCE OF THE UNCANNY

'Things are what they seem to be, or maybe something else'. This unsettling statement, which was the theme prescribed for a photography competition (Kalvar, 2011), captures how the uncanny both does and does not belong to everyday life. It is an ambush, making what should be familiar feel suddenly spooky and dislocated. Such eerie moments are not quite part of ordinary experience, and yet the feeling is recognisable. This is normal abnormality. When Freud wrote a book dealing with 'unintentional' slips of the tongue, 'mistaken' actions, and so on, he called it '*The Psychopathology of Everyday Life*' (Freud, 1981a). The paper he wrote about the uncanny shows him fascinated by it as a phenomenon, but in the end it seemed to him a similar intrusion of pathology into ordinary life (Freud, 1919b).

Freud admired and appreciated the deliberate use of the uncanny for artistic purposes, and a fascination with this continues today, often linked specifically to Freud's paper. In 2008, a collection of short stories appeared, entitled *The New Uncanny: Tales of Unease* (Eyre and Page, 2008). It was generated by the editors' idea of sending a copy of Freud's paper to a number of authors and inviting them to write a story prompted by their reading of it. Where the visual arts are concerned, Caterina Albano's (2008) article, 'The uncanny: a dimension of contemporary art', is an example. A book with the intriguing title, *The Architectural Uncanny: Essays in the Modern Unhomely*, again draws on Freud's paper, describing the uncanny as 'a disquieting slippage between what is homely and what is definitively unhomely' (Vidler, 1992: ix–x). In certain urban architectural environments, says the author, 'subjectivity is rendered heterogeneous, nomadic, and self-critical in vagabond environments that refuse the commonplaces of hearth and home in favour of the uncertainties of no-man's-land' (Vidler, 1992: xiii). One may also be vagabond and nomadic, with commonplace assurances lost, in certain internal, psychic environments, and the quotation rings true for the experience of the uncanny to be described later in this chapter.

E.T.A. Hoffmann's story 'The Sandman' (1817) was a paradigm example for Freud of the uncanny being creatively deployed as an aesthetic device. He wrote of 'the quite unparalleled atmosphere of uncanniness' which it evokes

(Freud, 1919b: 227), and it is evident that he admired it greatly as a work of art. When it comes to the uncanny in real life, however, Freud is still fascinated but somewhat disparaging of the experience. 'The uncanny as it is depicted in *literature*, in stories and imaginative productions … is a much more fertile province than the uncanny in real life' (Freud, 1919b: 249). Psychologically mature people, Freud believed, should not be subject in their own lives to uncanny experiences. He comments as follows on the weird coincidences which kept appearing in the Rat Man's life.

> There can be no doubt that the patient felt a need for finding experiences of this kind to act as props for his superstition, and that it was for that reason that he occupied himself so much with the inexplicable coincidences of everyday life with which we are all familiar, and helped out their shortcomings with unconscious activity of his own.
>
> (Freud, 1909: 231)

Freud thought that for the uncanny to enter one's personal experience revealed a failure to surmount primitive modes of mental functioning, and he considered such happenings to be essentially a mark of immaturity (Freud, 1919b: 247–9; see the quotations on p.11).

This negative view was queried in Chapter 1 (pp.11f) and the present chapter continues this critique. In the first place, Freud's distinction between the admissible uncanny, as an aspect of a literary text, and the inadmissible uncanny, as an element of subjective experience, is hard to sustain. A text cannot be considered in isolation from its readers. Not only will texts look different according to the lenses (feminist, post-colonial, psychoanalytic etc.) through which they are viewed and read, but individuals also bring to them their own perspectives, conscious and unconscious. The aesthetic qualities of a text cannot be separated from the reader's experience of it. Frank Kermode's (2010) essay 'Eliot and the shudder' makes it especially clear that to call a piece of literature uncanny, as Freud did 'The Sandman', is to say that the reading of it is an uncanny experience. In it the uncanny is encountered. It is not in the end possible to divide, as Freud wished to, the uncanny as an aesthetic attribute of a work of art from the uncanny as a subjective experience in real life.

Neil Hertz (1985) has discussed the complex relations between writer, reader and characters in 'The Sandman'. He examines Freud's readings of the story in 'The Uncanny', considers what those readings did not include, and how, as a piece of writing, 'The Sandman' resists the kind of reading Freud proposed.

The central character of 'The Sandman', Nathanael, is trapped in a repetitive cycle of destructive relationships. He is a student who used to be frightened by the nursery story of the Sandman; a terrifying figure who steals children's eyes out of their heads. Now grown-up, he does not of course believe in this monster any longer. But Sandman-like figures, in various guises, appear and reappear in his life, threatening to destroy his eyes, until he is eventually driven to kill himself. Freud linked the uncanny to the overt reappearance of something that was supposed to be kept hidden. In his analysis of Hoffmann's story, Nathanael's recurrent quasi-psychotic episodes of terror that his eyes will be destroyed represent the re-emergence of his repressed dread of castration at his father's hands. The fact that Nathanael's suicide occurs while he is preparing for his wedding is a further signal that the roots of his psychic disaster are to be found in the oedipal triangle.

Freud's evident fascination with Hoffmann's story invites the following questions, as must any account of a text: why this reading, of this text, by this reader, at this time? Hertz points out that, alongside writing 'The Uncanny', Freud was developing the idea of repetition, not just as an occasional manifestation with various possible causes, but as a compulsive phenomenon in its own right. The concept of the repetition compulsion would appear fully fledged a year later in *Beyond the Pleasure Principle* (Freud, 1920). Hertz suggests that Freud could analyse 'The Sandman' as he did because he found links in it to this theme with which he was already occupied theoretically. It may have meshed also with concerns that were occupying Freud personally. Making use of Paul Roazen's book *Brother Animal: The Story of Freud and Tausk* (1969), Hertz draws a parallel between the destructive triangular relationships in 'The Sandman' and certain events in Freud's life at the time. Shortly before 'The Uncanny' was published, Freud's gifted student, Victor Tausk, committed suicide on the eve of his wedding. This real-life catastrophe also followed a repeating pattern of triangular relationships which were problematic, to say the least. Tausk was a lover of Lou Andreas-Salome. She was also close to Freud, and she and Freud would discuss together Tausk's intense and ambivalent feelings towards Freud. Tausk wanted to be analysed by Freud, but Freud sent him instead to Helene Deutsch, who was herself in analysis with Freud. The analyses became intertwined when Tausk, in his sessions with Deutsch, could talk about nothing but Freud, and Deutsch, in her analysis with Freud, became more and more preoccupied with Tausk. Freud broke the triangulation by insisting that one or other of the analyses must be terminated, whereupon Deutsch broke off her analysis of Tausk. Three months after this, on the eve of his marriage, Tausk committed suicide. Hertz (1985: 114ff; 247, endnote 12) is judicious in his treatment of this material, and of Roazen's account of it. He does not exaggerate its possible connections with Freud's paper, but it does undermine further any idea that the uncanniness Freud found in 'The Sandman' could belong to some self-contained realm of artistic technique, remote from personal experience.

Hertz also draws attention (1985: 101f) to a significant discrepancy in Freud's comments about what it is that provokes a feeling of the uncanny. In 'The Uncanny' Freud postulates 'the dominance in the unconscious mind of a "compulsion to repeat" ... a compulsion powerful enough to overrule the pleasure principle, lending to certain aspects of the mind their daemonic character' (1919b: 238). He then says that 'whatever reminds us of this inner "compulsion to repeat" is perceived as uncanny'. This ascribes the uncanny feeling to an awareness of being in the grip of an unconscious inner process over which there is no control. The point is not what is reproduced by the process of repetition, but the eeriness of the unconscious process itself. Similarly, in *Beyond the Pleasure Principle,* Freud writes:

> It may be presumed that when people unfamiliar with analysis feel an obscure fear—a dread of rousing something that, as they feel, is better left sleeping—what they are afraid of at bottom is the emergence of this compulsion with its hint of possession by some 'daemonic' power.
>
> (Freud, 1920: 36)

This passage could imply not only dread of the compulsive unconscious process itself, but also dread of the something that might be roused. Elsewhere in 'The Uncanny' Freud does attribute uncanny feelings to the nature of the repressed element which the process threatens to bring back to life: for example the son's dread of castration by his father, re-emerging in the threats of destruction to Nathanael's eyes.

The distinction is important. If uncanny experiences are a result of the resurgence of a specific developmental anxiety, such as fear of castration, then Freud's view that they indicate regression to archaic forms of psychic functioning is valid. If, on the other hand, what produces them is the intimation of some powerful unconscious process calling for attention, this carries the potential for greater self-awareness, for being more, not less, in touch with one's inward life. Perhaps this explains why experiences of the uncanny, however disturbing, may also feel significant and enriching, as the following story illustrates.

I have led seminars at the Institute of Psychoanalysis, the training organisation of the British Psychoanalytical Society, with the title 'Listening to ourselves listening to others'. The theme of these seminars is that we hear more sensitively what is going on in another person by learning to be sensitive to the responses which this person stirs up in ourselves (a central topic of Part III of this book). The seminar group explores this experientially in various ways. For example, we read poems aloud and discuss how the external music of the poem arouses an internal music in ourselves (see Chapter 10, pp.158ff). This illuminates the clinical situation, where the internal music aroused in a listening analyst helps the analyst understand more of the external music that is the patient.

Participants are disconcerted, then intrigued, by another idea. I invite them to go outside at night and stand alone in the dark, keeping still and silent for at least half an hour, just listening. The object is to observe how much more they are hearing at the end of the half-hour than at the beginning. If they can find a field to stand in, away from traffic and other sounds, so much the better. On a still night in open country what seems at first like silence gradually yields up a world of sounds. After ten minutes or so there is a certain amount to be heard: leaves rustling; an animal moving about; someone whistling in the distance. Twenty minutes of silent, motionless listening produces a surprising amount and variety of noise. After half an hour, what started out as silence has become an extraordinary polyphony. If seminar members cannot get into the countryside like this I suggest they find whatever situation they can in which to be still themselves while they listen. Even in an urban setting they find subtle variability and unexpected combinations in familiar kinds of noise, and they discover new sounds, previously unheard, gradually revealing themselves. (On one occasion a participant, despairing at the city traffic surrounding him, gave up trying to listen and spent half an hour looking at the bark of a tree. He gave a remarkable description in the seminar of the visual detail that could slowly be perceived in an ordinary tree trunk.) As with the poems, we link this experience to a kind of listening in the clinical situation that is able to hear, over time, much more going on in a patient than was detectable to begin with.

In the seminar I join in with whatever I ask the others to do, and the following week we share our experiences as a group. The weekend after I had suggested this exercise, I was visiting the village where I had grown up from the age of twelve. Nearby is an area of several square miles of rough open country and woodland where I often used to roam. I needed to find a time before the next seminar to do my listening to the night and, remembering from my teenage years the deep stillness and mysterious nocturnal sounds of this place, I thought that here was an opportunity.

I parked my car and set off up a bridleway through the woods for a couple of hundred yards. I thought that should be far enough from the road to provide the silence I was looking for. But the sounds of the night were obscured by a noise that had not been there in my adolescence: the repeated drone of aircraft overhead. *Murmur, crescendo, sky full of sound, diminuendo, fade-out, brief silence, murmur, crescendo …* I listened in exasperation, then laughed to myself as I saw how tied I can be to my preconceptions. I had once heard that someone would be taking part in the seminar by telephone link. I was not happy with the idea. I thought an anonymous voice through a loudspeaker would spoil the quality of emotional interchange in the group, and that the person on the other end of the phone would feel excluded from the experience. How wrong I was! In a room in central London we listened enthralled to a woman in Scotland telling us how she and her two dogs sat in the dark beside a loch, listening to the sounds of the water and the land around. The dogs, one either side of her, were intensely alert to the surroundings. She knew they could hear things that she could not. They seemed like extensions of her own listening, and we talked about how they represented unconscious areas of her mind, able to perceive things she was not consciously aware of, but which might eventually become audible. So now I thought, 'All right, I didn't want that telephone link and look what happened. If aircraft noise is what I have to listen to, let's see what I can hear in it'.

There was more detail in the sound of the planes than I expected. The steady, apparently uniform drone had various components: deep rumbles and high-pitched whines that I only heard because I was listening as I did not normally do. Sometimes there were subtle differences between the noise of one plane and the next, but the sounds did not seem to develop any further, and soon enough I thought I had heard as much as I was able to.

Looking up I noticed that the plane whose lights I could see was well ahead of where its sound appeared to come from. This familiar observation struck me in a new way. I was perceiving the plane at two separate moments of its existence at the same time. The present moment of the plane was where its lights showed it to be. The point from which the sound seemed to come was in its past. Both these moments in the life of the plane were presented to me together. Again, I thought how this related to the analytic situation. Patients talk about what is going on in their lives at the moment. For the analyst, listening to this narrative of the present, the patient's history is simultaneously audible.

Pondering this amongst the trees, I knew all at once that I was not alone. I looked around. Nobody was there. The vivid sensation persisted, however, of another presence. Then I understood. Beside me, watching, listening, was my adolescent self. I knew, of course, that there was nobody there. I was not hallucinating. But the sense of another human presence was distinct. This was more than just fantasy. It seemed apt that, in the wake of my thoughts about the plane, two parts of my own life should encounter each other. How real the imaginary can be, I thought, and we settled down—myself as I am now and myself as I was then—to savour the night together.

Some people came walking along the path. I turned away to be less visible and moved further into the trees. Facing now into the depths of the wood, I was assailed by its smells. A rich, moist earthiness was dominant. But there were all sorts of overtones: a fresh, green smell of foliage; something dense and woody like soft bark; then a whiff of something acrid. Fox? The sound of the aeroplanes had drowned out whatever else I might have attuned myself to hearing. What had not happened in my listening, however, started happening now with my sense of smell. The longer I stood, letting an inner silence occupy me as I breathed in the night air, the more fascinated I became by the subtle variety, the richness and texture in the tapestry of scent that slowly unfolded. There was vivid discussion in the following seminar about what it might be like to listen to a patient in the same way that I had gradually been able to open myself to the smell of the woods.

Eventually, it felt time to leave and I walked back to my car. I drove up the empty country road, and had gone about half a mile when it suddenly came to me that I was not wearing a seat belt. This produced an extraordinary sense of shock. I felt poleaxed. But why? Forgetting to put on a seat belt is not so remarkable, after all. Then I realised it was not that I had forgotten. If I forget to put on my seat belt, when I notice I am not wearing it my mind goes back to when I should have put it on, and I recognise that I forgot. This was nothing like that. I had no sense at all of any forgetting, of failing to do something that I should have. There I was with no seat belt, and not because I had omitted to put one on. There must not have been one for me to put on in the first place. I gradually put it together that when I got back into my car I had got into a car that did not have seat belts.

This was a deeply uncanny moment. I learnt to drive before seat belts were introduced and for some years afterwards there were still no such things. The 'I' that got into the car and drove away from the woods had not been my present-day 'I', but the other one, the 'I' that was standing beside me in the night. That 'I' naturally got into a car without seat belts, started the engine and drove off. My moment of total disorientation and bewilderment was not just because I was not wearing a seat belt. The separation of past and present had collapsed, and my present-day 'I' suddenly found itself in a car that it did not know. I had become a vagabond in my own life history. After a while, I put on the seat belt of the present-day car and drove on, shaken by the experience, but grateful at the same time for its astonishing richness.

There was a coda. For the final evening of the seminar I suggest another approach to 'listening to ourselves listening to others'. There is a traditional practice in Western Christian monasticism known as *lectio divina*. This phrase means 'spiritual reading', and it refers to a technique of reading that is applied to an especially significant text. In the Christian monastic tradition this would typically have been the Bible, but the same way of reading can be practised with any text which, for whatever reason, is charged with meaning for the reader. The method consists of reading contemplatively at a deliberately slowed-down tempo, not attempting to understand the words but simply receiving them, letting them sink into one's awareness. A moment may come when the reader is stopped by a sense of something being encountered. It is not obvious, perhaps, why the passage in question should seem significant, nor what meaning it may contain for the reader, but there is a recognition of an inward resonance. The reader will then pause to stay with the words that have produced this response, and wait to see what they evoke. This involves a meditative awareness, an inward listening to associative responses which may continue for some time. When this feels sufficiently completed the slow, word-by-word perusal of the text is resumed. Mark Barrett, a contemporary Benedictine monk, gives a fine description of the process (Barrett, 2001: 81ff). He emphasises how the words coming from outside reveal their significance through the responses they elicit within the reader, and he extends the method to a contemplative 'reading' of the evolving patterns of one's own life history. Candidates in training find it surprising and refreshing to have such apparently non-analytic material on a seminar reading list, and then to discover how psychoanalytic it is.

The first evening of the seminar traces the early development of Freud's listening capacity (see the discussion of *Studies on Hysteria* in Chapter 8, pp.113–5). For the last evening we return to Freud. I invite the members of the group each to choose any work of Freud's they want, to read it in this particular way, and see what happens. Again, I do the same myself. We had all felt powerfully engaged in the experience of the seminar, and I was very aware of its ending. Perhaps this was why I decided to read one of the last papers Freud wrote. So two weeks after standing in the woods listening to the night, I was practising *lectio divina* on 'Constructions in Analysis' (Freud, 1937a).

I had not read this paper straight through for many years. Slowly pondering, sentence by sentence, its opening pages, I did not hear much by way of response from myself. The text struck me as intellectually immaculate, with its categorisation of patients' material in terms of dreams, associative sequences, and unconscious repetition in the transference, and with its breakdown of the work into two parts: the patient's task being to recover repressed memories, while the analyst's is to construct what has been forgotten from the traces it leaves behind. Then came the analogy with archaeology, and Freud's careful dissection of its similarities to and differences from psychoanalysis. This was a model of limpid exposition, and it was interesting for the way it reflected its period in analytic thinking. I admired it, but its measured detachment left me feeling somehow untouched. Nonplussed by my lack of response, I was wondering how I could bring this failed example of *lectio divina* to the seminar. All at once I was brought up short.

> Indeed, it may, as we know, be doubted whether any psychical structure can really be the victim of total destruction.
>
> (Freud, 1937a: 260)

This sentence made a sudden, powerful impact on me. I did not know why, but as I contemplated it there seemed an intriguing contrast between the cool objectivity of the text so far and this almost incidental declaration that the whole of our psychic life always, through no matter what vicissitudes, remains present in us. To come across this affirmation of persistence, just as I was despairing of my responsiveness, was unexpectedly moving.

I read on slowly through the text, arriving finally at its discussion of delusions and hallucinations. Freud suggests that the sense of conviction these arouse in those who experience them stems from fragments of historical truth which they contain.

> The delusions of patients appear to me to be the equivalents of the constructions which we build up in the course of an analytic treatment—attempts at explanation and cure ... Just as our construction is only effective because it recovers a fragment of lost experience, so the delusion owes its convincing power to the element of historical truth which it inserts in the place of the rejected reality. In this way a

proposition which I originally asserted only of hysteria would apply also to delusions—namely, that those who are subject to them are suffering from their own reminiscences.

(Freud, 1937a: 268)

It was poignant to find Freud himself exemplifying the statement that had so affected me eight pages earlier. The 'proposition' he mentions is part of his own psychic life. It dates back to his first psychoanalytic writing—'*Hysterics suffer mainly from reminiscences*' (Breuer and Freud, 1893–5: 7)—and here it still is, newly fruitful for him, two years before his death. Freud's nomadic journeying in his own mind has brought him, like Eliot, to the place where 'in my end is my beginning' (Eliot, 1969 [1940]: 183).

As I finished the paper, a penny dropped. There was a link between the impact on me of the sentence about no psychical structure ever being destroyed, and my feeling poleaxed when I realised I was not wearing a seat belt. What had felt so uncanny that night was the direct encounter with my own undestroyed psychical structures. Knowing I was in a car that did not have seat belts was, indeed, a momentary delusion containing a fragment of historical truth. It felt uncanny now, at this moment, to find I had chosen a paper that would ambush me with this connection.

Does this whole story simply confirm Freud's view that uncanny personal experiences amount to a regressive failure of reality-testing on the part of one who has not 'completely and finally rid himself of animistic beliefs' (Freud, 1919b: 248)?

This might be so according to one of Freud's two accounts of where uncanny feelings come from. If specific repressed memories are what trigger uncanny feelings as they re-emerge, there is no doubt that I was on fertile ground for regression. The territory I had chosen was redolent of my early life. Adolescent recollections were in my mind and the memory of learning to drive a car may have been full of unconscious symbolism. Perhaps I was sensitised also by the rather odd nature of the exercise I was engaged in. As to why I selected 'Constructions in Analysis' to read … maybe I had a greater memory of its content than I was consciously aware of. Does my response reflect not so much what is in the text as the state of mind I brought to reading it?

Perhaps 'yes' to all of the above. But Freud's alternative statement about what produces a sense of the uncanny offers a better explanation for what these experiences actually felt like. Of course, my subjective contribution was an inextricable part of them. The purpose of the seminar, and my own endeavour also, was to learn to hear more in what is outside us by listening more subtly to our inward responses to it. To analyse these experiences away, using a reductive understanding to master them and set aside their uncanny quality, would be an impoverishment. The potential value of uncanny experiences lies precisely in the way that they escape the boundaries of our habitual world view. It may be eerily disturbing to find oneself in the grip of a process operating outside one's awareness, but it may also open new inward horizons. The impact on me of Freud's declaration of psychic indestructibility came apparently out of the blue. In the triangle, however, of this statement, the shock of my experience two weeks earlier, and the unexpected linking of the end of Freud's analytic life to its beginning, there was a welcome, though startling, coherence. What happened with my adolescent self was not some piece of theoretical conceptualising but an encounter, which gave me a richer and more complex awareness of who I am. And the comparison between the layering of smells in the wood at night and the unconscious texturing of a patient's material left us, in the seminar, not more knowledgeable *about* analytic listening but different analytic listeners from whom we had been before.

What made an impact on me in 'Constructions in Analysis' was how the end and the beginning of Freud's life as an analyst map on to each other. In the wood at night my past and present also mapped on to each other, although in a manner that felt more like a collision. It is deeply uncanny to become suddenly aware that the present moment contains one's entire life. To give meaning intellectually to this idea is one thing, but if what T.S. Eliot called 'a lifetime burning in every moment' (1969 [1940]: 182) becomes not a literary turn of phrase but living reality, familiar boundaries are lost and normal points of reference disappear. The sense of uncanny dislocation may be profound.

Freud implies that a return to archaic modes of thinking is in itself undesirable. This seems too global. Regression may indeed be defensive and can amount to a failure of reality-testing: no question about that. And children may get stuck at certain points in their development. But to feel safe in taking a step forward children have to know that they can step backward when they need to. Otherwise they may be imprisoned in a kind of pseudo-maturity. Eliot's line has already been quoted in Chapter 2 (p.21), where it was emphasised that aliveness involves a freedom of imaginative movement up and down the trajectories of one's life. This movement extends back into the past, and from the past up to the present, forwards into the future, and back again to the present, encompassing whatever lies between death and the primal scene. Throughout the whole of life, a flexibility of movement between ways of engaging with the world—between various psychic repertoires, so to speak—is part of what it means to be fully alive. A child's revisiting of earlier ways of being is not a retreat if it helps the growing child link up with its past and gain a sense of psychic continuity. Even supposing, with Freud, that uncanny experiences stem from a return to earlier ways of being, this need not be a withdrawal from reality, but may serve a purpose similar to the child's apparent regression. César Botella (2011) has spoken of 'the structural incompletion characteristic of so-called normal psychic life which ... tends constantly towards the creation of wider psychic networks'.[1] Unconscious processes can produce shifts and elisions along the timeline of one's life which, in their unsettling way, make for a broader and deeper sense of identity.

The question of psychic repertoires, and the need for flexible movement between them, is treated by Iain McGilchrist from a neuropsychological perspective (2009: 350f). He emphasises the different ways of operating which characterise the brain's right and left hemispheres. While the functioning of the left is logically orientated and language-based, that of the right hemisphere is not grounded in the same linear rationality. McGilchrist postulates that a sense of the uncanny arises when the left hemisphere tries to make sense, in its own terms, of something coming to it from the right, but is unable to do so. McGilchrist also suggests that in Western society the mode of thought belonging to the left hemisphere is overvalued, leading to a disproportionate emphasis on scientific objectivity, along with rejection of anything not subject to rational explanation. 'At the Enlightenment the promptings of the right hemisphere, excluded from the world of rationalising discourse in the left hemisphere, came to be seen as alien' (McGilchrist, 2009: 350). The literary and cultural historian Terry Castle argues in similar vein that the notion of the uncanny came into being in the years between 1650 and 1800, as the reverse face of the intellectual ideology of the Enlightenment. In a series of essays, she elaborates the idea that the 'aggressively rationalist imperatives of the epoch' (Castle, 1995: 8)—what Andrew Lang (1897: x) called its 'cock-sure common sense'—meant that anything which could not be comprehended rationally took on an aura of bizarre mystery and estrangement.

In his *Essay Concerning Human Understanding*, one of the founding texts of the Enlightenment, John Locke expressed a hope with which Freud might have concurred.

> Were the capacities of our understandings well considered, the extent of our knowledge once discovered, and the horizon found which sets the bounds between the enlightened and dark parts of things; between what is and what is not comprehensible by us, men would perhaps with less scruple acquiesce in the avowed ignorance of the one, and employ their thoughts and discourse with more advantage and satisfaction in the other.
>
> (Locke, 1690; Bk.I, ch.1, sec.7)

The idea of a boundary needing to be maintained between 'the enlightened and dark parts of things' is worth noting. Analysts may think of certain patients as having an insecure sense of their boundaries, or not having a clear boundary in their minds between themselves and other people. The therapeutic hope will then be to strengthen these boundaries, helping such patients to keep themselves and their own thoughts distinct from what goes on in other people and the world outside them, and thus to develop a stronger sense of their individuality. However, it is possible for the boundary between self and not-self to be overvalued as a touchstone of psychic health. If the integrity of this boundary is taken too automatically as an obligatory standard of well-being, the boundary can become a confinement. It may then be difficult for us to put out feelers beyond our own edges, to explore the 'dark parts' beyond the boundary, and discover what more there may be to ourselves than we know so far. I think certain experiences of the uncanny represent unconsciously mounted explorations of this sort. The boundary between self and other, which provides the sense of ourselves as individual human beings, is essential, and there are undoubtedly people who need help in strengthening it. But it needs to be not totally impermeable.

Bion describes the 'contact-barrier', as he calls it, between conscious and unconscious in similar terms. If there is no barrier, nothing can be kept out of consciousness. If the barrier is absolute, nothing new from the internal world can be admitted into consciousness. 'The term "contact-barrier" emphasises the establishment of contact between conscious and unconscious and the *selective passage* of elements from one to another' (Bion, 1962: 17; italics added). The biological cell wall is an example of what is called a 'semipermeable membrane'. It keeps out, and keeps in, those molecules which must not be allowed to cross it. Other molecules do need to have free passage, and these move back and forth. Like the contact-barrier between conscious and unconscious, the boundary between self and other needs, in just this sense, to be semipermeable.

Freud's view of uncanny experience as regression to a more primitive mode of thought has a historical and cultural context. His disparagement of the uncanny, as a matter of subjective experience, belongs to a general attitude of denigration towards non-rationalistic mental processes which, according to McGilchrist and Castle, followed the Enlightenment. Even before Freud's time there had been a resurgence of interest in the uncanny. The Romantic Movement, reacting against the Enlightenment's pure rationalism, embodied culturally the idea that refusing any value to uncanny personal experience is not an index of maturity but an impoverishment. Freud, though, identified with the Enlightenment rather than Romanticism. I refer to his 'disparagement' of uncanny experiences because, in passages such as I have quoted (p.11), he does seem unmistakably to devalue them. But the story is more complicated. There is a polarity in Freud's thought, and in his character, between what we might call 'Enlightenment' and 'Romantic' values. Robert Holt, for example, and Madeleine and Henri Vermorel have investigated this in their articles 'Freud's mechanistic and humanistic images of man' (Holt, 1972), and 'Was Freud a Romantic?' (Vermorel and Vermorel, 1986). Aspects of Freud's personality were certainly in conflict with the empirical materialism of his scientific training. Ernest Jones quotes him as saying: 'As a young man I felt a strong attraction toward speculation and ruthlessly checked it' (Jones, 1954: 32); and Freud himself wrote: 'In the works of my later years … I have given free rein to the inclination, which I have kept down for so long, to speculation' (Freud, 1925b: 57).

Robert Snell observes that 'Freud's conflict echoes the great cultural battle of the earlier part of the nineteenth century' (Snell, 2012: 34). This again refers to the clash of values between the Enlightenment and the Romantic Movement. Snell elaborates in detail links between the values of Romanticism and the 'analytic attitude'.

> Latter-day Lockeans, practitioners of cognitive therapy in various forms, also regard the substitution of 'true' ideas and perceptions for 'false' ones as the mainspring of psychotherapy. Departure from a mechanistic, Lockean view in favour of doubt, imagination and relationship is what distinguishes both Romanticism and psychoanalysis.
>
> (Snell, 2012: 31)

In fact, according to Snell, 'a recognisably analytic attitude began to take shape in European culture one hundred years before Freud' (Snell, 2012: 37). One of Snell's heroes is the poet Samuel Taylor Coleridge. In 1805, fifty-one years before Freud's birth, his coinage of the very word 'psycho-analytic' was anticipated by Coleridge. Reflecting on the overlap of classical and Christian references in fifteenth-century poetry, Coleridge wrote in his *Notebooks* that to appreciate, from a later perspective, 'the reality of the passion' of the Greeks and Romans for their gods 'requires a strong imagination as well as an accurate psycho-analytical understanding' (Coburn, 1962 part 1: para. 2670; Eng, 1984).[2] In a sentence whose controlled meandering is worthy of Coleridge himself, Snell remarks:

> Confrontation with art of the Romantic era demands an emotional stance, a mental and emotional availability, which contemporary analytic psychotherapists might recognise: an openness, through a readiness to day-dream and free associate, to ambiguities and multiple meanings, to enigmas and encodings, to the indeterminate; to the unrepeatable quality of the present moment, as well as to the allure of the past; to feeling, to the fleeting, fragmentary and subliminal, to dream, desire and terror, the erotic and the life of the body.
>
> (Snell, 2012: 3)

Not for nothing does Snell claim that Romanticism intuitively prefigured essential aspects of a psychoanalytic attitude.

The Romantic Movement subverted the values of the Enlightenment, and the kind of teaching I have described may perhaps recover something of the subversive quality of psychoanalysis. At the Institute of Psychoanalysis it is expected that seminar leaders in the training curriculum should report, at the end of a seminar, on the performance of those taking part in it. The seminar described here, however, challenges participants (as well as the seminar leader) to risk sharing their emotional experience without knowing in advance where that will lead.[3] It is only possible to invite people into this thoroughly psychoanalytic position on a basis of confidentiality. I therefore had to tell the

Curriculum Committee that I could only do this seminar on the understanding that I would make no report about any of the participants.

Like psychoanalysis, the uncanny too is subversive. Its nature is to waylay us, destabilising habitual modes of seeing both the world and ourselves, and offering up new ones. It carries the potential to open fresh perspectives that are closed to experience which stays, or is kept, too safely within existing frameworks of understanding.

Notes

1   This passage is more fully quoted in Chapter 13 (p.232), in relation to the termination of analysis.
2   Coburn (1962: part 2, para. 2670) noted that the *Oxford English Dictionary* did not, at the time of her writing, record this occurrence. The *OED* Online, however, does now cite Coleridge's use of the word 'psycho-analytical'.
3   Compare the discussion of clinical seminars in Chapter 13 (pp.216–21).

Part II

CONCEPTS ON THE MOVE

Streams that are drawn from the springheads of nature
do not always run in the old channels.

Francis Bacon, *Novum Organum*
(1620: aphorism 109)

5

SEXUALITY AND PERVERSION

Discovering what Freud discovered

The previous chapters have shown the importance of a freedom of imaginative movement up and down the trajectory of life: backward into the past and up to the present again, finding new meanings in one's cumulative experience to date; and forward into the future and back again to the present, enlarging the possible ways of giving meaning to the rest of life. Not only individuals, but intellectual and artistic disciplines as well, need the same ability to keep understanding their history afresh, questioning how their concepts and practices have come to be the way they are, so as to broaden the possibilities of future development. About philosophy, for example, John Cottingham has written:

> The philosophical illumination we get from ideas of the past is dependent on our placing them in the context of more recent developments; and conversely, any more than superficial understanding of our present predicament requires us to enter into a continuing dialogue with what has gone before. Adapting an idea loosely derived from Freud, one might say that fruitful philosophising operates at the locus of a dynamic interplay between *Nachträglichkeit*, the past that we struggle to recover and reinvent, and *Zukünftigkeit*, the 'futurality' towards which we strive, and which will bestow the 'meaning to come' on what we do now.
>
> (Cottingham, 1998: 7)

Psychoanalytic theory likewise needs to be considered *après-coup* so that creative apperception may give it new meaning in the present. If it can be considered *avant-coup* as well, so much the greater chance for it to find new meaning in the future.

The next three chapters take such an approach to the concepts, central to psychoanalysis, of sexuality, the Oedipus complex and narcissism.

The main themes of this chapter are the way that Freud's original formulation of sexuality has evolved, and its potential to go on evolving. This is exemplified specifically by the development of psychoanalytic thinking about perversion, but it is worth setting the topic in a larger frame by considering how concepts in other fields as well evolve in their social and historical contexts. An example from the visual arts may provide a starting point. Figure 5.1 shows *Le Déjeuner sur l'Herbe* by Manet, and Figure 5.2 the sculptor Anthony Caro's revisiting of it. Manet's painting was a scandal when he showed it, because of how he himself was reworking a traditional theme. Figure 5.3 shows a detail from an engraving after a drawing by Raphael of *The Judgement of Paris*. The engraving is shown in its entirety in Figure 5.4. Raphael's conventionally pastoral image poses no threat or challenge. Manet's use of this same material confronts and disturbs the viewer. The stylistic provocations, such as the flatness of space and the harsh frontal lighting, are part of how Manet is questioning what pastoral itself consists of. These are not country folk in some ideal classical age, but contemporary townspeople on a day out. Nudity has become a matter of irony, as well as of beauty, and the 'in-your-face' quality of the sexual theme goes with Manet's overall refusal to idealise. Without losing touch with the pastoral tradition, indeed with clear delight in being part of it, he makes it impossible to view it with the same innocent eyes as before.

There is a parallel between the reactions to Manet when he showed *Le Déjeuner sur l'Herbe* in 1863, and the reactions to Freud when he published *Three Essays on the Theory of Sexuality* in 1905. Something familiar was subverted. What people were accustomed to, and had ways of dealing with, suddenly

Figure 5.1 Edouard Manet, *Le Déjeuner sur l'Herbe*.

Figure 5.2 Anthony Caro, *Déjeuner sur l'Herbe II.*

Figure 5.3 Marcantonio Raimondi, *The Judgement of Paris*: engraving after a drawing by Raphael (detail).

Figure 5.4 Marcantonio Raimondi, *The Judgement of Paris*: engraving after a drawing by Raphael.

became more complicated and dangerous. But the point of the parallel lies in the Caro sculpture (Figure 5.2). This, in turn, subverts Manet's view. Caro's work is not even a painting. It is in three dimensions, and abstract rather than figurative. It shocks, but differently, with its opening up of the woman's body and its concern with inward spaces and volumes. Just as Manet confronted the viewers of his day with a contemporary challenge, so Caro challenged the viewer in 1998. If the engraving after Raphael stands for the view of sexuality that people had been used to, and Manet's painting stands for what Freud did to that view with the *Three Essays*, the question to be answered is: what does the Caro sculpture stand for? How has psychoanalysis reworked Freud's conceptualisation of sexuality, to give us our own contemporary understanding of it?

To raise this question implies that sexuality is a concept whose meaning can develop and evolve, as the culture it belongs to develops and evolves. The relation of Freud's discoveries to their social and historical context has been used to trivialise psychoanalysis; for example, when his observations are disparaged as being about a few women in a narrow sector of Viennese society at a particular time, with no relevance outside that group. Superficialities of this sort should not deter analysts from recognising that psychoanalysis does have a socio-historical context, and that it developed in relation to its own cultural setting. Freud was part of his intellectual generation. In 1897, he was sent a book about child psychology (Baldwin, 1895), which he later referred to in the *Three Essays* (Freud, 1905: 173–4fn). He mentions the book in a letter to

Wilhelm Fliess, commenting ironically on the widespread current interest in the subject: 'So one still remains a child of one's age, even with something one had thought was one's very own' (Freud, 1954 [1897]: 228).

That concepts which appear to us as objective aspects of reality are in fact socially constructed is a familiar and well-debated idea in the social, and even the natural, sciences (Berger and Luckmann, 1971; Latour and Woolgar, 1979; Pickering, 1984, 1992; Searle, 1996; Hacking, 1999). Social anthropologists have developed a view of childhood, for example, as a concept whose meaning varies between cultures, and can evolve over time. The French historian Philippe Ariès claimed that 'in mediaeval society the idea of childhood did not exist' (Ariès, 1962: 125). Ariès contended that the idea of children occupying a category in their own right, with a different order of being from adults—the concept, that is to say, of childhood—was not fully established until the mid-eighteenth century. Others argued that Ariès was implicitly using the concept of childhood current in his own age as a touchstone. Even though past ages did not have our concept of childhood they might still have had a different one of their own. What emerged undisputed from the debate, however, was a recognition that childhood has not always been the same thing.

In the Puritan ethos of seventeenth-century England, children were seen as the carriers of original sin. They were subject to wicked impulses and childhood was the time of life when control of these had to be instilled. In the following century, this gave way to a more tolerant and liberal attitude which saw children as vulnerable, requiring protection, and with needs of their own to be considered (Hockey and James, 1993: 63–72). The point is not just that children had different sorts of experience in these periods, but that they were understood as different kinds of creature, and what childhood meant, as a period in a person's life, was differently construed.

Anthropologists have shown the same thing across cultures. A striking example is the contrast between the Chewong people of Malaysia and the Hausa of Nigeria (James, Jenks and Prout, 1998: 63). Among the Chewong, adult status is not just a matter of age. It has to be achieved, and for a woman this is not until the birth of her first child. For the Hausa girl, childhood ends at the age of ten, when she is betrothed. From then on she begins to assume the adult responsibilities of a wife. What it means to be a child is different in these two cultures. 'This variability in what childhood means reflects how … the immaturity of children is conceived and articulated in particular societies into culturally specific sets of ideas and philosophies, attitudes and practices which combine to define the "nature of childhood"' (James and Prout, 1990: 1).

The practical importance of this is shown by sociological studies of international aid. If aid agencies, operating on the basis of a European or North-American urban view of childhood, assume that childhood is the same thing everywhere, they may consider as criminal or deviant ways of behaving which, in the cultures receiving the aid, are in fact expected of children. This can be seriously disruptive to those cultures (Boyden, 1990). In the words of James and her colleagues: 'childhood is less a fact of nature and more an interpretation of it' (James et al., 1998: 62).

The same is true of sexuality. The parallel offered by this view of childhood is helpful because in both instances there is an irreducible biological given, which can be made sense of and dealt with in all sorts of different ways. Like the anatomical and physiological changes that children go through as they mature, the sexual impulse is a biological fact, to which different societies, and the same society at different stages of its development, can attach different meanings. 'Sexuality', like 'childhood', is a concept, determined by how a society interprets the biological fact, and what meanings it attaches to it. A useful survey of the social construction of sexuality is provided by Archer and Lloyd (2002: 99ff).

Heading off possible misunderstandings tends to be a lost cause, but it may be worth emphasising that this is not a matter of turning psychoanalysis into some kind of social psychology. Psychoanalysis is specifically to do with unconscious mental processes, and these are what analysts listen out for in their consulting rooms. But when an analyst listens to how patients unconsciously deal with their sexuality, what the patients are unconsciously dealing with is comprised both of their innate biology and of the meaning given to that innate biology within the social and cultural environment to which they belong.

The question of constructing reality is debated most contentiously where the natural sciences are concerned. There is an assumption that scientific facts are truths about a pre-existing reality, which are impersonally discovered by the rational evaluation of objective evidence. Observers of how science is conducted in practice, however, have claimed that the eventual presentation of scientific facts bears not much relation to the institutional and intellectual hurly-burly out of which they emerge. 'The negotiations as to what counts as a proof or what constitutes a good assay are no more or less disorderly than any argument between lawyers and politicians' (Latour and Woolgar, 1979: 237). Andrew Pickering (1984), surveying the development of particle physics from the 1960s to the 1980s, asserts likewise that decisions about methodology were constantly influencing which scientific facts were decided on as being true.

> Theoretical entities like quarks [a kind of sub-atomic particle], and conceptualisations of natural phenomena like the weak neutral current [a force governing interactions between particles], are in the first instance *theoretical constructs*: they appear as terms in theories elaborated by scientists. However, scientists typically make the realist identification of these constructs with the contents of nature, and then use this identification retrospectively to legitimate and make unproblematic existing scientific judgements.
>
> Most scientists think of it as their purpose to explore the underlying structure of material reality, and therefore it seems quite reasonable for

them to view their history in this way. But from the perspective of the historian the realist idiom is considerably less attractive. Its most serious shortcoming is that it is retrospective. One can only appeal to the reality of theoretical constructs to legitimate scientific judgements when one has already decided *which* constructs are real. And consensus over the reality of particular constructs is the outcome of a historical process.

(Pickering, 1984: 7)

Such a position has been strongly contested (see, for example, Latour's (2005) arguments for a constructivist viewpoint, and Boghossian's (2006) critique from a realist perspective). Without prejudice to this ongoing debate, however, some of Pickering's comments are certainly relevant to psychoanalysis. Analysts think of it as their purpose to explore the underlying structure of psychical reality, and the same processes that Pickering points out also apply to them. Freud warned repeatedly against reifying psychoanalytic constructs. Sexuality is a construct, and it would be a mistake to settle into thinking of one interpretation of it as being a final, objective description of the facts as they are. There is always the possibility of, and sometimes the need for, reworking.

How valuable such reworking can be is shown by Melanie Klein's concept of a 'position'. Freud's (1905) *Three Essays on the Theory of Sexuality* and Abraham's (1924) *Short Study of the Development of the Libido*, with their description of oral, anal and phallic stages, leading to an end point in genital maturity, might have seemed to be statements of the facts as they had been discovered by psychoanalysis. Klein, however, found that this account did not offer the conceptualisation she needed in the late 1920s and early 1930s. The framework she did need came from reworking the concept of 'developmental stage' into that of 'position' (Klein, 1928, 1935). She says clearly that this was not intended as a more correct description of the *facts* of development than Freud's and Abraham's theory. It is a question, as Bernardi (1989) has pointed out, of incommensurable paradigms, and the point is not which is closer to the truth, but what is the particular fruitfulness of each one.

Klein's concept has turned out to be one of the most important advances in psychoanalysis. In saying this, I am not referring specifically to the paranoid-schizoid and depressive positions. It is the concept of a position, in itself, that is so fruitful. A position is a psychic constellation of impulses, fantasies, anxieties, defences and object relationships, with an overall quality related to the point in development at which it arises, but without a definitive end point at which it disappears. Instead it remains present, active or latent, so that someone's unconscious relation to this aspect of their internal world may continue to evolve throughout the whole of life. This allows developmental processes to be conceptualised in a more mobile, open-ended way, than was available before. Previous concepts are not thereby falsified. They remain fruitful in ways that they are fruitful; especially, for example, with regard to the body-ego, which the notion of a 'position' does not address very powerfully. However, the concept of position is fruitful in new ways. It has been extended by Steiner (1993: 11) to the idea of a borderline position. Originally, Klein herself also thought of manic and obsessional positions. The latter is related to the concept of 'anal organisation', which Shengold (1988) has elaborated in detail. He shows it to be a constellation comprising developmental tasks, the conflicts and defences aroused by them, and archaic affects and fantasies, all in a context of increasingly complex and ambivalent object relationships. The anal organisation could be regarded as a position, in the sense of being a complex psychic formation whose elements are interrelated, and which continues to present itself in various ways throughout life. Another example is Green's (2000) hypothesis of a 'central phobic position'. Evidently, the concept of a position extends beyond the bounds of any single theoretical orientation. With it Klein has enriched the thinking of all psychoanalysts. Particular instances aside, it is the abstraction of psychic structure inherent in the concept that so usefully opens up new ways to conceptualise the internal world, just as the abstraction of Caro's sculpture enables him to open up the structure of Manet's figures, and reveal new aspects of their internal volumes and spaces.

This reworking of 'developmental stage' into 'position' offers new ways of thinking about maturity. A striking feature of late twentieth-century psychoanalysis was the move toward seeing personality development as a lifelong process. Erikson's (1950) *Childhood and Society*, with its chapter on 'The Eight Ages of Man', was a landmark. Jaques' (1965) paper 'Death and the mid-life crisis', the writings of Pollock (1982), Hildebrand (1988) and Limentani (1995), and comments on the lifelong nature of the Oedipus complex (Parsons, 2000: 123ff) are other examples of increasing attention to the developmental challenges of later life. A static view of maturity as a goal arrived at through certain phases of development which, once achieved, is simply dwelt in and made use of, is no longer adequate. Today, there is a more dynamic, developmentally mobile, view of the human life cycle, with implications for the role of sexuality throughout the whole of it. The concept of a position, as something open-ended, always able to re-present the underlying constellation in fresh forms, revisits earlier accounts of development in a way that makes possible a more contemporary conceptualisation of maturity.

A contemporary conceptualisation of sexuality depends likewise on revisiting: in this case, a revisiting of the *Three Essays* (Freud, 1905). Their central organising idea is that drives, and specifically the sexual drive, have a source, an aim and an object. This is a powerful concept, and it is worth noticing how Freud's own description of the book emphasises that concepts are what he is working with. The preface to the 1920 edition speaks of 'enlarging the concept of sexuality', and refers to 'the "stretching" of the concept of sexuality which has been necessitated by the analysis of children and what are called perverts' (Freud, 1905: 134). What Freud highlights here is not his discovery of new facts about sexuality, but the change that is needed in our understanding of what sexuality means. This reveals itself in the very structure of the book. It seems odd, at first glance, for a book about sexuality in general to begin with a long discussion of perversion. One reason is that in order to discuss childhood sexuality Freud needed to describe how the multiplicity of component instincts was brought together under the primacy of genitality; and his best way of getting to the component instincts was through the multiplicity of the perversions. Another, and very important, reason for bringing perversion into the foreground is that what is thought of as perverse sheds light on how the nature of sexuality itself is understood.

The source of a drive remains a mysterious idea throughout Freud's writing. The elements in his scheme that he makes active use of are the object of a drive and its aim. In principle, these two are on a reciprocal footing and either one could be taken as primary. The aim of a drive implies the kind of object required for its fulfilment. The nature of the object, on the other hand, determines what kinds of aim it can serve. In practice, however, Freud was not so even-handed. He says: 'What distinguishes the instincts from one another and endows them with specific qualities is their relation to their somatic sources and to their aims' (Freud, 1905: 168). He sets out to classify perversions by aim and by object, and does consider deviations in respect of the object, but then he writes:

> The most general conclusion that follows from all these discussions seems, however, to be this. Under a great number of conditions and in surprisingly numerous individuals, *the nature of the sexual object recedes into the background*. What is essential and constant in the sexual instinct is something else.
>
> (Freud, 1905: 149, italics added)

Ten years after the *Three Essays* he was even more explicit.

> The study of the sources of instincts lies wholly outside the scope of psychology. Although instincts are wholly determined by their origin in a somatic source, in mental life *we know them only by their aims*.
>
> (Freud, 1915a: 123, italics added)

It is the aim that Freud regards as the essential, constant and defining factor, and it has since become habitual to think of drives firstly in terms of their aims, and then to consider the choice of object that will serve those aims. Freud's fundamental idea, however, was that a drive comprises source, aim *and object*. To see the aim as primary, and the object as subservient to the aim, is the construction Freud placed on his idea, but it is not intrinsic to the idea itself.

Freud's stress on the aim of an instinct and his subordination of the object seem one way in which he was 'a child of his age'. *On the Origin of Species* (Darwin, 1859) was published when Freud was three years old, and *The Descent of Man* (Darwin, 1871) when he was fifteen. Darwin revolutionised not only biology but also the entire cultural climate, and no scientist in Freud's time could avoid presenting his ideas against the background of Darwin's influence. It was not yet possible to see round the edges of Darwin, as biologists nowadays are trying to do, and as our present task is to see round the edges of Freud. Darwin's two fundamental principles were those of natural and sexual selection. Natural selection meant the selecting of characteristics that enabled members of a species to survive more effectively, while sexual selection favoured characteristics that gave an advantage in attracting or finding a mate. Darwin saw these two as independent of each other and, behind them, he posited two independent instincts as the basis for all animal behaviour. These were the instinct for self-preservation and the sexual instinct. By the turn of the century, this view of instinct had become part of the intellectual repertoire of any progressive biological scientist. The dualism of Darwin's self-preservative and sexual instincts was reflected in the dualism which pervaded Freud's instinctual theory throughout its various manifestations.

In Darwin's scheme, those who are involved either in supporting the subject's existence or as mating partners are not taken account of as individuals. They are there simply to promote survival and to enable reproduction. Such emphasis as Freud did give to the object was, therefore, a significant advance; but what mattered for him was still the function of the object in fulfilling the aims of the sexual and self-preservative instincts.

This functional view of the object was challenged by Fairbairn. He declared that objects are not sought simply for libidinal discharge or instinctual aim-fulfilment. Instead they are sought in their own right, and they matter to the object-seeker for themselves. To quote from Fairbairn's own summary of his views:

1) Libido is essentially object-seeking;
2) Erotogenic zones are not themselves primary determinants of libidinal aims, but channels mediating the primary object-seeking aims of the ego.

(Fairbairn, 1952: 162)

Fairbairn still refers here to libido, but he also expressed very directly his scepticism about drive theory (Fairbairn, 1952: 84), and in revising Freud's ideas in terms of object relations he came to be seen as having effectively abandoned it.

Fairbairn's arguments are compelling. However, they lead to the abandonment of drive theory only if we limit ourselves to viewing drives according to the particular use Freud made of his framework. Fairbairn can be seen as challenging not so much the idea of drives in themselves, but rather the subordination of object to aim. Freud's genius was such that his conceptual framework allows a larger view than he, in his own time, could arrive at. If aim and object are placed truly on the equal footing he postulated originally, so that either one may be taken as primary, the concept of drive appears in a new light.

As was mentioned above, the way perversion is conceptualised reflects how sexuality in general is understood. Theoretical accounts of perversion have evolved in a manner that suggests there has, in fact, been a revisiting of sexuality along the lines I am putting forward.

An important shift in Freud's own view of perversion took place between the *Three Essays* and 'A child is being beaten' (Freud, 1919a). In the former he saw perversions simply as residues of the pregenital component drives, which had neither been sublimated nor transformed into neurotic symptoms. By 1919, he saw the beating fantasy as having a defensive function, and wondered whether this might be true of perversions in general. Since then, the idea of perversions as defensive has remained central. One question about a defensive structure concerns the mechanism of defence employed. Much has been written about this aspect of perversion. Disavowal, splitting of the ego, aggression, regression, sadistic control of the object ... the list of what form perverse defences may take would be a long one. Another fundamental question is: What is being defended against? How analysts have answered this question sheds light on the larger one of how they have construed sexuality in general.

Freud explained the beating fantasy as a defence against guilt aroused by oedipal wishes. Oedipal guilt, and the need to repress the Oedipus complex, became dominant motifs in the literature. Perversions were understood as defences against the castration anxiety aroused by oedipal wishes, and against attacks from the superego with its oedipal origins. A perversion might be the sexual formation least likely to provoke criticism from the superego that a person was able to develop. Another strand of thought was that, when projection of aggressive impulses gave rise to paranoid anxieties, a perversion might protect against psychotic breakdown (Glover, 1933). Gillespie's (1956, 1964) surveys of this period up to the 1960s are invaluable.

The theories just mentioned all rest, eventually, on the idea of perversion as a defence against drive derivatives. In more recent literature the idea of perversion appears, in one form or another but consistently, as a defence against object-relatedness.

In the view of Robert Stoller (1975), for example, what chiefly characterised perversion was the wish to harm the object. The misgiving that this shift aroused in some analysts is shown in a review by Charles Socarides, who wrote:

> While these observations are correct and describe some aspects of the meaning of the perverse act, Stoller lessens this important contribution by concluding that whether something is a perversion or not is determined by 'one's attitude toward the object of one's excitement' (p.6). When he states that he will 'accept' as perversion '... [an act] in which there is hatred' he does not give equal emphasis to the

observation that in perversions both libidinal and aggressive drives are at war with each other.

(Socarides, 1977: 331f)

The hostility towards the object was primarily, in Stoller's view (1975: 4), a vengeful response for harm inflicted on the subject in infancy, converting childhood trauma into adult triumph. It was also, however, an attempt to dehumanise the other person, so as to avoid the risk of intimacy (Stoller, 1985: 31). This new emphasis on the object relationship in perversion, and the dissension that it aroused, were highlighted at the 1985 Congress of the International Psychoanalytical Association in Hamburg.

Mervin Glasser (1986) and Joyce McDougall (1986) presented papers on identification in the perversions, which were discussed by Jacob Arlow (1986). Glasser outlined his concept of the 'core complex', with its important distinction between aggression and sadism, and the need to defend against a maternal object that has been experienced as engulfing and annihilating. Glasser expresses clearly and succinctly the function of the perversion as follows:

Clinical and social observation shows us that both sadism and masochism have the characteristic of engaging the object in an intense relationship but on the uncompromising condition that intimacy and union are never present. Through sado–masochism the individual establishes a firm grip on the object but this grip also entails keeping the object at arm's length.

(Glasser, 1986: 10)

On the same panel McDougall pointed out that what is called a perversion may be the only system of survival a person has been able to devise that safeguards, at least to some extent, a sense of sexual, and also personal, identity. She argued that to consider this structure simply as a bit of pathology that the person would be better off without, did not get near meeting the complexity of the situation.

Perhaps in the last resort only *relationships* may aptly be termed perverse. From this standpoint, therefore, the pertinent question is not which acts and which preferences are to be deemed deviant, but when is deviancy to be regarded as a simple variation or version of adult sexuality in the context of a significant object relationship, and when is it to be judged symptomatic?

(McDougall, 1986: 20)

Both Glasser and McDougall thus characterised perversion in terms of the quality of the relationship to the object.

Arlow disagreed strongly in this respect with both of them. Criticising Glasser for making sexual identity dependent on a sense of autonomous personal identity, he said:

> ... the fact remains that, according to most observations in the literature, perversions constitute a phase-specific problem, related aetiologically primarily to the conflicts arising during the oedipal phase (Hartmann, 1950). The essential problem of most male perverts, at least, appears to be how to achieve phallic sexual gratification in the face of overwhelming fear of danger.
>
> (Arlow, 1986: 247)

That Arlow refers here to a paper dating back to 1950 seems to confirm the theoretical shift I am describing. In discussing McDougall's paper, Arlow likewise rejected her emphasis on the quality of the object relationship. Not that he thinks this is unimportant, of course, but for him it is nothing to do with what characterises something as perverse. He said that McDougall's 'attempted redefinition' of perversion missed the point:

> For Freud the question of what should be considered normal as opposed to perverse sexuality posed no particular problem. He used a biological criterion. Based on nineteenth century biological theories and Darwinism, he saw the role of sexual activity as the union of the genitals of members of the opposite sex for the purpose of continuing the race. Any deviation of aim or object which compromised the achievement of that goal could be considered perverse.
>
> (Arlow, 1986: 249)

It is hard to imagine a drive more explicitly defined in terms of its Darwinian aim than that.

Heinz Lichtenstein (1983 [1961]) approached the question from the opposite direction, pointing out that the very thing Freud showed in the *Three Essays* was that sexuality is *not* essentially linked to procreation. The multiple aspects of sexuality are only placed secondarily at the disposal of the genital organs. Lichtenstein went on to argue that the non-procreative aspects of sexuality had their own function in helping to mediate an individual's sense of identity, personal as well as sexual. The close relation between this and McDougall's ideas is evident. An essential element in the sense of personal identity is the capacity for reciprocal object-relatedness; that is to say, the acceptance and enjoyment of the personal identity of another. If someone is unable to tolerate this, then as Glasser points out, a perversion may be developed to defend against it. Lichtenstein's article is a milestone, especially for its date of 1961.

77

Many discussions of perversion make the point that it aims at two things together: depersonalising the object, and merging with it. What is unbearable is a relationship to a person who has their own otherness. The personhood of the other is avoided by turning the person into a thing, while the otherness of the person is avoided by the merging. ('Personhood' is an awkward word, but it carries the precise meaning required here, which is 'the quality of being a person'.) Even analysts whose theoretical orientation is very classical now take these issues into account. Janine Chasseguet-Smirgel's contributions, for example, are centred on the concept of an anal-sadistic universe. Discussing De Sade's writings, she shows them to be dominated by the idea of nature as a melting-pot, where difference is obliterated in a general process of fusion and merging. 'Regression to the anal-sadistic phase brings about the erosion of the double difference between the sexes and the generations, of all differences in fact, and this regression seems to me substantially the same as perversion' (Chasseguet-Smirgel, 1985: 2).

McDougall's 'pertinent question' begins to look like a question about whether non-procreative sexuality is used to serve and promote object-relatedness, or to impede and obliterate it. Masud Khan introduced his book, *Alienation in Perversions,* as follows:

> The basic argument of this book is that the pervert puts an *impersonal object* between his desire and his accomplice: this object can be a stereotype fantasy, a gadget or a pornographic image. All three alienate the pervert from himself, as, alas, from the object of his desire.[1]
>
> (Khan, 1979: 9)

Khan is interested in what he calls a 'technique of intimacy'. This is a mode of object-relating which produces the appearance of intimacy and concern for the other, but which is unable to surrender to the experience and instead needs always to maintain control. Khan found in his patients an inconsolable, although perhaps unconscious, knowledge of their isolation. 'The pervert tries to use the technique of intimacy as a therapeutic device and all he accomplishes is more expertise in the technique itself' (Khan, 1979: 24). Khan captures in his formulations how the perversion is, at one and the same time, a person's best effort at intimacy and their defence against it. The 'technique of intimacy' calls to mind a sado-masochistic patient described by Sheldon Bach (1994: 7). This man felt that he had only a 'technical' relationship to other people, including his analyst. He said he did not know about people as human beings; all he knew was how to get them to meet his emotional needs. Another patient (Bach, 1994: 9) liked to be blindfolded during sex so that she could stay with the fantasy of her partner being perfectly attuned to her, and not have to see the uncertain reality of what he might actually be feeling.

A possible contemporary definition of perversity would be that it occurs when, impelled by the kind of anxiety just discussed, a person, firstly, places something (in fantasy or material reality) between themselves and their object, so as to prevent a relationship based on respect for, and pleasure in, the otherness and the personhood of the object; and when, secondly, they turn doing that into an occasion for sexual excitement. If this is too cumbersome, perversion could be defined more epigrammatically as *the sexualisation of the avoidance of mutuality*.

This shift in analytic thinking about perversion reflects a shift with regard to sexuality in general: a shift, but not a break, as the following passage shows.

> 'Falling in love' as such is certainly no perversion; but it is a perversion if the only possible sexual excitement consists in the feeling of one's own insignificance as compared with the magnificence of the partner.
>
> (Fenichel, 1946: 352)

It is striking to find so archetypally classical an analyst as Fenichel saying that heterosexual falling in love can be a perversion, depending on the quality of the object relation that it serves. There is a continuity from Fenichel to, say, McDougall, just as there is from Raphael to Caro.

Underlying this evolution in analytic thinking about perversion, and about sexuality in general, is a theoretical development in conceptualising what it means for something to be an object. Freud's original paradigm of source, aim and object indicates an object to be anything that a drive may cathect for the purpose of discharging its energy. Klein's development of Abraham's (1924) ideas on introjection, in her landmark paper 'A contribution to the psychogenesis of manic-depressive states' (Klein, 1935), inaugurated a new understanding of objects, not just as passive terminals for the discharge of drive energy, but as psychic entities in their own right. They have been variously understood as being mental structures, phantasies, representations and developmental capacities (Perlow, 1995).[2] But whatever their status, they are now seen as existing *in relation to each other* in a person's conscious and unconscious mental landscape. That objects should be internalised gave rise also to the concept of the 'internal object', an entity whose nature has also been much debated (Sandler, 1990a, 1990b; Hinshelwood, 1997; Sandler and Sandler, 1998). The concepts of object relations and of internal objects mark a development in psychoanalytic understanding, such that it is no longer possible to think of an object in the external world without also thinking about what relation that object bears to the subject's internal world. My objects are not just things, or people, out there. They also represent aspects of my fantasies, carry my projections, provide me with identifications, and so on. The development is from thinking that an object makes it incidentally possible for such psychic events to take place, to thinking that what it means to call something an object at all is to imply this kind of connectedness to the subject's internal world. By virtue of what being an object means, *an object cannot be conceived of separately from the quality of relatedness that the subject brings to it.* This is the theoretical advance that underlies the evolution in psychoanalytic understanding of sexuality and the perversions.

Other theoretical developments point in the same direction. Affects were classically seen in psychoanalytic theory as by-products of drive activity. Kernberg (1995), however, proposed that drives should be understood as developing through the organisation of affective experience. This reversal posits an integral, not an incidental, connection between drive and affect. Given, in addition, that affects arise in relation to an object, Kernberg's view implies that the concept of a drive must include, not just an object, but object-relatedness (Kernberg, 1995: 15–22).

On revisiting Freud's paradigm in the light of these developments, it is no longer possible to see the object as being there simply to serve the aim of the drive. The object now demands the reciprocal status which, earlier in this chapter, I said belongs to it in principle. If an object cannot meaningfully be considered apart from the subject's relatedness to it, Freud's paradigm should be rephrased, to say that a drive consists of source, aim and quality of relatedness to object.

Freud's own presentation of his paradigm implies a construction of sexuality according to the question: what kinds of object serve the aim that is demanded by the bodily source of the sexual drive?[3] Another view of Freud's paradigm, however, leads to a different construction of sexuality, according to the questions: what kinds of aim may be fulfilled by what different qualities of object-relatedness? And how does the body play its part in this? Sexuality remains rooted in the body, in the conscious and unconscious accumulation of the experience of the body, and in the intercourse of the parental couple that is the origin of the body. All of this belongs to the irreducible biological given. The shift, where perversion is concerned, lies in defining it not by the nature of the external object or of the behaviour aimed at, but in terms of the quality of object-relatedness, and whether sexual excitation is used in the service of, or to obstruct, object-relatedness. This offers a broader and more nuanced view of perversion in which it becomes possible, for example, to think meaningfully about whether a particular homosexual relationship is a perverse one or not.[4]

This construction also offers a fresh approach to issues of gender. Freud describes the sexual aim in a man as 'the discharge of the sexual products' (Freud, 1905: 207) or 'penetration into a cavity of the body which excites his genital zone' (222), while in a woman it is 'to bring about the formation of a new living organism' (208). The former happens to serve the purpose of the latter, and the latter provides an opportunity for the former; but considered in their own right, these male and female aims operate in a different register from each other. If the nature of sexuality is defined by the aim of the sexual drive, Freud's argument implies male and female sexualities whose fundamental natures will be different. If sexuality, on the other hand, is seen in terms of how sexual excitation serves the quality of object-relatedness, this brings men's and women's sexualities into closer relation with each other.

Freud's accentuation of the aim of a drive also goes some way to explain why female perversion has been harder for psychoanalysis to conceptualise than male perversion. The male phallic gratification which Freud describes is easier to define behaviourally than the woman's aim, more nebulous in external terms, of bringing about the formation of a new organism. This has led to a clearer view, on the face of it, of what is perverse for men than for women. From the present standpoint, however, this apparent contrast results from an oversimplified attention to the aim of the drive at the expense of object-relatedness. If sexuality is characterised by its quality of object-relatedness, perversion can be understood, not as a matter of contrast between the sexes, but in terms of what is common to them.

Finally, the conventional analytic construction of sexuality does not help us connect sex with love. When Freud introduced the death drive in *Beyond the Pleasure Principle* (Freud, 1920), his dualist outlook required the existence of a complementary drive. He identified this as 'the Eros of the poets and philosophers which holds all living things together' (Freud, 1920: 50). Freud then tried to equate Eros with the sexual drive. It does seem that Freud was looking for a theory that would relate love and sexuality to each other; but this would have involved a radical review of drive theory along the lines proposed in this chapter. The equation of Eros with the sexual drive, in the form Freud had been conceptualising it since the *Three Essays*, is full of problems, as Jonathan Lear (2003: 157ff) observes. In proposing the death drive Freud defines an instinct as 'an urge inherent in organic life to restore an earlier state of things' (Freud, 1920: 36). This is a new description of what an instinct consists of; a departure from any definition Freud had given before. With some effort Freud manoeuvres it to encompass the self-preservative instincts.

> They are component instincts whose function it is to assure that the organism shall follow its own path to death, and to ward off any possible ways of returning to inorganic existence other than those which are immanent in the organism itself … The organism wishes to die only in its own fashion.
>
> (Freud, 1920: 39)

But the sexual instincts simply cannot be fitted into the new definition. Having just asserted that the urge to restore an earlier state is 'a universal attribute of instincts' (Freud, 1920: 36), Freud has to declare that one half of his duality is an exception.

Even allowing for this, the attempt to identify Eros with the sexual instinct does not work. Freud published *Beyond the Pleasure Principle* in the same year as the fourth edition of *Three Essays on the Theory of Sexuality*. In the former he refers to the speech about love by Aristophanes in Plato's *Symposium* (Freud,

1920: 57f), while the latter has a new preface, which states 'how closely the enlarged sexuality of psychoanalysis coincides with the Eros of the divine Plato' (Freud, 1905: 134). Freud is repeating his identification of sexuality with the 'Eros of the poets and philosophers', but Lear shows that this is a revisionist rewriting by Freud of his own history. In the *Three Essays,* Freud was not concerned with Eros, and the same passage from Plato that occurs in *Beyond the Pleasure Principle* is referenced in the *Three Essays* (Freud, 1905: 136), not to confirm the 'popular view' that sexuality and love are essentially related, but to distinguish them and imply their separateness (Lear, 2003: 160).

Two new concepts are introduced in *Beyond the Pleasure Principle*: Eros, and the death drive. It is the wrong one that has been seen as revolutionary. Lear (2003: 158) comments that the death drive 'fits [Freud's] old conception of the psychic apparatus as aiming to reduce stimulation; and the death drive only extends this idea by suggesting that the ultimate reduction is towards zero'. He also quotes Loewald's remark that 'the death drive is really nothing new, not a conception that should have taken analysts by surprise' (Loewald, 1980 [1971]: 62). The truly revolutionary concept is Eros.

The perspective of this chapter allows us to see that, as with the concept of the sexual drive, Freud was saying more than he realised. The equation of Eros with sexuality does not hold in the form in which he stated it. To call Eros a drive, however, highlights the idea of an impulse of love that is naturally bound up with sexuality, but is not reducible to it. This is the radical conception to which Lear gives the name of 'Love as a drive'.

This chapter proposes an account of sexuality, rooted in biology but balanced also between the aim of a drive and its quality of object-relatedness. It also has in it the makings of an account of Eros. The *Three Essays* were published just over 100 years ago. For psychoanalysis to offer our culture a construction of sexuality which opened into a view of Eros would be not a bad start for the next 100 years.

Notes

1   A sign of the change in theoretical climate which I am discussing is how much less common it is nowadays to refer to 'the pervert' as a generalised description of a particular type of person. When Arlow refers to the essential problem of 'most male perverts' (see p.77), he is operating from a distinctly old-fashioned perspective. When Freud mentions 'the analysis of children and what are called perverts' (see p.72), his reference to 'what are called' perverts seems to indicate his awareness of the labelling, and a desire to distance himself from it.

2   Klein attached a specific conceptual meaning to the word 'phantasy', which is indicated conventionally by the spelling 'phantasy', instead of 'fantasy', which I use elsewhere in this book.

3   Although Freud said that the concept of instinct lies 'on the frontier between the mental and the physical' (Freud, 1905: 168), where the source is concerned he referred to it explicitly as 'somatic', as in the passages quoted above (p.73).

4   This reference to homosexuality has a historical context. In 1998, when I was writing the paper on which this chapter is based, there was a vociferous public debate in Britain

about the status of homosexuality. This had been prompted, in large part, by the visit to London, in 1995, of Charles Socarides, an American psychoanalyst who is quoted on pp.75f. Socarides was something of a standard-bearer for the view of homosexuality as pathological by definition; an illness which psychoanalysis should attempt to cure. He wrote, for instance, of 'the severe sexual disorders such as homosexuality and the other sexual deviations' (Socarides, 1976: 371). His lectures in London provoked a furious reaction from those who found his views socially unacceptable. However, while opposition to him was mounted on ideological grounds, there was no adequate debate in theoretical terms (see www.qrd.org/qrd/religion/anti/protesters.storm.antigay. psychs.lecture-04.29.95). Against this background it seemed useful to point out that the ideas presented here make it possible to think psychoanalytically about the perversity or otherwise of *any* relationship, including a homosexual one, on the basis not of the gender of the object, but of the quality of relating.

6

OEDIPAL DISIDENTIFICATION

Au nom du fils, au nom de la fille

The natural history of the Oedipus complex has been debated since Strachey (1961), editing Freud's (1924) paper on its 'dissolution', raised the question of whether such dissolution in fact occurs. In Chapter 5, reference was made (p.72) to discussion of the Oedipus complex as a lifelong developmental process (Parsons, 2000: 105–27). Just as that chapter revisited psychoanalytic concepts of sexuality in order to develop them further, so this one is a revisiting and fresh exploration of the Oedipus complex.

Newly qualified analysts naturally base their way of working on their experience in their own analyses. They tend to do what their analysts did, and this identification is a necessary springboard for the development of an analyst's identity. Then comes the important moment of deciding to do something differently: to deal with fees, or holiday dates, in another way; to make the sort of interpretation that never happened in one's own analysis, or not to interpret what one's own analyst certainly would have done. The identification with one's own analyst has been essential, but this moment is a threshold of freedom. Likewise, in the early stages of their careers musicians play, artists paint, scientists design experiments in the kind of way that their teachers did. This is inevitable and, as with analysts, it is how they begin to form themselves as musicians, painters and scientists. However, to develop their individual identities they have to free themselves from this identification. More accurately, they have to free themselves from its inevitability. Doing things the way one's teacher, or one's analyst, did needs to become a matter of choice, which implies the freedom to do them differently. From having been a functional necessity, identification becomes a constraint from which liberation is needed, so that it can finally be made use of autonomously.

It is a revelatory experience to listen to the piano sonatas of Beethoven in chronological order. From 1795 to 1800, he writes eleven, all in conventional sonata form, composing in identification with his predecessors. But one can hear him pushing at the limits of the form and suddenly, in 1800–1801, come three sonatas unlike any that he or anyone else had written before. Opus 26 in A flat has a first movement in variation form, a funeral march for its slow movement, and contains no movement in the standard sonata form. Beethoven gives both the two Opus 27 sonatas the title *Sonata quasi una fantasia*, subverting the idea of what a sonata consists of. One of these is the well-known 'Moonlight' Sonata. This does have an energetic movement in sonata form, typical of a conventional opening movement, but it is placed by Beethoven at the end of the work. The first movement refuses the usual sense of contrast and development. It is serene and contemplative, pointing mysteriously towards the finale with whose unexpected sonata form the work closes. The musicologist Wilfred Mellers writes that the experiential relationship of the movements in this sonata 'is more "organic" than anything in Beethoven's previous work' (Mellers, 1983: 77). Having thus emancipated himself from identification with his predecessors, Beethoven returned, in his later sonatas, to conventional structures, but with unprecedented freedom in his use of them.

An active process of disidentification is required for this shift. A patient was appreciating his analysis and benefiting from it, but when he came across a paper I had published, and saw the notice of a lecture I was giving, he found this difficult. My professional success, as he interpreted it, gave rise to a conflict in him between gratitude and envy (Klein, 1957). He dealt with this by a somewhat idealising admiration and a wish to be just like me in his own field of work. This was at first constructive, in that it allowed him a relationship to me in which the analytic work could progress and the identification be interpreted. But it was also obstructive to his autonomous development. Then he saw another paper of mine which had a long list of references. He talked about the hours I must have spent in a library digging out all those journals. 'I couldn't bear to spend my time doing that!' he said, in a tone that implied nobody in their right mind could bear it. Then he said, 'But maybe it just shows that you and I are different sorts of people.' To be able to have this thought implied a psychic separation from me, where previously he would have found any idea of dissimilarity between us an unthinkable contradiction in terms. This freedom to be different from me opened a way for him to take what he found valuable in me and make constructive use of it for himself.

Octave Mannoni (1988) emphasised the interplay between identification and disidentification as an essential factor in psychic development. His examples indicate, though, that he is mostly concerned with defensive aspects of identification, and with the ongoing need to extricate oneself from counterproductive identifications. My concern is rather with the biphasic quality of identification, which is first necessary and productive for development, but then blocks its progress, so that disidentification is needed for forward movement to continue. Mannoni also maintains that the fact of becoming conscious of an identification means in itself that disidentification takes place: the very process of bringing the identification into consciousness is what disidentification consists of. This may apply to the defensive identifications that Mannoni is primarily dealing with. However, in the case of those identifications that have been essential to development, the subsequent disidentifying will involve substantial psychic work, of which the previous example begins to give an indication.

This has a specific importance in sexual development. According to the standard oedipal narrative, a child is involved in relationships of desire with the parent of the opposite sex, and of rivalry with the parent of the same sex. Both relationships are conflictual: the first because the desire is unfulfilled and leads to frustration; the second because the rivalry arouses guilt and fear of retaliation. What moves the situation forward is a shift from object relating to identification. Daughter and son give up their relationships of rivalry—she with her mother, he with his father—and identify with those same parents instead. This elision of duality in the child's mind between itself and the parent means that competition between them as separate individuals disappears. The relationship of desire towards the other parent becomes manageable because the child is identified with the parent for whom this relationship is legitimate. A son's identification with his father, and a daughter's with her mother, open the way for them to find, in due course, mature sexual relationships of their own outside the family. So goes the familiar story. What is not so often mentioned is the further need for a process of disidentification from the parent who has been identified with.

The dilemma for adolescents, as they move into adulthood, is not just whether they can achieve a sexual relationship, however gendered, but what kind of sexual relationship in emotional terms is psychically possible for them. If their relationships remain based on their identifications with the parent of the same sex, the choice of object open to them will be limited by the range of object choice that that parent was able to make. When sons marry women like their mothers, and daughters men like their fathers, this is not just the continuation of an oedipal attachment to the parent of the opposite sex. It is a continuing identification with the object choice of the parent of the same sex. The identification with that parent is essential to a child's development but, if it is not to limit the young adult's internal freedom in choosing a partner, it must eventually be given up. This does not signify a rejection of that parent's qualities nor imply that a son, for example, should necessarily choose someone unlike his mother. The point is not to make a different choice from one's parent for its own sake, but to arrive at freedom in the choice of object.

Here are two illustrations of what may happen when this disidentification is not achieved satisfactorily.

A patient in his early thirties was considering whether to emigrate. Both his parents seemed to have felt defeated by life and the home atmosphere as he grew up was bleak. He described his father as a chronically depressed and phobic man, who avoided social contacts and any kind of intimacy. He was hard to relate to emotionally, and could not offer any real closeness to his wife or son. The patient's mother had been an academic. She gave up her work when he was born and resented never having found her way back to it. Stories suggested that she was more cheerful earlier in her life, but he mostly remembered her as unhappy and irritable. She might have had a breakdown of some sort during his early childhood. Sometimes she was able to enjoy life and could be quite funny, but such moments were rare and unpredictable. There was a sad sort of excitement for him in trying to get these livelier reactions out of his mother at the risk of annoying her.

When this patient was a child his father would never ask what he thought about anything. His mother, however, did think he had a mind. She could be interested in his school projects, and sometimes she would listen to him and discuss his ideas. He felt close to her at these times, but they were also complicated. They were special, and when his mother collapsed back into her usual moroseness he felt frustrated and miserable. On the other hand, these moments never happened when his father was around, and he was uncomfortable at the way his mother denigrated his father and so obviously preferred to be just with her son. As he approached puberty, these special times with his mother began to feel wrong, and they stopped quite suddenly. During his teens he became depressed and anxious. He avoided going out and socialising and, although the idea of a girlfriend appealed to him, he was too inhibited to risk trying to find one. It was clear that when puberty made desire for his tantalising mother feel too dangerous, he dealt with this by identifying with his socially phobic and depressed father. Unfortunately, the identification his father offered was not helpful for his development.

In his twenties this man began a relationship with a woman whom initially he found stimulating and exciting. She was chronically dissatisfied with her life, however, and when he did well in his work he did not feel she took pleasure in his success. He came to think, in fact, that she was not really interested in him, and did not get much enjoyment from being with him. Their relationship became rather flat, and seemed to be continuing by default. She did not appear to want emotional intimacy and he thought she was irritated by feeling dependent on him. At the same time, he recognised that he had given up hoping for anything better, and was drifting along in the relationship in an emotionally closed-off way himself. This man's choice of a woman who seemed at first to offer something lively but then withdrew into dejection and resentment, and the mode of relating into which he himself retreated in response, showed how subject he still was to the identification with his father. His idea of emigrating—something his father could not have conceived of doing—was a desperate attempt both to think about, and not to have to think about, his internal situation.

This man's problems were not just because the persisting identification with his father was an unsatisfactory one. To be imprisoned in any identification, even an apparently good one, is a limitation of freedom.

The second of these examples is of a woman in her mid-sixties. She occupied a high position in her professional field and came into analysis because of issues stirred up by the ending of her career. Her father had been a larger-than-life character who worked in the performing arts. He was well-known and successful, but self-centred and vain about his achievements. His wife was a good-natured schoolteacher and he was contemptuous of her easy-going enjoyment of day-to-day reality. At the same time, he was emotionally dependent on her. He readily felt slighted by his friends, and would take setbacks in his artistic life very personally. He was often in a depressed, somewhat paranoid state for days on end, until he could be helped to feel that he occupied centre stage again. My patient had memories from her young childhood of her father taking her backstage in theatres where he was working. These were exciting occasions, but usually he was too self-absorbed to have much time for her, and she was often in a muted fury about the way he oppressed the family with his unpredictable moods. She admired her mother's tolerance and the apparently non-masochistic way she coped with her difficult husband. Her mother enjoyed her teaching, had activities and friendships of her own and seemed to live a reasonably satisfying life. When her mother died this woman thought, *the wrong one went first,* and when her father died not long afterwards she felt guilty at the relief of not having to look after him.

The mother taught English and an identification with her seemed to have been what steered the daughter towards a field of work involving language. Early on, she was offered what looked like an outstanding career opportunity, but the results were unexpectedly traumatic. After committing herself to a major practical upheaval in her life, she found her new work environment not at all congenial and, before long, the project she had been invited to work on was closed down. She was left, as she put it, 'stuck with nothing'. Soon after this she got married.

The point of this example is that the husband she chose to marry, at this moment in her life, was a more benign version of her father. He also was a performing artist, and eventually quite successful, but he was a prickly, irritable character, often reacting to frustration with a childish kind of petulance. His engagements meant he was sometimes away from home for long periods, but he used to take it badly when his wife was away on her own work assignments. As her career recovered and went on developing, she had to calculate how much independence on her part he could tolerate. Nevertheless, she said it had been a good marriage. Her husband was basically a kind and caring person. She could be exasperated by his regressive demands, but on balance she found their life together rewarding. Sometimes, over the years, she had questioned the marriage, but her feelings swung back, like a compass needle, to the conviction that what she and her husband meant to each other mattered more than the difficulties between them.

This woman's father, like the previous patient's mother, seemed potentially interesting and exciting, but in fact proved frustrating and disappointing. Just as that man's solution was to identify with his father, this woman dealt with her conflicted feelings about her father through an identification with her mother. Such an identification with the parent of the same sex is, as I have said, a normal aspect of development, but the quality of this identification will inevitably be variable. This woman's mother offered her a better identification than the previous patient's father was able to offer him, and it allowed her to make a good enough marriage. The marriage took place, however, at a moment when she was vulnerable to a regressive pull towards the identification with her mother. If this woman, having made use of that identification when she needed it, could have subsequently disidentified more thoroughly from her mother, she would have had greater freedom in her choice of object. This might have helped her to find a relationship that offered her greater emotional mutuality.

This disidentifying does not mean repudiating the parent who has been identified with. It is a matter of no longer being subject to the identification. There is, all the same, an act of negation involved. An existing prohibition is being abrogated.

In Jacques Lacan's (2006 [1953]: 230) vivid and epigrammatic phrase, the original identification with the parent is instituted 'in the Name of the Father' —'*au nom du père*'. There is a play on words. In French, the word '*nom*' ('name') has the same sound as '*non*' ('no'). When '*le nom du père*' is spoken, we also hear '*le "non" du père*'. This represents a necessary paternal interdiction. To be capable of this 'No!' ('*Non!*') is an essential aspect of what it means to be a father: the name (*nom*) of the Father. The father's 'No!' is spoken twice. First, there is the 'No!' directed at the early dyadic fusion of the infant, of either sex, with the mother. On the one hand, the father is a containing presence for the mother–infant couple. On the other, his interposition of himself, as a third term, disrupts what Freud (1923b: 31) called the infant's 'primary' identification. This '*non*' *du père* impels the infant to form an object relationship with the mother as a separate being. The father's second 'No!' is directed at the son who has discovered the mother as an object of desire. It is this interdiction of desire which initiates the son's oedipal identification with the father.

I am playing here with Lacan's idea. This pun between '*nom*' and '*non*', which I am emphasising, is not part of Lacan's own thinking, or at any rate is not spelt out by him. How Lacan himself conceived of the *nom du père* is well summarised by Malcolm Bowie.

> For Lacan as for Freud the primal Other is the father within the Oedipal triangle, who forbids incest, threatens castration, and, by placing an absolute prohibition on the child's desire for its mother, becomes the inaugurating agent of Law. Lacan is concerned not with the real or imaginary fathers of a given individual but with the symbolic father whose name initiates and propels the signifying chain: 'It is in the *name of the father* [*nom du père*] that we must recognise the support of the symbolic function which, from the dawn of history, has identified his person with the figure of the law'. The original encounter with the legislating *nom du père*, and the abiding lack and non-satisfaction to which the subject is thereby condemned, produce the

complex pattern of intermingled aggression and subservience which is to mark the subject indelibly in his dealings with others.

(Bowie, 1979: 134f)

Evidently, the concept extends far beyond the oedipal context of the family, and the overtly sexual arena, to pervade all aspects of an individual's relation to society and the world. To foreclose the meaning of a concept, however, limiting it to what its creator has said about it, would be contrary to Lacan's own thinking. For him, meaning consists of a relation between words and what they denote, between a 'signifier' and the 'signified'. The meaning of a signifier is never fixed. It is always liable to be displaced, so that the precise nature of any signified—that is to say, what it is that any given signifier signifies—can never be finally pinned down. Lacan's paradigm example is the 'Purloined Letter' in Edgar Allan Poe's short story of that name. The letter shifts from person to person through the story—from the queen who received it, to the thief who steals it, to the detective who recovers it—without its content ever being revealed. It exemplifies, according to Bowie, 'a pure migratory signifier'.

As it passes from hand to hand, and moves from point to point within a complex web of intersubjective perception ... it attracts different meanings to itself, mediates different kinds of power relationship and determines subjects in what they do and are.

(Bowie, 1979: 141)

Lacan's famous, or notorious, wordplay is a calculated evocation of the continual play of signifiers, with any presumed meaning always disappearing behind the next one. The deliberate intention not to allow the meaning of his ideas to be captured definitively is what makes an attempt to understand Lacan both intriguing and infuriating. Personally, Lacan was much identified with by his followers; but his view of psychoanalytic concepts implies the importance of a continual process of disidentifying. My playing with Lacan's idea, to do *au nom du père* what Lacan did not do, is in response to his own view of how psychoanalytic concepts work. The phrase *'le nom du père'* is itself a signifier, which I am accepting Lacan's invitation to purloin and displace.

The mother, as well as the infant, is the target of the first *nom du père*. Greenson (1968) discussed the importance, for infants of either sex, of disidentifying from the mother. He thought this mattered particularly for boys, in order to avoid the risk of their sexual identities being feminised. This disidentification out of the mother–infant dyad is also discussed by Marcus Johns (2002). He describes a father who wanted his wife and son to remain as a dyad, subservient to his own authority, rather than supporting 'the appropriate distancing of a son from his mother'. The case shows the essential role of the father 'in securing the son's disidentification from the mother' (Johns, 2002:

190). Greenson and Johns refer particularly to boys, but this first *nom du père* applies to the pregenital infant of both sexes, boy and girl.

The later *nom du père*, the father's negation of the son's oedipal desire for his mother, is what inaugurates a son's active identification with his father. When the son eventually determines that he is no longer subject to this identification, an unconscious act of negation on the son's part abrogates the *nom du père*. This filial disidentification may be considered, I suggest, as the '*nom du fils*'.

Corresponding to the *nom du père* there is a '*nom de la mère*', directed by the mother at her daughter, which negates the daughter's oedipal desire for her father, and institutes the daughter's oedipal identification with her mother. And there is likewise a '*nom de la fille*'; the daughter's act of negation when eventually she abrogates this identification.

This concept of the *nom du fils* and *nom de la fille* may help to clarify the debate about whether or not the Oedipus complex has an end point. The father's and mother's interdictions, of the son's desire for his mother and the daughter's for her father, initiate identification, as I have said, with the parent of the same sex. There are two aspects to this identification. As a defensive response on the child's part, it runs its phase-specific course, and when the need for the defence has been superseded, it concludes in the disidentification that I am describing. What is instigated by the *nom du père* and the *nom de la mère* is ended by the *nom du fils* and the *nom de la fille*. This brings an element of closure to the process of oedipal development, in conformity with Freud's (1924) account of the 'dissolution' of the Oedipus complex.

But does the complex disappear so absolutely (Strachey, 1961)? A second aspect of oedipal identification reveals the Oedipus complex to be a developmental process continuing throughout life (Loewald, 1980 [1979], 1985; Parsons, 2000: 105–27). As well as being a defence against the threat of castration, the identification with the parent of the same sex has a constructive developmental function. It enables the child to explore, and begin to enter into, its own experience of adult sexual identity. This is why it is important that the child should experience castration anxiety. Oedipal development can go wrong, broadly speaking, in either of two directions. On the one hand, if a child does not experience a safe boundary between fantasy and reality, in its own or in the parent's mind, then the anxiety that fantasy could become reality may be too great, inhibiting the child's essential use of fantasy to explore and develop its sexuality. On the other hand, if a daughter's relationship with her father, for example, does not provoke *sufficient* anxiety in her, not much need for defence will be felt and a strong identification with her mother may not be produced. This matters because the oedipal mother is not just a rival to her daughter. She is also the woman who shows her daughter the way to a womanhood of her own. The daughter needs this identification to gain a sense of what being a mature sexual woman means for her mother. Then she must free herself, by disidentification, from the limitation of seeing womanhood only through her mother's eyes. Without both these stages she cannot find her own way towards being whatever kind of woman she has it in herself to be. All this applies as well, of course, where son and father are concerned. Seen from this angle, the disidentification marks not the close of something that has run its course, but the opening of a new horizon.

It is schematic to present any developmental process as a linear progression. The distinction between pre-oedipal and oedipal identification is real, but in clinical practice pre-oedipal and oedipal do not appear in pure culture. Work with one always involves, to some degree, work with the other as well. Likewise identification does not give way to disidentification all at once. A child's identification with its parent has many aspects, and disidentification happens piecemeal, involving some elements at one time, some at another. Nor is it immediately stable. There will be swings back to identification before disidentification is consolidated. As with all developmental processes, there are eddies and countercurrents within an overall tidal flow.

Identification can be difficult for children if their parents are physically absent or not emotionally available for it. Disidentification may also be problematic if parents consciously or unconsciously find it hard to consent to it.

A woman with a son and daughter in their twenties was in psychotherapy twice a week. She had always had clear ideas about the kind of people she wanted her children to become, the careers they were to pursue and the marriages they would make. She found it difficult when they did not follow suit. With the help of her therapy she became more able to accept how they differed from her preconceptions of them. One day, she said she had nothing on her mind and did not really want to talk. After some silence she said that yesterday had been her son's birthday. She and her husband had had dinner with him and his wife, whom she disliked and who was not the kind of woman she hoped her son would marry. He had a new job, less prestigious than she had hoped, but he seemed to find it rewarding. She said she thought she could accept his not being as brilliant as she had wanted. The dinner was surprisingly relaxed. She and her husband had disagreed about politics with their daughter-in-law, but it was a straightforward argument without a hidden emotional subtext.

Then she spoke of her daughter, who had just undergone a traumatic experience. This was being dealt with adequately and, rather to my patient's surprise, she did not feel she needed to get involved. She thought she really was letting her children move away from her. Then she mentioned shifting a photograph of her son, taken in his teens, to a new position in her house. 'It's strange,' she said. 'I've always thought of it as a recent photo, but it's a long time ago now.' I said, 'You mean he's shifted in your mind, as well.' There was a silence of several minutes and she said again that her mind felt empty. She did not seem bothered by this, and I said that one thing I thought she felt emptier of, was a kind of anxious concern to monitor her children and check that they were getting on as she thought they should be. After a moment, she said she knew it was trivial, but the hardest thing to let go of was to do with her daughter. She was attractive and always looked good, but my patient knew that if she herself could be the one to dress her daughter, taking her to the right shops and showing her what to wear, then she could be absolutely stunning. I could hear the sadness of this mother as she told me she had never been allowed to do that. Since puberty, in fact, her daughter had never wanted to wear anything but jeans and sweaters. I said she might call it trivial, but I thought she found it very painful to give up the idea that she could make her daughter more attractive than her daughter herself knew how to.

This woman was struggling bravely with the recognition that she had regarded both her children as extensions of herself. With her son it seemed to be mainly a pre-oedipal disidentification that was in question. No doubt there was a sexual element in her rivalry with her son's wife. Parents have to contend with sexual jealousy towards the partners of their children, and I have written elsewhere of the parent's downwardly directed oedipal conflict of later life (Parsons, 2000: 123). But this woman's negative reaction to her son's marriage seemed mostly to be a narcissistic grievance that he should marry someone so unlike the sort of woman she would have chosen for him. She was reluctant for him to make any choice, of career or wife, independently of her. With him, her difficulty was more in letting him differentiate out from a dyadic fusion with her than in giving him up to a rival object relationship.

With her daughter, on the other hand, while a dyadic element was no doubt present, the question at issue was who would control the daughter's attractiveness to a man, and what kind of mature sexual woman the daughter should be. In this case, it was the oedipal identification that the daughter was abrogating. As with the previous examples, this shows that for a woman to be truly a daughter (the *nom de la fille*), and not simply a carbon copy of her mother, necessarily involves a disidentification (the *non de la fille*). It is worth emphasising again that for this daughter to disidentify from her mother as a sexual woman did not signify a rejection of female sexuality. It meant not being bound to her mother's version of what it was to be a sexual woman, and that is what her mother found hard to bear.[1]

Earlier in the chapter I set out the sequence:

1 Identification begins as a functional necessity which helps psychic development forward.
2 It then becomes a constraint from which it is necessary to liberate oneself by a process of disidentification.
3 If this is successful the original identification may be taken up on fresh terms so as to make new creative use of it.

Disidentification allows identification to be made use of in a state of freedom. Beethoven's piano sonatas offer one example. Here is another illustration, from Greek tragedy, of the essential relation between the *Non du fils* and the *nom du fils*.

In Sophocles' play *Trachiniae* the dying Heracles believes that his wife Deianira is responsible for killing him. He commands his son Hyllus to 'show himself a true-born son' (Sophocles, *Trach.* 1064ff) by bringing her to Heracles for him to kill her in revenge. This instruction to collaborate in the murder of his mother is a grotesque perversion of what it means for Hyllus to be a son to his father. It arises, in the play's complicated plot, from Heracles' wish to marry Iolē, a young princess who would in fact be a more appropriate bride for Hyllus. Heracles is blocking his son's disidentification from him by taking for himself the kind of woman that Hyllus might marry. Hyllus, however, rejects the identification demanded by his father as a distortion of what it means to be a son, and refuses to bring his mother to be killed. Later, in a different state of mind, Heracles gives Hyllus another command, again in the name of being a true son to his father. After his father's death, Hyllus himself is to marry Iolē (1224ff). There is a crucial ambiguity to this. Heracles insists that Hyllus should marry the woman he himself had wanted, apparently locking his son's identification with him into place. But the same command is also Heracles' renunciation of Iolē in favour of Hyllus. He has recognised that she is the right object choice for Hyllus, not himself, and his command is an acknowledgement of his son's necessary disidentification from him. Hyllus' *non du fils*, his declaration of independence, has become a step on the way to his *nom du fils*, a true sonship that can make creative use of the father's identity.[2]

The following clinical example shows a son trying to liberate himself from a compulsive identification with his father that hindered his development, so as to be free to identify with aspects of his father that he can use constructively.

An opera singer was in analysis four times a week. Although successful professionally, he was afraid this must somehow be a sham and he would be shown up as an impostor. His father was a politician, renowned as a public speaker. According to the patient, he was also narrow-minded and intolerant, and in the family there was an oppressive sort of morality, with the father constantly on the lookout for transgressions. The patient's childhood was dominated by his father's explosive rages. He dreaded his father's return home in the evenings, wondering every day what he would be punished or beaten for. But he also felt compassion for his father whom he saw as a tormented, insecure man. He thought that being admired for his speeches was the only way his father could feel any confidence in himself. With an extreme ambivalence he both hated his father and had deep sympathy for him. The patient's mother was intelligent and creative, but deprived of education. She was indulgent to her son, and when she knew he was doing things his father would disapprove of she shared his excitement in a conspiratorial sort of way. This man avoided confrontation. Although he often thought people were deceiving or trying to exploit him, he would let himself be taken advantage of rather than risk an argument. Apparently minor incidents, however, could suddenly provoke him to uncontrollable fury.

His mother's seductiveness brought out both rivalry and identification with his father. The continuing identification was evident both in the episodes of rage and in the satisfaction he gained as a singer from using his voice to hold an audience. The latter had the potential to be a rewarding part of his life, but only if it were not limited to the defensive function that he had seen performance serve in his father's life. He needed to be free to explore the identification with his father instead of being locked into it. How significant these issues were for him is shown in the following clinical material.

He thought that a friend might be trying to cheat him out of some money. He could not bring himself to confront his friend, or even ask him to clarify the situation. If this friend did turn out to be swindling him, he insisted, he would have no difficulty in forgiving him. I interpreted that he was confused about what the deception, if it were the case, would mean to him. If he reacted to it as something dishonest or unethical, he would feel identified with a moralistic aspect of his father from which he was trying to escape. His concern not to get into that position meant that any sort of negative response was disallowed. This prevented his seeing the situation in terms of a personal relationship, where the sense of betrayal would matter and anger would be legitimate.

The next day, he spoke of his fear of his wife's criticism. When he had shown their teenage son how to put in some electric wiring, she had just been angry he had not done more of it. This made him feel wretched. Then he said that after yesterday's session he was able to be more assertive with his friend. It seemed odd to him now that he had not kept a closer eye on what his friend was doing. I said it seemed he did not think he had the right to ask, and linked this to the helpless feeling which his wife's criticism evoked. He agreed, and said his feeling of being able to confront his friend had soon begun to seep away. He asked his son how he would react if he thought he had been swindled and his son said he would be furious.

I said he was letting me know that discussing the situation with me had helped him stand up for himself, but not for very long. I thought that in asking his son how he would react, he wanted to know what sort of father he had managed to be. Had he helped his son to feel that he could stand up for himself? 'Standing up' for himself was not an accidental figure of speech. It was an implicit reference to the castration anxiety that underlies this material. My comment implied a transference interpretation about his wish to use me as a different sort of father from his own, so as to help him become a different sort of father himself.

He said he realised suddenly why his confidence disappeared when he was trying to confront his friend. His body language and tone of voice must have shown that he did not trust him, but he had not been able to say this in so many words. He thought it was very wrong to reveal his feelings indirectly like that, without confessing his distrust openly to his friend. His shame at this was what had made his confidence vanish. He turned to thinking about what sort of father he was, and said he did not believe he was much of one. For one thing his work had meant he was not there for his son as he should have been. 'So your son,' I said, 'might have enjoyed having his father show him how to install an electric circuit.' 'Oh!' he said, sounding surprised. 'Yes, maybe he did.'

I did not understand at first why he should feel so guilty about the discrepancy between the words he spoke and his tone of voice and body language. It struck me as odd that an opera singer, whose work involved conveying the truth of feelings by the expressivity of his voice and body, should criticise himself for doing exactly that. Then I thought of the identification with his father, a man whose narrow rigidity would insist that, on all occasions, one must automatically tell the whole truth without any concealment. A moral straitjacket of this sort seemed to be leading the patient to interpret the actual honesty of his voice and body as a failure of integrity.

This man wished for an identification with his father that he could put to good use in his own life and be grateful for. To an extent this was happening in his operatic career, and my last comment had picked up his desire, as a father, to offer a good identification to his own son. But he could not identify freely with his father as a fine vocal performer while he was locked in identification with his father the oppressive moralist, and the father whose anger erupted in uncontrollable outbursts. His own performance was still constrained by what performing had meant where his father was concerned, and he could not yet be confident in the fathering he was offering his own son. If he could continue with his disidentification, then identification with his father might no longer be something he was subject to, but a resource for him to draw on and make use of for his continuing development, both as an artist and as a father.

Late in his life the poet Rainer Maria Rilke wrote to a young man who had asked for advice:

> When I think now of myself in my youth, I realise that it was for me absolutely a case of having to go away at the risk of annoying and hurting ... What I write as an artist will probably be marked, to the end, by traces of that opposition by means of which I set myself on my own course. And yet, if you ask me, I would not want *this* to be what emanated above all from my works. It is not struggle and revolt, not the deserting of what surrounds and claims us that I would wish young people to deduce from my writings, but rather that they should bear in a new conciliatory spirit what is given, offered ...
>
> (Hass, 1987: xliii)

Rilke was brought up as a girl by his mother, and then sent to a brutal military academy by his father. Whether or not this passage may be linked to the problems of his oedipal situation, it captures well the developmental movement delineated in this chapter.

Notes

1 The paper which is the origin of this chapter was presented in Athens, in March 2002. Afterwards, some women expressed particular appreciation, saying it was liberating, in their traditionally minded and male-orientated culture, to hear that a woman could be expected to disidentify from her mother so as to find an identity that was truly her own. The paper treated the *nom du fils* and the *nom de la fille* symmetrically, as the present chapter still does. This conversation made me reflect, however, that in many parts of the world it is more acceptable for a son to disidentify from his father than a daughter from her mother.

2 For a detailed psychoanalytic discussion of *Trachiniae* see Parsons (2000: 115–27).

7

NARCISSISM AS PRISON, NARCISSISM AS SPRINGBOARD

A Reading of Sophocles' *Ajax*

Narcissism is one of the more complicated and confusing ideas in psychoanalytic theory. In his landmark paper introducing the concept Freud linked it to psychosis, which he thought was characterised by the withdrawal of libido from external reality into a narcissistic cathexis of the ego (Freud, 1914c: 74f).[1] A year later, he classified schizophrenia as a 'narcissistic psychoneurosis' (Freud, 1915a: 124). Not surprising then that narcissism has tended to be discussed in terms of pathology. When Ronald Britton (2003: 145ff), for example, set out to clarify the concept, he found it used in three ways: as an observable lack of interest in others and preoccupation with oneself; as a force or tendency in the personality that opposes relationships with others; and in reference to a group of conditions known as the 'narcissistic disorders'. Britton's discussion centres largely on these latter cases, and the part played in them by libidinal and destructive narcissism. This focus on pathological aspects of narcissism typifies much of the literature on the subject. So it is important to remember that the statements by Freud just mentioned are balanced, in his writings, by other passages such as these:

> All through the subject's life his ego remains the great reservoir of his libido, from which object-cathexes are sent out and into which the libido can stream back again from the objects. Thus narcissistic libido is constantly being transformed into object-libido and *vice versa*.
>
> (Freud, 1925b: 56)

> In rare cases one can observe that the ego has taken itself as an object and is behaving as though it were in love with itself. Hence the term 'narcissism', borrowed from the Greek myth. But that is only an extreme exaggeration of a normal state of affairs. We came to understand that the ego is always the main reservoir of libido, from which libidinal cathexes of objects go out and into which they return

again, while the major part of this libido remains permanently in the ego. Thus ego libido is being constantly changed into object libido and object libido into ego libido.

(Freud, 1933: 102f)

Freud saw ego-libido not just as a retreat from object-libido, but as a necessary counterpart to it. There is a continuous oscillation between investment in the ego and investment in external objects. Narcissism only becomes pathological when this free mobility of libido breaks down.

Lichtenstein (1983 [1964]) stressed the qualitative change which the concept of narcissism brought into Freud's view of psychic development. He remarks how close Freud's thinking is to biological, especially embryological, concepts of development. He draws attention, for example, to Freud's comparison between an infant's 'psychical system shut off from the stimuli of the external world' and 'a bird's egg with its food supply enclosed in its shell' (Freud, 1911: 219–20fn). Such a view of development implies progression from a simple primary configuration to a complex, individualised and highly structured end condition. The unidirectional nature of this process means that any retrograde movement must involve disintegration of what has been achieved developmentally. Lichtenstein observes that narcissism introduces into development the crucial idea of reversibility. He acknowledges that regression in the sense of disintegration is certainly possible, but his central point remains: the oscillating ebb and flow of libido between objects and ego, between external and internal reality, is henceforth understood as an essential aspect of the developmental process.

The importance of appropriate withdrawal from the external world is seen most obviously in sleep. Freud wrote: 'In a sleeper the primal state of distribution of the libido is restored—total narcissism, in which libido and ego-interest, still united and indistinguishable, dwell in the self-sufficing ego' Freud (1916–17: 417). Bertram Lewin (1955) drew a comparison between the nature of the mind's activity during sleep and in the psychoanalytic setting. Censorship and resistance, for example, play a large part in clinical work, while in sleep they are the psychic mechanisms behind dreaming. In each case there is a withdrawal of cathexis from external reality. In Lewin's words, 'the narcissism of sleep … coincides with narcissism on the couch' (1955: 171f). Lewin is not using 'narcissism' here to denote pathology. It is a metapsychological description of a self-absorbed state of mind which is necessary for a certain kind of psychic work: dreaming on the one hand, analytic work on the other. These are both avenues of access to the unconscious, and they both illustrate the double need for narcissistic withdrawal into the self, and for the ability to re-emerge from this. Self-absorption is not in itself pathological. What is damaging is imprisonment in a narcissistic state of mind.

This recalls a discussion by Gregorio Kohon (2011) of John Steiner's (1993) concept of 'psychic retreats'. These are modes of psychic functioning to which someone may retreat if their psychic equilibrium feels threatened. Different individuals will retreat in different ways, according to what feels safe and familiar to them. Steiner (1993: 5) claims that such habitual retreats amount, by definition, to pathological organisations, while Kohon wants to make a case that withdrawing into the core of the self may, at times, be needful.

> While we undoubtedly depend on others to develop our sense of identity and need their recognition in order to derive personal meaning and satisfaction, we need to acknowledge and maintain 'a non-pathological, indeed a necessary, silence at the core of psychic life' (Cohen, 2010: 3). This silent core in us is connected to the possibility of creating and nurturing a private self (Modell, 1992), a self that can ignore and at times actively reject the cultural narratives that are imposed on us.
>
> (Kohon, 2011: 50)

In Kohon's view psychic retreats are only pathological when they become fixed and rigid. More than this, he sees it as a necessity to establish and make use of an inner psychic space that is isolated from outside contact. This, says Kohon, 'makes the subject feel real. It allows him to experience the continuity of his self, helping him or her to become creative. For the subject, periods of non-relatedness are as vital as periods of relatedness' (Kohon, 2011: 51). The importance of this during adolescence was stressed by Winnicott. 'This preservation of personal isolation is part of the search for identity, and for the establishment of a personal technique for communicating which does not lead to violation of the central self' (Winnicott, 1965 [1963]: 190). The freedom, at times to withdraw into such inward solitude, at other times to reach out and make contact with the world, and the interdependence between these two, reflect in terms of object relations what Lichtenstein described in the language of libido theory. It is only if libido becomes fixated on the ego, or the psychic retreat becomes a bunker, that development stops and disintegration may follow.

Psychic development tends nonetheless to be viewed in terms of progression from the ego being narcissistically invested in itself, to being able to invest itself in contact with others, and so develop a capacity for object-relating. The narcissism may be primary, or secondary if there has been a later retreat from object relationships, but narcissism and object-relating are essentially seen as alternatives; with swings no doubt between them, as Lichtenstein emphasised, but with the former, in normal development, gradually giving way to the latter.

Heinz Kohut developed a fresh conceptualisation of narcissism, which did not involve this oscillation of investment between ego and objects. Kohut's first step was to make a clear distinction between the ego and the self. The ego is an element of the psychic apparatus. It is a high-level metapsychological abstraction, inferred theoretically but not experienced subjectively. The self, on the other hand, is part of the individual's subjective experience. It is 'experience-near', as Kohut put it, while the ego is 'experience-distant' (Kohut, 1971: xivf). Joseph and Anne-Marie Sandler, in commenting on the work of Hartmann and Jacobson, also distinguished the self as the mental representation of the person that one is, from the ego as an element in the structure of the mind (Sandler and Sandler, 1998: 125f). In Kohut's thinking, narcissism is a matter of a person's relation, not to their experience-distant ego, but to their subjective sense of self. This radically shifts the relation between narcissism and psychic development. To give up attending to who one is as a person, would not be an index of maturation. Continuing attention to one's sense of self is as important an aspect of psychic maturity as is concern with object relationships. Kohut does not see narcissism and object-relating as being in a kind of psychic competition. He refers to the narcissistic 'sector' of the psyche, implying an object-relating sector also, with the two existing alongside each other (Kohut, 1971: 42). Each of these has its own parallel line of development. Kohut is clear that the mature self requires a sufficient and reliable supply of narcissistic investments, and that 'narcissistic sustenance' is necessary for cohesion of the self and a rewarding relationship with one's ideals (Kohut, 1971: 19, 21). Where regression is concerned Kohut does not see narcissism as a way station in a retreat from object-love. Instead there is 'the disintegration of higher forms of narcissism [and] the regression to archaic narcissistic positions' (Kohut, 1971: 6). 'Higher forms of narcissism' is a noteworthy phrase. For Kohut the achievement of qualities such as humour and wisdom depends on successful development of the narcissistic sector of the psyche (Kohut, 1971: 324–8).

Kohut's conceptual framework remains controversial, and more detailed exploration of it is beyond the scope of this chapter. It is clear enough, though, that he insists on the essential and continuing role of narcissism in normal development and healthy mental functioning.

Sophocles knew about this, as about so much that is important in psychoanalysis. His tragedy *Ajax* shows narcissism operating both as the source of psychotic breakdown, and as a necessary aspect of normal psychic life. The setting is the Greek camp at Troy after the death of Achilles. The dead hero's armour has been presented to Odysseus. For Ajax, who considers himself the greatest of the Greeks after Achilles, this is an unbearable humiliation. He sets out to murder Odysseus and those who awarded him the armour. In order to protect them, Athene has sent Ajax mad. He has attacked the sheep and cattle of the Greeks, torturing and killing them in the belief that the animals are Odysseus and the other Greek generals. At the beginning of the play he appears in this deluded state, surrounded by dead animals and triumphing in his supposed revenge. He recovers from his madness and is overcome with horror at what he has done. Despite all the pleas of his wife Tecmessa he commits suicide. The second half of the play amounts to a debate, in which Menelaus and Agamemnon, outraged at his attempt to murder them, forbid the burial of

Ajax's body, while Odysseus, up till now the arch-enemy of Ajax, shows an unexpected generosity of spirit and persuades them to allow Ajax the ritual honours due to him.

For a long way into the play, Ajax's madness is ascribed only to external causes. Athene needed to prevent him murdering the other Greek generals, and making him insane is how she did it. This is the Sophoclean equivalent of biological psychiatry. No connection is made between Ajax's psychotic breakdown and his inner mental life or character structure. The goddess has simply altered his brain chemistry. In the first half of the play, the only hint of another viewpoint lies in one remark by Ajax's wife. When Ajax has recovered from his delusion Tecmessa says that, now being sane again, he has to suffer the pain of realising that he himself has been the cause of his own disaster (Sophocles, *Ajax*: 258ff). On the surface this refers simply to Ajax's discovery that he is the one who slaughtered the sheep and cattle that he now sees around him. But Tecmessa's words may also suggest that, at some level, Ajax bears responsibility for his madness.

When Ajax realises what he has done he is horrified and says the only thing to do is to kill himself. His overwhelming feeling is of shame at the disgrace to his reputation. He seems to feel no guilt about the murders he was trying to commit nor concern at the damage his vengefulness has caused. He thinks only of the indignity and mockery he will suffer, especially by comparison with the fame of his father Telamon, who had accompanied Jason as one of the Argonauts. To be concerned for his honour and glory was the normal state of mind for the Homeric hero. Shame, in the sense of having the image he presents to the world damaged, is what he avoids at all costs, and the worst thing possible is to have his reputation diminished in the eyes of his peers. An inner ideal, that he tries to live up to, regardless of what the world thinks, is not part of the Homeric hero's makeup. Ajax shows no concern for the economic and emotional disaster that killing himself will cause his wife and child, but this seems at first not so much a matter of callousness as the expression of a standard social attitude.

Later in the play this will appear in a new light. First, however, there is Ajax's suicide. Here Sophocles gives the audience a remarkable bit of psychiatric realism. Ajax, full of shame and hopeless about his future, leaves the stage with the idea of ending his life (595). The Chorus sing a despairing ode, and then Ajax reenters, apparently in a very different state of mind (644ff). His hopelessness has gone; he does have concern for his wife and son; he can think about the future; and instead of using his sword against himself he is going to bury it. He goes off on his own to do so, while the Chorus sing of their delight at his recovery. A messenger arrives with instructions from the prophet Calchas that Ajax must not go out alone. He must be looked after for the rest of the day by his brother Teukros (749–84). But Ajax has already left his tent. He appears alone by the sea shore and the audience sees him fix his sword in the ground and kill himself by falling on it.

This reversal has baffled commentators, who offer various explanations. Was Ajax's apparently positive speech just a piece of cynical deception? The richness and emotional resonance of its language belie this. If the speech was genuine, must the audience assume some reversal in Ajax's state of mind which Sophocles leaves unexplained? Was he intending to die all along, but trying to reconcile himself with the gods? Anyone who has worked in a psychiatric hospital, however, knows that the time of maximum risk for suicide is not when a patient is most depressed. At that stage, mental and physical lethargy make any form of activity, even suicidal activity, difficult. The most dangerous time is when recovery has begun and the patient is capable of some initiative. Should suicidal thoughts recur the patient is now capable of acting on them. This is what seems to happen with Ajax. Calchas knew, and after the body has been discovered the Chorus say how heedless they were not to have gone on keeping watch over Ajax (908–14), just like psychiatrists or nurses realising too late that they should not have allowed the patient home for the weekend.

At this point, a crucial aspect of Ajax's character is revealed for the first time. The messenger who reports the words of Calchas says that the prophet also gave an explanation for Athene's treatment of Ajax. When Ajax left home for the Trojan War, his father advised him always to seek the help of the gods in battle. Ajax replied that even a worthless man could win with the gods on his side. He would seek his own triumphs without help from the gods. When Athene did stand by Ajax on the battlefield to encourage him he sent her away, saying he had no need of her and she should go and look after the other Greeks instead.

In the light of this we look back over what has happened with fresh eyes. Ajax's behaviour now appears not simply to exemplify the standard attitudes of the epic hero, but to show the disturbance of his particular character. It always made sense that it should be Athene who drove Ajax mad and thwarted his murderous attack because, of all the gods and goddesses, she is the most concerned to protect the Greeks from harm. But now her involvement has a deeper meaning. It is not that Athene is taking personal revenge for Ajax's insult to her on the battlefield. Euripidean divinities might be driven by wounded *amour-propre*, but not the Athene of Sophocles. What Calchas' story reveals is that Ajax's psychosis is the consequence of a grandiose omnipotence which denies the dependence on others that is part of the human condition. To Greek sensibilities, his dismissal of the goddess would be grotesque. It demonstrates how far the narcissistic attempt to see himself as totally self-sufficient has put Ajax out of touch with humanity. The audience might think back, at this point, to the *Kommos* (348–427); the long lyric exchange between Ajax and the Chorus in which, having recovered his sanity, he curses the ridicule and indignity to which he will now be subject. Unconsciously, Ajax reveals how dependent he really is on other people's opinion of him. His image of himself was shattered when the armour of Achilles was awarded to someone else, and it is psychologically accurate that Athene, who represents the dependent relationship that Ajax deluded himself he did not need, should be responsible for his breakdown.

In the face of Ajax's impersonal harshness his wife maintains a striking warmth and humanity. When he makes clear that he intends to commit suicide (430–80), Tecmessa asks him to consider the effect of this on herself, their son, Eurysaces, and on Ajax's parents. She would be mocked and enslaved, Eurysaces would have no family to bring him up and protect him, and Ajax's father and mother would live out their old age in misery. Tecmessa evokes vividly her own future suffering, and her care for her son and parents-in-law makes her plea the more touching.

So far, Ajax has shown no guilt or concern about what he has done or was trying to do, but only shame at the failure of his murderous project. Tecmessa is pleading for Ajax to discover an imaginative capacity to put himself in another person's position—her own, their son's, his parents'—and to think what it will be like for them if he does what he is planning. However, when the Chorus supports Tecmessa and asks Ajax to agree with her, he replies that his approval of her depends on her obedience to him. He does not seem to have heard a word she has said. No dialogue with him is possible. Tecmessa keeps trying, and tells Ajax that killing himself would be a betrayal of her and of their son, only to be told she is becoming tedious (589). To her final heartfelt entreaty that he should relent, Ajax replies that she is a fool if she thinks she can change his mind (594f). He does manage to think of Eurysaces to the extent of asking that his brother Teukros should take care of him, and there is one moment when he is touched by compassion for what his wife and child will suffer when he is gone. But he rejects the feeling. Pity takes the sharp edge off his spirit, he says, and makes his speech 'womanish' (650–53). His sense of masculinity depends on his selfcontained omnipotence, and the experience of caring about someone else is a threat to it. In his final speech before killing himself, he feels again a momentary pity, this time for his parents. He imagines what it will be like for them to hear the news of his suicide. Immediately, however, he has to stifle his 'idle weeping' and 'get on with the business quickly' (852f). He seems afraid that he might lose his resolve, and makes himself rigidly unfeeling so as to push away any such possibility. Ajax's overpowering desire to possess the armour of Achilles symbolises his compulsion to maintain a rigid character armouring that will protect him against human encounters which he is not able, at an emotional level, to deal with.

Compare Ajax, as Sophocles presents him to us, with a man who did know he needed help, but still had great difficulty in receiving it.

Jacques, a social worker from another country, was training as a counsellor. He found the experience disturbing, but hated to acknowledge how out of his depth he felt and how much support he needed from his supervisor. He was referred to me for psychotherapy and came once a week for about a year.

Jacques came from a well-to-do professional family. He had a brother who was two years younger. A pattern developed of this brother being the 'naughty' child, while Jacques was the 'good' one; the family diplomat who smoothed out difficulties. He told me this with pride, but seemed uneasily aware that it might also need some thinking about. He began school aged five. At first things went well, but then his classmates turned against him. He claimed not to know why, but it seemed they were reacting against how he boasted and bossed them around. From then on he was miserable. Either he would be the leader of a gang, or else rejected and bullied. The issue seemed to be about humiliation: would he be the humiliated one, or the one to humiliate others? In his teens the family emigrated. He said this was difficult because in their new country the family had a lower social position. They were less well-off and had to live in a crowded flat. He found it unbearable that classmates at his new school were more advanced than he was and that many came from wealthier families.

In his social work training he had been held up for a year because he failed an exam. He was astonished that this meant he could not go forward, and complained that the regulations had not been made clear. This was plainly not the case, but he insisted nonetheless that it was true. I wondered if he had needed to think he was so special that such a humiliating rule could not possibly apply to him. He understood my thought, but only intellectually. He felt shamed when other students could answer questions that he could not. He grew withdrawn and isolated, came to be seen as a 'problem student', and eventually took a year out of the course to go travelling. During this time he formed a relationship with Tessa. She went back with him to this country and they married. He completed his training, after which they came to London for his counselling course. When he was referred to me he had about a year of this left, and their son Yuri, born in London, was one year old.

Both at work and at home Jacques was dominated by a desire to be the centre of attention. When he was not admired as he wished he became depressed and anxious, to the extent of fearing a breakdown.

At work he took on multiple projects. When his tutors, instead of praising him for this, told him to slow down and take his time, he could not reflect on what they said. Instead, he became angry because they did not appreciate his efforts. He was full of anxiety about being humiliated in seminars. Once when he had to speak after a woman had presented a case very well, he could hardly get a word out and thought he was going to have a panic attack. He nearly stayed away from an important exam because he could not bear the idea that he might fail it. When he was reprimanded for being late in writing up notes and sending letters, he was angry at the lack of sympathy for his difficulties. He could not think of the clients' and the institution's needs, or consider that he might have a problem he needed to look at.

His contempt for his wife and their child was painful to listen to. He constantly complained about Tessa's differences from himself. She did not care as much as he did what other people thought. She did not pay attention to how she dressed, while for him clothes were very important. The idea that Tessa might have wishes and needs of her own seemed meaningless to him. It was likewise unbearable to him that his son had needs, and he could only perceive him as a nuisance. When Tessa got up in the night to feed him, Jacques was angry at being left alone. When Tessa was trying to wean Yuri, Jacques did agree to get up himself and feed him because he was glad that the intimacy of breastfeeding was coming to an end. He thought doing this made him feel like a father, but if he had to look after Yuri while Tessa was out of the house, he was annoyed at having to spend time with the child. Once Tessa and Yuri went away together for a week, and Jacques was shocked to find he could not cope on his own. He had looked forward to being rid of them, but in fact he sank into a miserable passivity, unable to do much except gaze at the television.

Jacques' grandiosity and his contempt for Tessa and Yuri were sometimes hard to bear. What was touching and painful, though, was that he knew there was something terribly wrong. He was aware of being cut off from other people. In some of his clients he saw an emotional flatness and shallowness that he could recognise in himself. The therapeutic relationship between us was complicated. He was willing to consider my interpretations, and I sometimes felt he had a real wish to look at himself. At other times, he seemed falsely compliant and concerned mainly to get me to like him. Sometimes he felt threatened and humiliated by my professional position and my ability to understand him, and he would become hostile and suspicious. He felt abandoned by me between his sessions (he could not bring himself to come more than once a week), and we could link this to the abandonment he felt by his mother when his brother was born, and by Tessa when Yuri was born. He could recognise his feelings of helplessness, and also his fear of discovering he was not brilliant after all, but he was afraid of becoming depressed if he stayed with such feelings. Then he would retreat into telling me how much better off he would be without Tessa and Yuri, or into thinking I was deliberately humiliating him. I thought there was a risk of both a depressive and a paranoid breakdown.

At the end of his year's therapy, he returned home with Tessa and Yuri. He seemed a bit more aware of his grandiosity and the terror against which it defended him, but not much seemed really to have changed. I put him in touch with a colleague in his own country, without great optimism.

The point of resemblance between Ajax and Jacques that I want to emphasise is not simply how narcissistic they are capable of being, but that they are not capable of being anything else. They are imprisoned in their narcissism.

To feel concern and gratitude for another person are capacities that have to be achieved. At first, an infant relates to others only in terms of their effects on itself. To realise that those others have thoughts and feelings of their own, and that the infant may have an impact on them for which it can be responsible, are specific steps in development. They make it possible to appreciate and be grateful for another's actions, and to think of one's own behaviour in terms of its effect on another. Ajax represents a character that has not been able to achieve these steps. Athene's offer of assistance implies that Ajax might have need of her strength. He cannot accept and be grateful because he cannot bear the desire of the goddess to do something for him that he cannot do for himself. When Tecmessa begs him to imagine the disaster his suicide will be for her, the idea does not register. Imagining his effect on other people is beyond him. It is the same with Jacques. He cannot imagine a situation at work from his colleagues' and teachers' point of view. His only concern is whether they support or threaten his inflated picture of himself. At home, he cannot recognise that a wife and small son have needs of their own, and that it could be rewarding for him to respond to these as a husband and father. All he feels is fury at being displaced from centre stage.

The discussion at the beginning of this chapter emphasised that narcissistic states of mind are not by their nature pathological. On the contrary, they are essential to psychic development, provided there is the necessary freedom of movement between an inwardly directed self-absorption and an outward-looking interest in the states of mind of others. Ajax and Jacques show how damaging is a developmental failure to achieve this freedom of movement.

When Sophocles' hero commits suicide half-way through the play, this divides it into two parts which may appear only weakly connected. After Ajax's death the play is peopled with characters, Teukros, Menelaus and Agamemnon, who played no part in the first half. Odysseus, who appeared only briefly in the opening scene, becomes dominant. Some scholars have thought the play falls apart in the middle while others, notably Kitto (1960: 179ff), contend that Sophocles knew his job as a playwright. *Trachiniae*, another of Sophocles' plays, also seems fractured by the death of the central character. As in that instance (Parsons 2000: 115–27), so here also a psychoanalytic perspective reveals the coherence of Sophocles' vision.

Along with Odysseus, Agamemnon and Menelaus were the primary targets of Ajax's murderousness. The latter pair react to the story of his madness and suicide with the same rigid vindictiveness and arrogance that Ajax himself displayed. All they can see is an insult to their kingship, and a threat to their positions of command. Menelaus forbids Ajax's body to be buried, saying that because Ajax would not obey him while he was alive it is a pleasure for him to govern Ajax in his death. When Ajax's brother Teukros tells Menelaus that to dishonour the dead is disrespect to the gods, Menelaus answers that respect for the gods does not apply where his personal enemies are concerned (1129ff). This placing of his own self-importance above the gods mirrors exactly the attitude of Ajax towards Athene. Agamemnon mocks Teukros for his lowly origins in speech that is full of brittle anxiety about the threat that Ajax's valour posed to Agamemnon's pride of place.

Then Odysseus enters, and Sophocles takes the audience by surprise. Odysseus was the object of Ajax's greatest hatred, but instead of continuing the vitriolic diatribe of Menelaus and Agamemnon he tells them they are wrong, and that Ajax should have a honourable burial. The dialogue between Agamemnon and Odysseus which follows (1346ff) is an emotional turning point. Agamemnon is amazed at Odysseus' attitude and asks him if he did not hate Ajax. Odysseus replies that indeed he did, but Ajax also had greatness and nobility, and should be recognised as the bravest of all the Greeks after Achilles. Agamemnon asks if Odysseus can feel pity for a corpse that he hates. There is evidently no distinction for Agamemnon between the person and the dead body. Odysseus answers that the greatness of Ajax means more to him than his own feelings of hatred. This line (1357) is the heart of the play. Odysseus' capacity to recognise what belongs to another person, setting aside his own feelings to do so, displays the emotional growth that was beyond Ajax's reach. The psychotic breakdown Ajax suffers reveals how desperately he needed the armour of Achilles to try and shore up, in external, material terms, his narcissistic defences. For Odysseus, on the other hand, the armour represents symbolically an internal structure of strength and security that he already possesses, which lets him respond to the world around him with generosity and openness.

Agamemnon then says that if he agrees for Ajax to be buried it will make him appear a coward. The self-involvement of this statement underlines the contrast between the two psychic positions. Odysseus says that he wants burial for Ajax because he recognises that he too will one day have the same need. Sophocles has already signposted this capacity in Odysseus for identification even with an enemy. The play began with Odysseus telling Athene of his hatred for Ajax, and recounting Ajax's attack on the Greek leaders, which turned into his mad onslaught on the animals. Athene explains that this was her doing, and Ajax in his madness appears, torturing a ram which he triumphantly declares is Odysseus. Odysseus responds:

> I am all pity for his wretchedness,
> enemy though he is, and for the evil
> doom that he is yoked to. Seeing his state,
> I see also my own, for all of us
> live only as dim shapes and shadows.
>
> (Sophocles, *Ajax*: 121–4)

This capacity for identification with a universal humanity recalls Theseus' statement to the blind, polluted, exiled Oedipus: 'I am a man too, and I know the difference between us lies only in the fortune of the morrow' (Sophocles, *Oedipus at Colonus*: 567–8).

My patient Jacques could not respond to his wife's need to be recognised as another human being in her own right. Ajax likewise had no way of responding to Tecmessa's plea for emotional growth on his part. Odysseus at the beginning of the play is terrified of Ajax's madness (74ff), and as a corpse Ajax becomes something still more absolutely 'other'. But Odysseus has been able to achieve the developmental step that Ajax could not. Even faced with the extremities of madness and of death he can identify with, and care for, the man he hated.

Alongside seeing Odysseus as representing an emotional growth that eluded Ajax, one might also take Agamemnon and Menelaus on the one hand, and Odysseus on the other, to represent twin aspects of Ajax, both present in his character, but with an unresolved split between them. The first half of the play could be viewed in terms of an oscillating struggle between these: Ajax gripped for the most part by the grandiose paranoia later represented in Agamemnon and Menelaus, and only occasionally finding the concern for other people exemplified by Odysseus. His suicide, from this perspective, would represent the triumph of the former over the latter.[2]

Back now in the consulting room, here are two patients who had the same thought: a narcissistic thought, one might say, but the results in each case were very different, illustrating further the difference between narcissism as a symptom that imprisons, and narcissism as a state of mind with a potential for evolution.

The first patient is a man who had broken up with his girlfriend and was beginning to recognise that he had not treated her with much consideration. He had let her think the relationship might work out, when he knew that really he wanted to end it. When he did end it he did so abruptly, while they were abroad together and she was out of contact with her friends. He talked of his 'weakness' in not being able to make a clean break when he should have done. I said there might also be some cruelty in his behaviour, belonging to a pattern of wanting women to suffer, which was linked to his relationship with his mother. He found this very difficult ('I wouldn't come to you for a character reference!'), but in the next session he commented that I had not been horrified or disgusted. I seemed to think the way he had behaved could be accepted and thought about. Then he imagined his girlfriend being my patient instead of him. He said there was plenty she needed to look at in herself, and I would be doing the same thing with her that I was with him. 'It's not because you are taking my side against her that you are accepting how I treated her. You're doing something different from that.' He did not fully understand what this was, but he was interested in what I was doing that could belong both to his girlfriend and to himself.

The second of these patients is a woman with little capacity for symbolic thought. She avoided fantasy at all costs, in case what she was imagining turned out not to be true, which would fill her with shame and humiliation. Her life was dominated by fear of getting things wrong or being tricked. She would ask me questions about myself and when, instead of answering these, I tried to understand what lay behind them, she thought I wanted to trap her into making mistakes about me. She wanted me to say she was the most complicated or most difficult patient I had ever had. This was not just a matter of rivalry with my other patients. My entire being had to be totally and uniquely involved with her. I might give her all my attention and try my utmost to understand and help her, but if I were doing the same for another person too, any worth it had for her would be lost.

Both these people have the same thought: 'What if my analyst is doing the same thing with somebody else?' The woman cannot give up her demand for an exclusive relationship, and the idea of sharing her importance to me with another person is unbearable. It would mean that she had no importance to me after all, and that would take away all value from what I am doing with her. A third person would threaten her very existence in my mind. When the man, by contrast, thought of my having the same relationship to his girlfriend as to him, he could accept the idea and be interested in it. It did not obliterate my relationship to him, but shed new light on what it consisted of. The woman's preoccupation with herself was absolute, while the man was capable of giving his up. Narcissism was for her a prison: for him, a state of mind he could make use of for further emotional development.

A secure identity depends on a capacity for self-absorption. This means withdrawing from engagement with external reality to make one's inner world both consciously and unconsciously the focus of attention. This is narcissism, not as a symptom, but as a state of mind. The crucial question is whether such self-absorption is used as a defence against the world, or as a catalyst for further engagement with it. For some, like Ajax, Jacques and the woman who insisted her relationship with me should be exclusive, their self-involvement must be protected at all costs, because other people can only be seen as a threat. Others, like Odysseus and the man who wondered about my seeing his girlfriend, are able to step out of the narcissistic state of mind. It remains necessary, however, as a base to return to. Developmentally mature, non-pathological narcissism implies knowing how to engage with the internal world and one's own being, while also knowing how to yield this up and engage with one's fellow beings in the outside world. A flexible, mobile capacity to shift back and forth between these positions makes narcissism not an affliction, but a springboard for growth.

Notes

1   The term had already appeared in passing in 1910, in a footnote added to the *Three Essays on the Theory of Sexuality* (Freud, 1905: 144–5fn).
2   I am indebted to Sotiris Manolopoulos for this suggestion.

Part III

THE ACTIVITY OF LISTENING

And still, even when he could do nothing for a sufferer,
he always conversed with him; not on higher matters, as
one might have hoped, but on very insignificant affairs
… Strangely enough, people went away happy, saying
that he knew how to listen, that by following your little
tale he uncovered the grieving thread of your soul.

André Schwarz–Bart,
The Last of the Just (1961: 26)

8

LISTENING OUT, LISTENING IN, LOOKING OUT, LOOKING IN

Psychoanalysts and psychoanalytic therapists have to listen in two directions at once: externally to their patients, and internally to whatever thoughts and feelings this stirs up in themselves. Psychoanalytic listening is a double process, directed inwards and outwards at the same time, both vectors essential, continuously active and interdependent. The evolution and the implications of this kind of listening are a thread running through this and the following chapters.

Freud was a doctor, a neurologist used to eliciting his patients' histories. Doctors know, by and large, the kind of information they need for the purpose of diagnosis and treatment. That is what they listen for, and it is taken for granted that the person under scrutiny is the patient, not the doctor. *Studies on Hysteria* (Breuer and Freud, 1893–1895), where the history of psychoanalytic listening begins, shows Freud well entrenched in such a mode. A long footnote to the case of Miss Lucy R. (112–14) reveals how insistently, not to say relentlessly, he would extract from patients what he was determined they should tell him. In the chapter on therapeutic technique, he says:

> It is of course of great importance for the progress of the analysis that one should always turn out to be in the right *vis-à-vis* the patient, otherwise one would always be dependent on what he chose to tell one.
>
> (Breuer and Freud, 1893–1895: 281)

Set that, however, against this comment during Freud's treatment of Katharina.

> I told her to go on and tell me whatever occurred to her, in the confident expectation that she would think of precisely what I needed to explain the case.
>
> (Ibid: 129)

Here, Freud does just the thing he had been so intent on avoiding. He explicitly makes himself dependent on what his patient chooses to tell him. The discovery of this different attitude begins with an observation of Breuer's about Anna O.

It turned out to be quite impracticable to shorten the work by trying to elicit in her memory straight away the first provoking cause of her symptoms. She was unable to find it, grew confused, and things proceeded even more slowly than if she was allowed quietly and steadily to follow back the thread of memories on which she had embarked.

(Ibid: 35)

Frau Emmy von N. was an instructive patient for Freud in this regard. He made the same mistake with her as Breuer had with Anna O., and with the same result.

When, three days ago, she had first complained about her fear of asylums, I had interrupted her after her first story, that the patients were tied on to chairs. I now saw that I had gained nothing by this interruption and that I cannot evade listening to her stories in every detail to the very end.

(Ibid: 61)

He observed, though, that her talk was not as aimless as it might seem.

On the contrary, it contains a fairly complete reproduction of the memories and new impressions which have affected her since our last talk, and it often leads on, in a quite unexpected way, to pathogenic reminiscences of which she unburdens herself without being asked to. It is as though she had adopted my procedure and was making use of our conversation, apparently unconstrained and guided by chance, as a supplement to her hypnosis.

(Ibid: 63)

This observation was vital, as Frau Emmy informed Freud.

She said, in a definitely grumbling tone, that I was not to keep on asking her where this and that came from, but to let her tell me what she had to say.

(Ibid: 56)

Of the cases described in the *Studies*, Frau Emmy was the first that Freud treated, probably in 1888–89 (Breuer and Freud, 1893–1895: 48 fn1; Strachey, 1955). By the time of his conversation with Katharina, in the early 1890s (Breuer and Freud, 1893–1895: 125), he had evidently taken Frau Emmy's lesson to heart. Freud trusted that, regardless of his own preconceptions, whatever emerged from Katharina's mind would reveal the hidden meaning of her symptoms. He had learned to listen for what he did not know he was listening for. The concepts of free association and the unconscious were still in the future, but Freud's listening was already psychoanalytic.

Besides learning to trust the patient's mind Freud also learnt to mistrust it. He discovered that as well as revealing hidden meanings, it was itself doing the hiding. Another patient described in *Studies on Hysteria* was Fräulein Elisabeth von R. She used all sorts of manoeuvres to avoid communicating her thoughts, so that Freud 'began to attach a deeper significance to the resistance offered by the patient in the reproduction of her memories, and to make a careful collection of the occasions on which it was particularly marked' (Breuer and Freud, 1893–1895: 154). Freud found he needed to listen in two registers. Where symptoms were concerned, he understood that they could, in one and the same act, both express and conceal a forbidden thought or wish. Now this turned out to apply to the verbal communications of patients as well. Analytic listening needed to encompass not only the unconscious meanings which a patient's words revealed, but also the defensive manoeuvres which, at the same time, concealed those meanings. When Freud found that dreams also operated in this way, the concept of 'compromise-formation' became fundamental.

Freud did not yet, at this early stage, mistrust his own mind. By 1910, however, at the second Psychoanalytical Congress at Nürnberg, he was saying that 'no psycho-analyst goes further than his own complexes and internal resistances permit' (Freud, 1910b: 145). He realised that analysts' objective understanding of their patients was liable to be disrupted by their own psychic irregularities. Rationality might not be expected of the patient, but neither could it be taken for granted in the analyst. So the analytic counterpoint acquired another voice. Analysts began to listen internally to their own reactions and responses to the analytic situation, and the concept of 'countertransference' was born.

The classical view of countertransference was as an obstacle to the analysis caused by unconscious factors in an analyst's psyche, which blocked the analyst's understanding of the patient. At first, therefore, the purpose of analysts' inward listening to themselves was to protect their analytic functioning against such interference from within. In the period around 1950, a new perception of countertransference emerged. Although that original view remained valid and important, it was also realised that the way in which analysts found their functioning disturbed could be a useful indicator, revealing unconscious aspects of the relationship between patient and analyst.

The historical development of the concept of countertransference has been well surveyed by T.J. Jacobs (1999), and the evolving understanding of it figures significantly in Parts III and IV of this book. It has become steadily clearer that the analyst's internal situation is continually in resonance with that of the patient. An analyst's interior listening needs to be just as continuous and free from preconceptions as the external listening to a patient's words.

This quality of analytic listening represents more generally a certain way of engaging with the world. The world presents itself to an analyst in the form of another person who, by making a certain connection with the analyst, becomes a patient. Analysts attend to the manifestation of external reality that is the patient, and attend at the same time to the internal resonances that this fragment of the world arouses in them. Analysts try to be inwardly sensitive to the relationships they get drawn into in this way: in analytic language, to transference and countertransference. Reflecting this awareness back towards the outside world, they try to understand their patients as creatively as possible.

The purpose of this perhaps unusual description of psychoanalysis is to indicate connections to other disciplines whose deep structure is similar. One might say of artists, for example, that they engage with reality by attending closely both to the outside world directly, and to the internal resonances that it arouses in them. They try to be imaginatively open to the kind of relationship that the world around them draws them into, endeavouring in this way to reach, and to reflect in their work, as creative as possible an understanding of it.

Andy Goldsworthy is an artist who creates structures within the landscape, using the natural materials of the landscape itself. In 1989 he spent six weeks making sculptures in the Arctic. To create these structures he had to learn a great deal about the material qualities of ice and snow. Equally important was a sensitivity to his own personal responses to the polar environment. The diary he kept shows the relation between his outward and inward kinds of attention.

> I have always considered snow and ice to be one of the most ephemeral of materials that I have ever worked with, but here it has a feeling of permanence and it makes me realise how rhythms, cycles and seasons in nature are working at different speeds in different places ... There are feelings that I have because of coming here, that I can't put into words and I don't understand, but are nonetheless very deeply lodged in my understanding, in my art. I think it will take a long time for me to be able to articulate those feelings ... the ice here has the same feeling of permanence as the rock does for me in Britain, and obviously the ice here is not permanent and that makes me realise that perhaps the rock at home is also in the same state of change. It is just a slower rate of change—but nonetheless changing.
>
> (Goldsworthy, 1989: diary entry, Wednesday, 8th April)

> North is an integral part of the landscape that I already work with. I can touch North in the cold shadow of a mountain, the green side of a tree, the mossy side of a rock ... Its energy is made visible in snow and ice ... I want to understand the nature of North as a whole ... It is more of a feeling than a place.
>
> (Goldsworthy, 1989: preface)

116

The North that Goldsworthy is exploring exists inside him, as well as outside.

Goldsworthy's work in the Arctic culminated in a piece made at the North Pole itself. Four circular arches, made of irregular slabs of ice fitted together, surround the very spot—as closely as Goldsworthy could calculate—at which the North Pole is located. By their enclosure of this space, the arches show an interior North. By their openness, however, and the expanse of the Arctic landscape seen through them, they reveal a North which is limitless.[1]

An artist came for analysis because his creativity was blocked. He felt he had lost his emotional responsiveness and was not generating any new artistic ideas. He said, as I recollected it later, that he had become 'a maker of *things* rather than an investigator of states of mind'. I remembered the impression his words made on me. They seemed an interesting description of what being an artist meant to him, and there were echoes in them of what I think it means to be a psychoanalyst. But when I looked back at my notes, I found my memory was mistaken. He had not said 'states of mind'. He said he had become 'a maker of *things* rather than an investigator of states of *being*'. His words must originally have evoked in me the thought that an analyst too could be an investigator of states of being, but it seems that I needed to repress this, and assimilate it to an apparently more manageable idea of an analyst as one who deals with states of mind.

What happened to my first response? What this man actually said gave me a momentary sense, not just of understanding, but of recognition. Then I let go of it, opting instead to deal with states of mind. In losing touch with myself as an investigator of states of being, I was enacting the very problem that the patient was bringing to me. Such introjective identification with a patient is familiar to analysts and, once recognised, may help in understanding a person's difficulties. My mistake, however, was more than just an interaction with this individual. For an analyst to retreat from the challenge of an artist's actual communication, back into what he knows already, is a familiar scenario …

Confronted in Rome by the *Moses* of Michelangelo (see p.12), Freud asked somewhat plaintively, 'Why should the artist's intention not be capable of being communicated and comprehended in *words*, like any other fact of mental life?' (Freud, 1914b: 212). To discover the artist's intention, he said, 'I must first find out the meaning and content of what is represented in his work; I must, in other words, be able to *interpret* it' (Freud, 1914b: 212). In 'The Unconscious' (Freud, 1915b), written soon after this passage, Freud discussed what he called thing-presentations and word-presentations. Thing-presentations consist simply of remote, unconscious memory-traces. Word-presentations consist of thing-presentations with the addition of words to refer to them. Only if something is available as a word-presentation, said Freud, can it become conscious and be thought about.

But works of art are things, not words. Even when made out of words they are still things. This was brought home vividly to me when I met the author of a remarkable novel, acclaimed for the quality of its writing and its portrayal of character. Having been intensely moved by the book, I was interested to ask the author about the experience of writing it. He was happy to talk, but what he had to say seemed to me banal compared to the power of the novel itself. I had expected something more profound, and was disappointed until I reflected that the profundity was, of course, in the work of art. This particular work had been created out of words, but that did not mean the artist should be expected to use words profoundly about it, any more than we expect painters, sculptors or composers to explain their work in words. The intention of the artist is a fact of mental life which, despite Freud, it may *not* be possible to represent in words or to interpret. It resides nowhere but in the work itself.

Freud struggled with the idea of artistic meaning. To think of an artist like my patient as an investigator would have seemed strange to him. He did see psychoanalysis as an investigation, one to be governed by the criteria of empirical science. He asserted this most strongly in 'The future of an illusion' (1927) and in 'The question of a *Weltanschauung*', the last of the *New Introductory Lectures on Psychoanalysis* (1933: 158–82). There he wrote that the three powers which might dispute the position of science were philosophy, religion and art. Of these he says 'Art … does not seek to be anything but an illusion … It makes no attempt at invading the realm of reality' (Freud, 1933: 160). Yet Freud called *The Brothers Karamazov* 'the most magnificent novel ever written', and said 'before the problem of the creative artist analysis must, alas, lay down its arms' (Freud, 1928: 177). This acknowledgement contains an implication of warfare between art and psychoanalysis which reveals the ambivalence behind Freud's admiration. Taking up arms himself, Freud attacks Dostoevsky for a narrow nationalism and submissiveness to the authority of State and Church. 'Dostoevsky threw away the chance of becoming a teacher and liberator of humanity and made himself one with their gaolers. The future of human civilisation will have little to thank him for' (Freud, 1928: 177). As a gift to humanity, the most magnificent novel ever written is evidently not worth much. No surprise if Freud thinks art is nothing but an illusion.

My patient, on the other hand, did consider art as a form of investigation; and here is Andy Goldsworthy again:

> I take the opportunities each day offers. If it is snowing, I work with snow; at leaf-fall, it will be with leaves; a blown–over tree becomes a source of twigs and branches. I stop at a place or pick up a material because I feel that there is something to be discovered. Here is where I can learn.
>
> I want to get under the surface. When I work with a leaf, rock, stick, it is not just that material in itself, it is an opening into the processes of life within and around it.
>
> (Goldsworthy, 1990: Introduction)

Melanie Hart (2007) has shown how Titian, in the very different visual language of his painting *The Flaying of Marsyas* (Figure 8.1), also sees the artist as an investigator. Apollo, flaying Marsyas alive, 'gets under the surface' of the musician in a concrete, psychotic way. The figure on the right, contemplating the scene, is a self-portrait of Titian. This emphatic inclusion of the artist's authorial presence establishes the painting as Titian's own creative scrutiny of what is 'under the surface' of the human mind, and of what it means to be an artist. If art is a form of investigation, the parallel between the artist's looking and the analyst's listening may broaden our conception of what kind of investigation psychoanalysis can be.

Why did I need to transpose my artist patient's reference to states of being into my own reference to states of mind? My mistake reveals a desire, like

Figure 8.1 Titian, *The Flaying of Marsyas.*

Freud's when faced with Michelangelo's *Moses*, to be dealing with aspects of mental life that I could interpret. The phrase 'states of being' seems to encompass all levels of a person's subjectivity, including those experiences of self that cannot be put into words. I had resonated momentarily to this, before altering it unconsciously to 'states of mind'. This phrase, by contrast, connotes for me those aspects of a person's intellectual and emotional condition that do have the possibility of going into words. Repressing my own recognition of this patient's meaning was a retreat, which illustrates the conflict between a wish for clinical psychoanalysis to be a matter of verbal interpretation, and the awareness, on the other hand, that it must also include the realm of the non-verbal.

What analysts are most used to dealing with is the interplay of symbolic representations. Condensation of representations, displacement of meaning between them, their repression in response to conflict: these are what analysts listen out for, in dreams, in symptom formation, in their patients' associations. And they do so by listening in, free-associatively, to their own symbolic representations. If this outward and inward free-floating attention detects distortion in a patient's representations, or signs that they have disappeared from the patient's consciousness, analysts will try, by interpretation, to put this into words.

This habitual mode of analytic understanding, however, leaves out what is not susceptible of verbal representation. When patients did not respond to intellectual explanations about their unconscious mental life, Freud was led to the concepts of resistance and intrapsychic conflict (see above, p.115 and Chapter 11, pp.171–3). The way to deal with these seemed naturally to be by further interpretation. This did advance the clinical process, until preoccupation with the person of the analyst turned out to impede the response of patients to interpretations. The obvious solution was to extend interpretation to encompass this as well, and transference interpretation became, as it remains, central to analytic technique. The unconscious processes that underlie conflict, defence and resistance can, in principle, take the form of word-presentations, and be articulated verbally in an interpretation. With transference, however, this is not always so. The transference experience in a session may relate to times in a patient's life when words were not available. Since pre-verbal experience cannot be expressed directly in words, interpretation in such cases can only represent what pre-verbal experience has been converted into by the analyst for the purpose of articulation.

One strategy has been to hold fast to verbal interpretation as the unique therapeutic activity of psychoanalysis, trying to extend its reach to encompass whatever the clinical situation may involve. Freud took this route. His clinical method, though, was linked to a theory centred around oedipal sexuality, and the interpretations consequently available to him could not easily deal with earlier levels of disturbance, as for example in the case of the Wolf Man (Freud, 1918; Gardner, 1972). Melanie Klein, following the same strategy, found a fresh approach to pregenital development from which new sorts of interpretation could be derived. These did apply to the earliest stages of development as she conceptualised them, and for some analysts this meant that pre-verbal experience could, after all, be brought within the reach of verbal interpretation.

Others have preferred a different strategy. This is to say that, although pre-verbal experience cannot be put into words, it may still be amenable to analysis because verbal interpretation is not the only agent for psychic change (Stewart, 1992). Self-psychologists with their emphasis on empathic attunement (e.g. Bacal, 1997; 1998), and intersubjectivists for whom countertransference enactment is a necessary part of analysis (e.g. Renik, 1993), both exemplify this view. Different again is the British Independent tradition, whose clinical approach, and the theoretical basis of that approach, are the subject of Chapter 12. Independent analysts generally take the view that regression during analysis to a pre-verbal state may be a necessary phase in the resumption of blocked developmental processes. During such periods of regression, the pre-verbal experience must be accepted without trying to convert it into a word-presentation that can be interpreted verbally (see pp.117f, 175f, 194). Regression, however, is not a simple concept, and what is meant by regression to a non-verbal level of experience needs to be explored and clarified.

Regression to a stage of development before words were available is temporal regression, and experience is non-verbal because it is pre-verbal. This is a matter of chronology. Comparable experience in an older infant with a more developed verbal capacity would not be non-verbal. Pre-verbal experience may become verbal by *après-coup*, when a child finds meaning retrospectively in happenings to which it could give none at the time, for lack of the necessary words. Analysts who respect temporal regression in analysis will try to articulate meaning for the experience in words when that becomes possible. Temporal regression is not the only form of regression. In *The Interpretation of Dreams* Freud also described topographic and formal regression (Freud, 1900: 548). He asks why dreams do not express their underlying wishes and anxieties as thoughts, but instead produce visual images. Freud's answer is that thought processes have a direction, moving from a perceptual stimulus, through different psychic agencies, towards a resulting activity. Since physical activity is inhibited in sleep, this direction of movement through the agencies of the mind is reversed, and what appear are direct perceptual images. This, in Freud's terms, is topographic regression. Resulting as it does in visual imagery, it might seem promisingly connected to the theme of art. But art as an investigation is not simply a matter of reproducing a perceptual stimulus. Artistic images are created by a process of psychic work. More relevant in this connection is Freud's third variety of regression, which he called 'formal', as it relates to the form taken by thought processes. In dreams, logical relations between one thought and another have no place. Different bits of mental content appear in various disguises, but the manner in which one is related to another cannot be represented. This constitutes regression as regards the formal aspects of thinking. Without logical connections the verbal articulation of meaning becomes impossible. Formal regression thus leads to an area of experience which is incapable of being put into words, but not because it belongs to a pre-verbal stage of life. The non-verbal is not limited to the pre-verbal, and a psychic domain which, by its nature, is not structured to allow of verbal representation, is present in everyone, adult as well as infant. This aspect of experience is unverbalisable in principle. It will not 'go into words' because it will not, so to speak, 'go into thought' in the first place.

After a long silence at the beginning of a session, a patient said he felt as though he were in a straitjacket, and however much he struggled he could not convey anything to me. This was a man in his forties, fairly successful in a responsible managerial job, but for whom emotional communication with others was very difficult. The situation between us was painfully familiar. We had laboured with its transference significance for a long time, and his words made me feel hopeless and exhausted. Despite all the analytic work … no progress. Listening inwardly to my reaction, I thought he was needing me to suffer the same thing that he was feeling. I considered why this might be: to communicate his experience to me; to punish or attack me; simply to know that he was not alone in his despair? But all I said was that he might want me to know the same hopeless impossibility of communicating as he did. He said he probably did want to impose the same feeling on me that he had. I said he wanted to put me into the same straitjacket. He said 'Yes'.

I had the thought at this point that we were getting too articulate. What we were saying seemed true enough, but the fact of putting it into words felt false. It implied that what this man had started with, the straitjacketed sense of incommunicability, could be communicated verbally after all. It felt as though the verbalisation were a denial of the reality that there was something which could *not* be put into words. I therefore said nothing more. After further silence, the patient said that coming to see me was like being in a box: I was on the other side of one wall of the box, but nothing could pass through the wall. What came to me then was not words but an image (see Figure 8.2). I remained silent. Later, the patient said he would like to have asked his father, when he was young, 'Why does it have to be like this?' I asked if he knew what he would have been thinking of, if he had said that. He answered 'Oh yes. The lack of contact with anyone, the complete absence.' I said then that we could see something about the nature of the straitjacket. He longed to be able to express that question, and to believe that his father, or I, could give an answer that would mean something to him. The very thing, however, that he was trying to ask about, the total absence of contact, made it impossible for words between us, or between him and his father, to have any meaning.

The French analysts César and Sara Botella have made a study of the role in analysis of experience that cannot be represented verbally. Their book is entitled *The Work of Psychic Figurability* (Botella and Botella, 2005), and the word 'figurability' ('*figurabilité*' in French) is a deliberate neologism. Its invention by the Botellas is a refusal of the word 'representability', the usual translation of

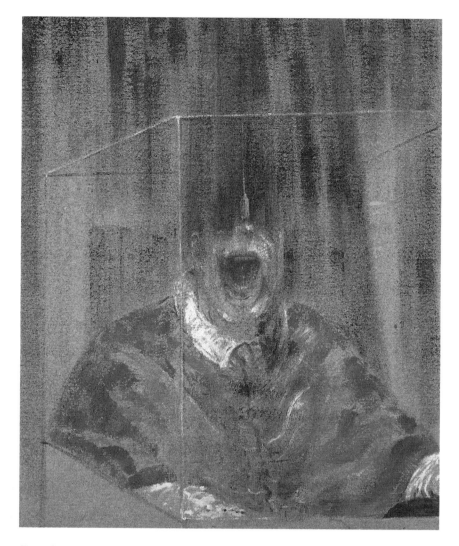

Figure 8.2 Francis Bacon, *Head VI.*

Freud's '*Darstellbarkeit*', in order to emphasise that what is not representable cannot be apprehended psychically by the same processes that allow representations to be understood.

At certain times in analysis, there may be a retrogressive movement in a patient's mind (in the sense of formal, not temporal regression) into a realm of non-representability. The analyst, picking up the patient's experience of non-representation, may follow the patient into this realm, and the term 'figurability' refers to a specific mode of internal perception arising from such a movement. The 'work of figurability' is the achievement of the analyst's mind opening itself to this retrogressive movement in order to accompany the patient's mind: 'achievement' because the experience can be disturbing and disorganising for the analyst as well as the patient. The analyst's own capacity for representation may be subverted, with an uncanny sense of derealisation, and of a disconcerting, even horrifying, void. The clinical examples given by the Botellas, one of which was described in Chapter 1 (pp.13f), illustrate this vividly. But the analyst's mind, through personal experience of analysis and the clinical practice of it, may be mobile along an axis between representability and non-representability, and able therefore to register an awareness of the irrepresentable void.

There is a state which the Botellas (2005: 102) call 'memory without recollection' ('*mémoire sans souvenir*'). This refers to an inchoate awareness of something having occurred, or having been the case, but an awareness that cannot be psychically represented. 'The absence of representable content does not mean the absence of an event' (Botella and Botella, 2005: 164). Instead of a mnemic trace, there is what may be called an amnesic trace. The idea of the negative is an important theme in French psychoanalysis (Green, 1999). Classically, analysts think in terms of drives leading to intrapsychic conflict, which may either be satisfactorily and productively sublimated or else, if it is too severe, may result in defensive fantasy and repression. The Botellas propose an additional line of evolution from the drives, which normally leads through object-representation, to thought. If the progress of this sequence is disturbed, the result is not repression but the negating of representation. Instead of being able to have an object and think about it, the person is left with a negative which by its nature cannot be represented. This seems to echo Winnicott's (1974) idea that 'clinical fear of breakdown is *the fear of a breakdown that has already been experienced*' (Winnicott, 1974: 104). Winnicott says that a patient suffering in this way needs to go on 'looking for the past detail *which is not yet experienced*' (1974: 105), because 'the original experience of primitive agony cannot get into the past tense unless the ego can first gather it into its own present time experience' (Winnicott, 1974: 105).

An object-representation is not simply the internal record of a perception. It is a representation not of the object alone, but of the significance that the object carries for the subject (see p.79). Object-representations comprise a network of meanings at different levels, 'thereby guaranteeing the constancy, the permanence of our psychic functioning' (Botella and Botella, 2005: 27). Loss of an object can be dealt with provided the capacity to represent the lost object remains. If the capacity for object-representation itself is lost, all that the object ever meant to the person disappears into a void.

The analyst's work of figurability is to make contact in this void with that which is not representable. This depends on the analyst's openness to a movement back from secondary process thinking towards non-verbal perception and non-representation. It is important that this work of figurability should originate 'in community with the patient's psychic functioning' (Botella and Botella, 2005:

71). The formal regression of the analyst's mind reflects the predicament of the patient's psyche. The analyst works, so to speak, as the patient's 'double' (Freud, 1919b; Green, 1986: 311–30; Botella and Botella, 2005: 67ff). Being someone's double, or *doppelgänger*, is 'uncanny' and disturbing, and there is a temptation for analysts to escape from their mirroring of the patient by converting the 'working as a double' into some more reassuringly familiar and transferentially manageable mode of analytic relating (Botella and Botella, 2005: 85). The task for analysts is to resist this and give themselves over to the work of figurability as doubles for their patients. The capacity of analysts to be aware of 'doubling', in their own psyche, the movement of formal regression that has taken over the patient's psyche, may awaken a capacity in patients for this same psychic work themselves, so that it eventually becomes possible, after all, for them to experience what has not been representable.

These are not simply issues of clinical technique. What is at stake is how the psyche grows. It is without question essential to find words that allow internal happenings to be understood verbally in new ways. But to think only in terms of states of mind is to think of psychic growth as resulting solely from understanding which can be put into words. This blocks a more radical opening of the horizons to new orders of experience, and new registers of psychic life.

Works of art, not being limited to the verbal, do have the capacity to open horizons and change the way we look at the world. After Picasso's *Les Demoiselles d'Avignon* and the cubist paintings that he and Braque created, the world looked different. Schoenberg's String Quartet No. 2 and his development of atonal music changed what other music sounded like as well. In John Cage's *4'33"* the audience in the concert hall is asked to listen for that length of time, while the musician on the podium plays … not a single note. The effect is to make the audience listen to the ordinary, taken-for-granted noises of people being together, as music. These works have the potential to change not just the viewer's and listener's states of mind, but their whole way of being in the world.

The word 'state', in the phrase 'state of being', begins to seem too 'static'. Engaging with the work of Picasso, Braque, Schoenberg or Cage is not a matter of shifting from one position to another. What these creations do is to open up potential. They are avenues of movement and exploration. The function of Cage's silent piece of music is to generate a new kind of listening in the audience. My artist patient's wish to investigate states of being was a wish to open qualitatively new avenues of growth for himself and his viewers, of a sort that words do not encompass. A regressed patient, who cannot at a certain moment communicate in words, may very much need *not* to be pulled back into the realm of the verbal. Despite, in theory, being aware of all this, I still let go of my recognition of the analyst as an investigator of states of being. Again, I ask myself why? The vilification that modernism in art provoked initially was driven by fury at its apparent disregard for reality-testing. This missed the point that the artists in question were not trying to make their representations more realistic, but were exploring new ways of seeing reality. Perhaps I too was subject to an anxious idea that reality-testing is what analysts are supposed to foster in their patients, not new visions that play havoc with ordinary perspective.

The way that artists explore new visions of reality, by directing their attention both outwards and inwards, is marvellously exemplified in Vincent van Gogh's letters to his brother. In the first place, there is Van Gogh's astonishing observation of the world around him.

> The broad-fronted houses here stand between oak trees of a splendid bronze. In the moss are tones of gold-green; in the ground, tones of reddish, or bluish, or yellowish dark lilac-grey; in the green of the cornfields, tones of inexpressible purity; on the wet trunks, tones of black, contrasting with the golden rain of whirling, clustering autumn leaves—hanging in loose tufts as if they had been blown there, and with the sky glimmering through them ...
>
> (Van Gogh, 1958: Vol. 2, 209)

> And then when twilight fell—imagine ... a few black triangular silhouettes of sod-built huts, through the little windows of which shines the red light of the fire, with a few pools of dirty yellowish water that reflect the sky, and in which trunks lie rotting; imagine that swamp in the evening twilight, with a white sky over it, everywhere the contrast of black and white. And in that swamp a rough figure—the shepherd—a heap of oval masses, half wool, half mud, jostling each other, pushing each other—the flock ...
>
> The sheepfold is again like the silhouette of a triangle—dark. The door is wide open like the entrance to a dark cave. Through the chinks of the boards behind it gleams the light of the sky. The whole caravan of masses of wool and mud disappear into that cave ...
>
> That coming home of the flock in the twilight was the finale of the symphony I heard yesterday ... What does one bring home from such a day? Only a number of rough sketches. Yet there is another thing one brings home—a calm ardour for work.
>
> (Ibid: 210)

Not long after he wrote this letter Van Gogh made the painting *Shepherd with a Flock of Sheep (After the Storm)*, Figure 8.3. It is unmistakably a representation of this scene, and evidences the impact that it made on him.

Van Gogh's passionate sense of relatedness to the world shines through his writing. He is also intensely aware of the internal experience which makes that relatedness possible.

Figure 8.3 Vincent van Gogh, *Shepherd with a Flock of Sheep (After the Storm).*

You will say that everybody has seen landscapes and figures from childhood on. The question is, Has everybody also been thoughtful as a child, has everybody who has seen them also *loved* the heath, fields, meadows, woods, and the snow and the rain and the storm? *Not* everybody has done this ... a peculiar kind of surroundings and circumstances must contribute to it, and a peculiar kind of temperament and character must help it to take root.

(Van Gogh, 1958: Vol. 1, 507)

The fusion of Van Gogh's outward and inward awareness, and how his work arises from that fusion, is shown in the way he sets about the practical business of making a painting.

I do not know myself how I paint it. I sit down with a white board before the spot that strikes me, I look at what is before my eyes, I say to myself, That white board must become something; I come back dissatisfied—I put it away, and when I have rested a little, I go and look at it with a kind of fear. Then I am still dissatisfied, because I still have that splendid scene too clearly in my mind to be satisfied with what I have made of it. But I find in my work an echo of what struck me, after all. I see that nature has told me something, has spoken to me, and that I have put it down in shorthand. In my shorthand there may be words that cannot be deciphered, there may be mistakes or gaps; but there is something of what wood or beach or figure has told me in it.

(Ibid: 448; Van Gogh's italics)

Van Gogh's writing is powerful, and it may seem strange to link it to a realm of non-verbal experience. In the end, though, he is writing about the limits of what he can put into words. '*I do not know myself* how I paint it'. The vision is in the painting. When he says to himself, 'That white board must become something', the white board is also his internal space where imagery can form. We may read the description of the sheep going into the sheepfold at sunset as Van Gogh's unconscious description of how he puts the experiences of the day to rest in a dark cave within himself, to wait and see what the processes of figurability may do with them.

Figure 8.4 Claude Monet, *The Studio Boat (Le Bateau-atelier)*.

There is a painting by Claude Monet which can be understood as representing this creative interior place. For Monet it was essential to paint out of doors, in direct contact with the landscape, and in the 1870s he converted a riverboat into a floating studio. It appears in several of his paintings, of which one in particular is striking for the relation that it shows between outward and inward space (Figure 8.4). The dark silhouette of the artist is a strong presence in the bright landscape of trees and river, but he is also detached from it in the enclosure of the cabin. The interior of the studio boat may be seen as an inner space in the artist himself, where the same kind of process that Van Gogh was writing about is allowed to do its work. This space, although secluded, is not cut off from the outer world. The opening at the far end of the cabin gives a view through the length of the boat, connecting its interior to the world outside it: outward and inward interpenetrate each other. This opening is also a frame, which sets the figure of the artist in relation to the river and trees beyond the boat. The artist at work in his inner, creative space is separate from the external world, but still belongs to it. Van Gogh's sheepfold, and Goldsworthy's ice arches, likewise enclose an inward space; and the ice arches, like Monet's studio boat, make the outer world visible through them. What is especially remarkable about Monet's painting is that it not only offers a representation of this inward space, but also reveals the manner in which an artist makes use of it. The river evokes the flow of the unconscious mind, whose imagery, like the image of the boat in the water, reflects the conscious world above it in unexpected ways. Beneath the river's translucent ripple there are depths on which the artist appears to drift, fishing quietly in the waters of his mind, alert to what may rise and break the surface. The link that connects the conscious and unconscious mind is what makes possible the work of both artist and psychoanalyst. Monet makes this link visible in the vertical line, reflected in the water, of the rudder on which the direction of the studio boat depends.[2]

Certain of John Constable's landscape paintings also reveal an artistic space in which both external reality and the subjective vision of the painter's inner world are represented. I have discussed his sketch for a painting of Hadleigh Castle (Figure 8.5) in relation to the topic of creativity (Parsons, 2000: 166), but it is worth revisiting in the present context. Constable observes intensely a stormy sky, a castle ruin in a rain-drenched landscape, and the fall of light on water. All these he skilfully records in paint. The picture has an emotional turbulence, however, which derives from elements that are not objective features of the landscape. There is a polarisation between brightness and darkness, and between the mass of the castle ruin and a vast emptiness. The sense of void is heightened by there being no clear sense of where the observer is situated. The viewer seems suspended in mid-air. The scattering of birds around the ruin is unusual in Constable's work, and emphasises the fragmented state of the two broken towers, with no link left between them. This painting

Figure 8.5 John Constable, *Sketch for 'Hadleigh Castle'*.

is not like Monet's picture of his studio boat or Van Gogh's evocation of the sheepfold. Those seem to be unconscious portrayals of an internal space in which a certain kind of vision can take shape. Here, Constable puts that space to use. He made this painting in the months following the death of his much loved wife, and the turmoil of its subjective elements shows us what his inwardly directed gaze found at this time in that creative space. In the way that this painting brings together both directions of Constable's looking, it embodies his investigation of a state of being.

The artist's outward and inward looking generate what goes into the picture frame. What happens within the analytic frame depends similarly on the analyst's outward and inward listening.

A man who comes to his analysis four times a week is finding it hard to trust me. Sometimes he can feel me as benign, but this easily gives way to a fear that I will reject any movement by him towards me. One day he allows me, with great trepidation, to see that what he really wants is for me to give him something of myself. The next session he comes in, lies down and is silent. There are not many long silences in his analysis. When they do develop, his conviction of being unwanted by me can give them a despairing feel, so that I think he needs rescuing from them. Today, though, there seems to be a calmness about the silence. After about ten minutes, he says he feels like just lying there and crying quietly to himself while I get on with something else. I say he might not really want me to turn away from him. Perhaps he wants me

130

just to be there quietly with him, and let him get on with crying to himself if that is what he needs to do. He says he thinks that that is exactly it, and falls silent again. This silence has a new quality of intense stillness. I find myself knowing I need to sit without any movement at all. Any sound from me might mean, to this patient, at this moment, that I am taking myself mentally away from him. I know from experience that patients may sense me shifting in my chair, or just turning my head, even when I think I am being completely silent; and sometimes they seem to pick up even psychic movement, an alteration in my attentiveness, without my saying a word or being aware of moving a muscle. I sense very clearly that this must not happen now. But it is not a question of staying motionless by an act of will. Tensing and relaxing, imperceptible to me, may still reach a patient's awareness, and a determination to immobilise my body will bring a psychic rigidity into my listening. The only thing is to let myself feel the silence inside me. As I become part of the stillness myself, time is suspended and the immediacy of the moment can extend itself as I think this person needs.

Later in the session we spoke at intervals:

He said I might read him a story, like a child in bed.

I said something about a comforting presence.

He said: a presence that would give meaning, so he would not have to do that himself.

A certain phase in this man's life was coming to an end, and I said (trying to respond to his request for meaning) that his crying might perhaps be to do with this.

He thought this was wrong. He was miserable because he felt he had no resources for the future.

I said he wanted so much not to have to be the one who had resources, but leave anything to do with that to me.

He said he should not push everything on to me.

There were long gaps between these utterances and no other words were said. The heart of the session was the absence of need for speech. These verbalisations were punctuation points in an extended moment of stillness.

In the account in Chapter 4 of a seminar on analytic listening (pp.51ff), I described the experiment of standing listening in a field on a still night. An apparent void can turn out to be full of sound; and in a session of profound stillness, movements in a patient's mind may become audible. What renders something audible, though, is not simply a background of silence, but the inward attentiveness of the listener. Here is an example of a much busier sort of session.

This patient, also in analysis four times a week, was a young man at the beginning of a professional career, just about to present his thesis for a doctorate. Somewhat obsessional and narcissistic, and inhibited in relationships with women, he suffered from panic attacks and psychosomatic complaints. His father was successful in his work but not a strong presence in the family, which the patient felt was run by his kindly but dominating mother. His older sister had had an illegitimate baby in her teens, which in this family's social milieu was considered a great stigma.

He spoke about a difficult working relationship with a senior woman in his office, who was both seductive and excessively demanding. He contrasted her with the director; a friendly and straightforwardly supportive man. The patient then said the director would be out of the office for the rest of the week. Today had been the last chance to go through certain bits of work with him, and the director was pleased with what he had done.

Looking through his printed thesis he had found a typographical error. He had checked the typescript over and over again, so it was extraordinary that he could have missed this, but it was not really important. He thought he had pushed his perfectionism far enough.

He had needed to phone a woman called Anna, who worked in a different office. He did not know her and one of the secretaries, Beth, told him she was a friend of Celia's, an attractive colleague whom he knew well. He and Anna got on well on the phone and he learnt quite a lot about her. Beth told Celia about this, and Celia asked him if he would like to know what Anna looked like. She showed him a photograph of her, and he thought Anna was even prettier than Celia. Then he remembered that some of the secretaries had been cross with him because he had recommended the film *Cold Mountain* to them and they had not liked it. He supposed he must have been too enthusiastic about it.

He described a nightmare. He was on a week's skiing holiday, and was afraid he would have a panic attack because the week was creeping by so slowly. With him in the dream were school friends from his home town, and he mentioned a real skiing holiday with these friends, where one girl had slept with several boys in the group. He thought she was a slut, but still found her very attractive. He had been unable to approach her himself, or any other of the girls on the holiday. He said he still found himself looking for excuses to go back to his parents' house, rather than make new friends in the city where he now lived.

All the members of the patient's family are transferentially present here. The supposedly benign but dominating mother appears in his female boss. His father—not as he was but as the patient wished he were—is represented by the supportive male director who outranks the woman (but who absents himself nonetheless). His sister is there in the girl on the skiing holiday, exciting but promiscuous, arousing both admiration and disapproval. Accepting the printing error in his thesis, he resists the obsessionality with which he habitually defends himself against sexual excitement, and allows himself some flirtatiousness around Anna, Beth and Celia. However, his offer of excitement about the film is rebuffed, and the nightmare of sexual failure returns. He dreams of skiing, presumably on the 'cold mountain' of the secretaries' rejection, and remembers his adolescent sexual timidity. The wait for the week to finish in the dream connects to the week-long absence of the director. If he can find, through his transference relationship with the analyst, a secure internal sense of the sort of father the director stands for, he may be able to leave home inwardly (see p.6), with confidence in his masculinity.

A session like this can be dealt with in different ways. The analyst could, at any moment, take up and interpret one element or another, as an investigator of the patient's state of mind. Working in this way may help the patient to investigate his own state of mind. If the analyst is more concerned to help the patient apprehend his own state of being, the complex unconscious counterpoint of the material has to reveal itself gradually. This is not just because the session takes time to evolve, but because the listening itself needs to be slow. Time is required both for the unconscious structuring of the material to develop, and for the analyst to observe the effect of this on his own internal silence. Listening in such a manner to a session even as busy as this one can feel like standing quietly in a field at night.

This chapter has various themes: the analyst's listening and the artist's looking; what kind of investigation psychoanalysis can be; experience that is non-verbal but not pre-verbal; states of mind and states of being. Running through all of these is the interrelation between outward and inward.

In Vienna's Art History Museum there hang two paintings in the same room. Figure 8.6 shows the Madonna and Child enthroned under a canopy and flanked by four saints. This is by Perugino, who worked in Umbria in the late fifteenth and early sixteenth centuries. It is a standard kind of composition, in which there is usually landscape visible at the back of the scene, while the figures either look towards one another, or gaze soulfully downwards or rapturously up to heaven. Here, however, Perugino has done something very different and deliberately unusual. The figures are completely enclosed, with nothing visible outside but the sky. There is a powerful sense of this group occupying an interior space, and the viewer too is drawn into the inwardness. The confines of this internal world are breached by the intent gaze of the figures, who look forward and to the side, out of the picture. This unified attention, focused on something beyond the enclosure that the viewer cannot see, tells us that the inside has an outside.

On the opposite wall hangs a painting by a student of Perugino's. This is Raphael's *Madonna of the Meadow*, one of the most famous images in Renaissance art (Figure 8.7). Raphael displays the expansiveness of the outside world. The vertical dimension is dramatised by the division between earth and heaven, with the Madonna belonging to both. The depth extends from the lovingly detailed wild strawberries at the very front of the picture plane, back through meadows, lake, hilltowns and mountains, into the furthest distance. In all this immensity sits the Madonna with the two infants. The family group forms a strikingly cohesive unity. This derives partly from its carefully planned geometry of interrelated triangles. The painting 'has often been singled out as the paradigm of the Renaissance triangular composition' (Oberhuber, 1999: 57). But the self-contained completeness of these figures is conveyed above all in

Figure 8.6 Perugino, *Madonna and Child with Four Saints.*

the way that none of them is aware of anything in this huge space beyond their own inwardly directed gaze. They are within the landscape and separate from it at the same time. The boys are intent on each other. The Madonna contains their play with her serene watchfulness, and her contemplation secludes the group in the inwardness of its private space. This vast outside has an inside.

Perugino shows an intense interior space by means of a physical enclosure, and powerfully conveys an external space by showing its impact, while not allowing us to see it. Raphael shows us an external space that seems boundless, and makes visible within it an interior space separated off by a purely psychological enclosure. These are investigations of a state of being marked by mutual

134

Figure 8.7 Raphael, *Madonna of the Meadow.*

permeation of inwardly and outwardly directed awareness. If analysts discover this in themselves, they may facilitate it in their patients. In their portrayal of this state of being, these paintings are an invitation. How to respond? Not by trying to constrain their meaning into words. Perhaps by letting them say to us, as Winnicott once said to a patient: 'So it seems that you have turned up, and you have an inside and an outside' (Winnicott, 1986: 134).

135

Notes

1 A photograph of this work, *Touching North*, is shown on the dust jacket of Goldsworthy's (1989) book of that name. It also appears in *A Collaboration with Nature* (Goldsworthy, 1990). Permission was, unfortunately, not granted for the image to be reproduced in this book.
2 I am grateful to Melanie Hart for drawing my attention to this painting, and for sharing her thoughts about it.

9

THE ANALYST'S COUNTERTRANSFERENCE TO THE PSYCHOANALYTIC PROCESS

The last chapter emphasised an inward listening by analysts to their own responses, in counterpoint to their external listening to their patients. This means more than being sensitive to thoughts and feelings that any given patient stirs up. There is countertransference, not only to individual patients, but to the process of psychoanalysis itself. Countertransference to the patient and to the process are not separate, since there can be no process without a patient. But as well as the responses that particular patients arouse in their analysts, there is the question of what it means to an analyst to be engaged in this work in the first place. Anyone who embarks on becoming a psychoanalyst is driven by deep personal motivations, conscious and unconscious. The practice of psychoanalysis, and the nature of the involvement that the work entails, are bound to evoke deep reactions. This remains true from start to finish of an analyst's working life.

To speak of 'the process of psychoanalysis' is already problematic. There is controversy even about the meaning of the idea. The sizeable literature on the concept is not very old. Few articles before the late 1970s focused specifically on the analytic process. The 1980s and 1990s, however, saw a proliferation of papers devoted to it. The lack of consensus in these is striking. Samuel Abrams commented that it was 'hard to imagine any term more burdened by ambiguity, controversy, and diversity of usage' (Abrams, 1987: 441). Running through many of these papers is a kind of conceptual *angst*; a desire to grasp the psychoanalytic process by pinning it down with a clear, specific definition. Is the analytic process something that happens, for example, in the analyst, or in the patient, or in both, or between them? Abrams (1987) gives examples from various authors of all these different viewpoints. Does the analytic process have any meaning apart from clinical technique itself? No, for Arlow and Brenner (1990). Yes, for Weinshel (1984). Several articles (e.g. Weinshel, 1990) attempt to describe observable aspects of an analysis that will indicate whether or not an analytic process is taking place. This concern with definitions and criteria, evident especially in the North-American literature, was linked by Weinshel (1984: 64) to the American Psychoanalytic Association's decision to make the ability to manage a psychoanalytic process a condition for Full Membership. The desire to operationalise the concept shows itself particularly among those interested in empirical research methodologies (Vaughan and Roose, 1995). The diversity of viewpoints is revealed in Ornstein's survey of the literature, where he found:

> ... an entire spectrum of views on the nature of the psychoanalytic process. At one end ... is an insistence on the importance and definability of the process ... On the other end is an insistence that there is no such thing as an analytic process apart from what the analyst does in order to bring about the desired change or 'cure'.
>
> (Ornstein, 2004: 17f)

In a debate at the French-Speaking Congress of 2004 in Milan, Dominique Scarfone pointed out that, in French versions of Freud, the single word *'processus'* translates various German words with different shades of meaning, such as *'Verfahren'*, *'Vorgang'* and *'Prozess'*. In English, the word 'process' has been used in the same way. Discussions of the analytic process generally treat it in unitary terms, as a single entity, about which it can be argued whether it exists or not, what its nature is, how to define it, and so on. But Scarfone's comment is a warning against this. The idea of a process may carry various connotations, and the analytic process is best understood as comprising several different strands. When Arlow and Brenner (1990) insist that the concept has no meaning beyond the interventions that the analyst makes, they seem to be using 'process' in the sense of a procedure, or method, by which something is carried out. One speaks in the same way of a manufacturing process, or a computational process. A different and familiar use of 'process' in psychoanalysis is to describe what goes on in a person's mind. Transference, repression, projection, internalisation: these are all 'psychic processes'. In Ornstein's spectrum of views, those who claim that the analytic process is what patients experience in analysis may be using the term to refer to the evolving psychic processes that analysis brings about. The procedures of psychoanalysis on the one hand, the intrapsychic processes it stimulates on the other, and the interrelational processes that are also evoked between patient and analyst, are equally essential parts of a whole. To argue about which of them is 'really' the analytic process recalls the blind men and the elephant.

The concept of an analytic 'process' might perhaps seem impersonal. Later I shall discuss how the notion of analytic 'material' risks abolishing mutuality in the relation between patient and analyst. If the analytic 'process' is taken to mean simply a procedure to be carried out, which the patient undergoes, this could be similarly depersonalising. An expression such as the analytic 'experience' might appear preferable. Experience, however, can be static.

Once over, an experience does not of necessity lead on to something new. The idea of 'process' is worth retaining for its connotations of movement, of evolution and development, which belong to the essence of psychoanalysis. The therapeutic effectiveness of the process does depend, however, on its being experientially alive.

The start of a new analysis brings a sense, for analyst as well as patient, of embarking on something. Imagine setting out to sail round the world, or dedicating oneself to the study of a language and its culture. One is not just beginning to do something, but engaging with something that extends far beyond oneself. We bring with us whatever nautical or linguistic knowledge we already have, but the process we have embarked on means putting ourselves into a relationship with ocean or language that will make demands on us. We do not yet know how mild or extreme those demands will be. The ocean, or the language, will test and challenge us, and we are committing ourselves to whatever the relationship with them will turn out to involve. The voyage that analysts embark on with a new patient is something that, over the years, they may have come to know quite a lot about. For all that familiarity, however, they also know that it exceeds their comprehension. The psychoanalytic process remains a conjunction of the familiar and the mysterious.

This perception of the analytic process as something with its own independent life and direction, something not to be controlled or predicted by either patient or analyst, originates with Freud.

> The analyst is certainly able to do a great deal, but he cannot determine beforehand exactly what results he will effect. He sets in motion a process, that of the resolving of existing repressions. He can supervise this process, further it, remove obstacles in its way, and he can undoubtedly vitiate much of it. But on the whole, once begun, it goes its own way and does not allow either the direction it takes or the order in which it picks up its points to be prescribed for it. The analyst's power over the symptoms of the disease may thus be compared to male sexual potency. A man can, it is true, beget a whole child, but even the strongest man cannot create in the female organism a head alone or an arm or a leg; he cannot even prescribe the child's sex. He, too, only sets in motion a highly complicated process, determined by events in the remote past, which ends with the severance of the child from its mother.
>
> (Freud, 1913: 130)

There is much to say, no doubt, about Freud's choice of analogy, but with the image of conception, pregnancy and birth, he certainly captures a process that is at once familiar and mysterious. Christopher Bollas (1999: 5ff) also suggests that the analytic situation has something unconsciously familiar about it. He describes the analysand's experience as that of being inside a process which is guided, for the most part, by the intelligence of another, but to which the activity of the analysand is also essential. This process holds analysands in a particular way that allows them to discover what it means to grow. Other human situations may be similarly described, and Bollas traces a line back to the beginning of life. The foetus is held and grows in an environment which is organised by the mother's physiological processes, but in which the foetus' own processes play an essential part. After birth the baby discovers existence within a world managed by another, but it is not a passive occupant of this world. Infants are aware of being held by an understanding that goes beyond their own, in a process where 'the alterations sponsored in the infant's psychosomatic states by this other contribute to the sense of this being a transformational situation: one that recurrently alters self-experience' (Bollas, 1999: 6).

The advent of a third figure brings a new set of processes. 'The logic of family structure', in Bollas' phrase, takes hold of the growing child, who continues to develop within a world whose organisation it does not comprehend, but to which it knows it belongs and contributes as much as do the mysterious organising others. A child does not just 'have' an Oedipus complex. Externally and internally the child inhabits the complex. In like manner, to say that a patient 'has' a transference to an analyst is thin shorthand for the experience of the transferential world in which the patient lives.

If these developmental situations share something of their underlying nature with the analytic situation, this invites crucial questions regarding the role of the analyst. Mothers and parental couples are in charge, but by no means in command, of their children's developmental environments. They themselves are subject to the processes of those situations. A woman, for instance, is aware of her pregnancy, but it is not under her control and she does not experience consciously the complexities of the process at work within her. To what extent does the process we call psychoanalysis also operate, in the analyst as well as the patient, at an unconscious level? Of course the analyst is aware of participating in it, as a woman is aware of being pregnant, and as parents know that they are bringing up children. The point at issue is how conscious the analyst is of the workings of the process and of the intricate elements that go to make it up.

This links back to the sense, on starting a new analysis, of embarking on something that as an analyst one knows how to do, but which will also go beyond one's knowledge. Psychoanalysis remains, of course, a task done with conscious attention to certain essential elements. The analyst listens, follows the feeling of the session, registers the transference, connects what the patient says to theoretical ideas, speaks at times, and observes how the patient responds. In the background are other things the analyst does, such as beginning and ending sessions on time, being clear about financial arrangements, and avoiding inappropriate contact outside the analytic situation. All these are part of the 'doing' of psychoanalysis.

Alongside all this runs the analyst's unconscious mind. Analysts need to sustain a creative tension between organised competence, operating at a rational level, and openness to the non-rational activity of their unconscious processes. Ferenczi expressed it as follows:

> On the one hand, [analytic therapy] requires of [the doctor] the free play of association and phantasy, the full indulgence of *his own unconscious*; we know from Freud that only in this way is it possible to grasp intuitively the expressions of the *patient's unconscious* ... On the other hand, the doctor must subject the material submitted by himself and the patient to a logical scrutiny, and in his dealings and communications may only let himself be guided exclusively by the result of this mental effort ... This constant oscillation between the free play of phantasy and critical scrutiny pre-supposes a freedom and uninhibited motility of psychic excitation on the doctor's part.
>
> (Ferenczi, 1919: 189)

Ferenczi conveys the tension between opposites very clearly, although I would query his reference to the analyst's 'indulgence' of his unconscious. Freud seems nearer the mark when he writes that the analyst needs to 'surrender himself to his own unconscious mental activity' (Freud, 1923a: 239; English versions of both Ferenczi and Freud are dependent, of course, on nuances of translation). Few analysts would disagree that analysis of a patient's unconscious depends on the analyst's access to his or her own unconscious. But what precisely does this mean? We might perhaps assume that Freud was referring to the analyst's preconscious: that area of the mind which, not being held in consciousness, is descriptively unconscious, but whose contents are available to bring back into consciousness without conflict. It is true that an analyst's work depends enormously on a free flow between conscious and preconscious. There are different views of how theory relates to clinical practice, but what is agreed is that analysts hold their theories preconsciously (Parsons, 2000: 54f). When Freud (1912b: 112) advised analysts to trust their unconscious memory, he was referring to memories that are available in the analyst's preconscious.

In that same passage, however, Freud introduces the idea of the analyst's evenly suspended attention, and he calls it the 'necessary counterpart to the demand made on the patient that he should communicate everything that occurs to him without criticism or selection' (Freud, 1912b: 112). The idea that free-floating attention has the same function for the analyst as free association does for the patient may have become familiar, but it still has radical implications. The function of free association is to allow access to unconscious areas of the patient's mind *in the face of resistance*. The analytic situation requires patients to put themselves at the mercy of their unconscious, trusting that the analyst will look after them in the face of whatever that leads to. Analysis then involves looking at how patients' anxieties stop them doing this. When Freud writes of the analyst surrendering himself to his unconscious mental activity, the word 'surrender' implies a similar conflict. To say that the analyst's free-associative process is a 'necessary counterpart' to that of the patient, is to recognise that psychoanalysis makes the same fearsome demand on analysts as on their patients; that they surrender to whatever they find inside themselves *in the face of resistance*. Analysts may take their wish to be analysts for granted and assume that, when patients lie on their couch, their desire is to analyse them. This calls, however, for analysts to lay themselves unconditionally open to their own selves: a challenge that is hard to meet without ambivalence.

Free-associative listening is bound to resonate beyond the preconscious mind of the analyst, evoking memories, thoughts and feelings that may be charged with conflict and anxiety. This calls for psychic work on the part of the analyst, and it is an analyst's job to be capable of this. These conflicts and resistances are not side issues, requiring self-analysis merely to avoid countertransference errors in the classical sense. Arising as they do in relation to the patient–analyst couple, they are a necessary element in the forward movement of the process. If analysts' listening does not stir up in them issues of their own which require analytic work within themselves, then they are in some way defending themselves against the power of a patient to disturb their equilibrium, and thus against the meaning of the analytic encounter. The only way to avoid recognising this, as Irma Brenman Pick has pointed out (1985: 158), is by claiming that the analytic function operates in a conflict-free, autonomous zone of the ego. Just such a clinical standpoint has indeed been held at certain times, and I think there is a continual temptation to revert unconsciously to that more comfortable position.

This tendency reveals itself in a piece of analytic terminology so automatic that it can go unnoticed. Analysts habitually speak of the patient's 'material'. Material is passive. It is the stuff on which we carry out an activity. 'Artists' Materials', says the shop window. Craftsmen speak of the material of their craft.[1] A patient's 'material' is what the analyst goes to work on. Embedded in this piece of analytic vocabulary is a conception of analysis as an activity that belongs to the analyst, while the patient's task is to provide the stuff that allows the analyst to analyse. The way analysts use the term so automatically is, I think, an unconscious defence, symptomatic of a universal countertransference resistance to the fact that the analytic process mobilises conflicts and anxiety in the analyst, not only at certain times or with certain patients, but by its nature.

Why *countertransference* resistance? The analytic encounter is transferential in both directions, and James McLaughlin (1981) has argued that countertransference is a redundant concept, since all that it refers to is the analyst's transference. He favoured dropping the term altogether, on the grounds that it skews perception of the analytic situation, and induces analysts to separate their experience as analysts from the rest of their psychic life and development. I think this last point is especially important, and I agree in general with McLaughlin's view. Nevertheless, I keep the term 'countertransference' for a particular reason. The concept of countertransference is associated with the historic shift, mentioned in Chapter 8 (p.115), from a limited perspective which viewed it only as an

142

impediment arising from the analyst's unconscious, to a broader one which could also see it as a source of understanding, produced perhaps by unconscious communication on the patient's part. Recognition of countertransference may correspondingly prompt analysts, on the one hand, to perceive distortions that their own transferences are introducing, and on the other, to discover fresh unconscious meaning in the quality of the analytic relationship. I use the phrase 'countertransference to the psychoanalytic process' so as to apply both of these, not just to an individual analysis, but to the analyst's relation to the process of psychoanalysis itself. As Howard Levine put it:

> I would like to look at a seemingly paradoxical feature of the countertransference that is not often emphasised in our literature. Schafer (unpublished) has argued that in the act of doing analysis, 'each therapist [is] inevitably acting on one or more basic, generalised, complex countertransferences' that 'will be more or less operative in each clinical encounter' and 'have gone into, if not dictated, the choice of a therapeutic career'. What I wish to add is that the very same infantile conflicts that give rise to these basic countertransferences, and that demarcate an analyst's areas of potential liabilities (countertransference interference), simultaneously serve as the wellspring for that analyst's unique intuitive capacities and analytic strengths. Perhaps Reich (1951: 31) had something similar in mind when she stated that 'countertransference is a necessary prerequisite of analysis. If it does not exist, the necessary talent and interest are lacking'.
>
> (Levine, 1994: 668)

This highlights the importance of McLaughlin's point that analysts should not split off their psychic activity as analysts from their personal psychic development as a whole.

Since use of the term 'material' is so pervasive, I called it a 'universal' countertransference resistance. Some aspects of the analytic process will, inevitably, evoke a countertransference response, even though the issues mobilised will be personal to every analyst, and specific with regard to individual patients. Termination is an obvious instance. Psychoanalysis draws two people into a relationship which is emotionally intense, and fated to come to an end. This cannot but have strong transference resonances for each of them. Whatever may have brought an analyst into analytic work in the first place, the fact of no longer being needed is bound to require working through. Throughout an analysis, analysts are transformational objects for their patients, to be made analytic use of in whatever way a patient is able, and their interpretations are another kind of analytic object, for patients to use and then leave behind when they have served their purpose (Bollas, 1987: 13–29; 1989: 93–113). All this will entail countertransference associations to those who have been transformational objects in analysts' own lives, and to how their offerings were received in different emotionally charged situations. Another example: as the once prevalent myth of the completed analysis has faded, analysts have had to realise that what they do is simply one element, at one particular stage, in a patient's lifelong psychic history. John Klauber wrote that 'psychoanalysis is a long process in which what happens after the patient has left the psychoanalyst's consulting room for the last time is more important than what happens during the analysis' (Klauber, 1981: xvi). Not to be able to know, after all that commitment, what difference they made in the end, tests analysts' faith in the analytic process, and may resonate with deep feelings about what they have really meant in the lives of those who matter most to them.

Detailed accounts of countertransference to the process of psychoanalysis are not common. McLaughlin (2005) offers a frank and engaging exploration of how his work as an analyst interacts with his sense of the person that he is. Ken Wright (2007) describes how analysts sometimes use theory to protect themselves against the disturbance that the analytic process arouses in them. This would amount, in terms of this chapter, to a failure to deal with their countertransference to the process; and it is bound, as Wright says, to be detrimental to their understanding of individual patients. Harold Searles did not spell out the distinction I am making, but much of his work seems based on the relation between his countertransference to the analytic process and his countertransference to the individual patient (see especially Searles, 1979). At first, he says, his idea of an analyst's identity was very rigid, and this blocked his view of what was going on between himself and a patient. As this rigidity 'dissolved in grief', Searles grew more able to let patients affect his feelings about what being an analyst meant to him.

> In a succession of papers I have described the process whereby my identity became sufficiently alive to change, open to symbiotic relatedness, aware of change through change in itself, so that it is now my most reliable source of data as to what is transpiring between the patient and myself, and within the patient. I have described, in effect, the 'use' of such fluctuations in one's sense of identity as being a prime source of discovering, in work with a patient, not only countertransference processes but also transference processes, newly developing facets of the patient's self-image, and so on; and, in supervision, of discovering processes at work not only between the supervisee and oneself, but also between the supervisee and the patient.
>
> (Searles, 1979: 68)

There is an extraordinary account by Ogden (2005: 1273–5) of his supervision with Searles, which shows two analysts shifting freely between, on the one hand, communicating at a deep level about what it is to be an analyst, and on the other, reflecting on their work with particular patients.

A candidate in supervision, after coming for some time, took to beginning his supervisions, not by getting out notes or necessarily referring to his patient at all, but by telling me what he happened to be thinking of. I would be interested in whatever this was and would respond. This was not pseudo-analysis, nor was it simply conversation. The candidate knew it was supervision and, sure enough, before long we were talking about the patient, but often without knowing quite how we had arrived there. Because of what he was coming for, there was always an unconscious connection between what was on his mind and the analysis he had come to discuss, and it was a question of waiting for this to reveal itself. We were trusting our unconscious minds to take us where we needed to be, without imposing preconceived ideas about how that should happen. This candidate's training was immersing him continually in unconscious psychic life, and showing him that this is what the work of an analyst involves. The supervision, as I came to see, was helping him to relate his feelings about one particular analysis to the larger impact of this discovery about the analytic process.

Freud himself offers interesting glimpses of countertransference to the process. His paper on screen memories was autobiographical (Freud, 1899; Jones, 1954: 27f). In it he interprets to himself, as to a patient, that a memory of playing as a child contains a displaced representation of an adolescent erotic impulse. Freud the patient asks why it should be a childhood scene that disguises such a wish, and Freud the analyst replies:

> For the sake of its innocence, perhaps. Can you imagine a greater contrast to these designs for gross sexual aggression than childish pranks? However, there are more general grounds that have a decisive influence in bringing about the slipping away of repressed thoughts and wishes into childhood memories; for you will find the same thing invariably happening in hysterical patients.
>
> (Freud, 1899: 317)

The interaction between Freud's self-analysis and his work with patients ran in both directions. Didier Anzieu (1986: 404–11) suggests that Freud's self-analysis of this screen memory led to important developments in his ideas about sexuality. The reciprocal dependence of his self-analysis on his clinical work appears when he writes to Fliess in 1897: 'My self-analysis is still interrupted. I have now seen why. I can only analyse myself with objectively acquired knowledge' (Freud, 1954: 234).

This interdependence between Freud's personal and analytic selves is striking in the case of Herr E, whom Freud mentions frequently in his letters to Fliess. This patient mattered to Freud because his earliest memories seemed to confirm Freud's ideas so well, and for a more personal reason.

> You can imagine how important this one continuing patient has become to me ... Buried deep beneath all his phantasies we found a

scene from his primal period (before twenty-two months) which meets all requirements ... I can hardly bring myself to believe it yet. It is as if Schliemann had dug up another Troy which had hitherto been believed to be mythical [see p.36]. Also the fellow is feeling shamelessly well. He has demonstrated the truth of my theories in my own person, for with a surprising turn in his analysis he provided me with the solution of my own railway phobia.

(Freud, 1954: 305f)

Three months later a lot had happened.

Prospects seemed most favourable in E's case, and it was there that I had the heaviest blow. Just when I thought I had the solution it eluded my grasp, and I was confronted with the necessity of turning everything upside down and putting it together again afresh, losing in the process all the hypotheses that until then had seemed plausible. I could not stand up to the depression of all this. I soon found that it was impossible to continue the really difficult work in the face of depressions and lurking doubts. When I am not cheerful and master of myself every single one of my patients is a tormenting spirit to me. I really thought I should have to give in. I adopted the expedient of renouncing working by conscious thought, so as to grope my way further into the riddles only by blind touch. Since I started this I have been doing my work, perhaps more skilfully than before, but I do not really know what I am doing.

(Ibid: 311f)

This is Freud's discovery of the analyst's need for free-floating attention. The episode confirms that free-floating attention requires the analyst to be open, when necessary, to his own disturbance. When Freud says 'every single one of my patients is a tormenting spirit to me', he reveals an intense negative transference, not to individual patients but to the analytic process, indeed to the fact of being an analyst. Working through this disturbed relationship to the process, however, brought a landmark advance in his understanding of it.

Anzieu (1986: 523–9) emphasises another important aspect of the story. The analysis of Herr E was drawing to its close at the same time as Freud's friendship with Fliess was becoming strained. According to Anzieu, the increased understanding of transference that Freud gained with Herr E, which let him bring the case to a satisfactory close, was linked to his being able to free himself from the transferential aspects of his friendship with Fliess, and bring that relationship also to an end.

This shows, like the writings of McLaughlin and Searles, that analysts' work evolves, not just as their theoretical understanding develops, but as their appreciation evolves of what being an analyst means to them personally. I said earlier that psychoanalysis calls on analysts, as much as it does on patients, to surrender to whatever they find inside themselves. Psychoanalytic listening is conflictual by its nature. It facilitates understanding and arouses resistance simultaneously in the analyst. The creative use of this conflict is what makes the analyst's work possible.

Here are two experiences of my own—a dream about an ex-patient, and my response to something that happened in a session—which caused me to reflect on my relationship with the analytic process. This was necessary for me both personally and as an analyst, and also for my understanding of these particular patients. The point of the examples is to show how these three are interconnected.

I had the following dream. *I was standing on the pavement outside my consulting room when a woman driving a big lorry pulled up beside me. She was a former analytic patient of mine.* Some time previously, I had moved both my home and my practice from one part of London to another. In the dream I was outside my new consulting room, and this woman was a patient who had finished her analysis before I moved. *She asked me how it was possible to move a particular armchair that had been in my old consulting room. This was a large, round, plastic armchair with a comfortable, containing feel to it.* I had never had such a chair. It existed only in the reality of the dream. *I told her that it was an inflatable chair. You could let the air out and then it was easy to take it to my new consulting room, blow it up, and there it was again. She laughed and said, 'That's a thing worth buying.' She was enjoying the idea that this solid-looking chair had all that unexpected space inside it.* The dream ended there and I woke up with an acute, vivid sense that I was in the house which had been my childhood home.

I grew up as an only child. This gave me a capacity for solitude, out of which the richness of emotional contact with others was something to be discovered. Like all analysts, no doubt, I see something of what led me into this work, and I think one meaning of the chair in the dream is that it relates both to my confidence and to my anxieties about being the kind of psychoanalyst that I am. This patient sees me as substantial and containing, and (I tell myself in my dream) she enjoys finding that her contact with me is based on an unexpected spaciousness that I have inside me. Her analysis was 'a thing worth buying'. There is an anxiety, however, that spaciousness might turn into emptiness, and an inflated capacity might be deflated. If I do have a capacity to help my patients discover what emotional relationships can mean for them, this analytic capacity depends on my continuing with my personal discovery of what emotional relationships mean, and never taking that for granted. My move was an upheaval, both practically and emotionally, and the dream reflects my anxiety, in all the turmoil, about staying in good contact with my personal and analytic identity, and with my emotional capacities. Beyond expressing this as an anxiety, the dream itself works to help me go on developing that identity and those capacities. This work is needed for my own sake and that of my patients; the two cannot be separated, as the case of Freud and Herr E shows.

The dream also relates specifically to the analysis of the patient who appeared in it. (As always with dreams, it has many facets and could be interpreted further, but I have stayed with aspects relevant to the theme of this chapter.) This woman gained greatly from several years of five-times-a-week analysis. She was faced with a terrifying internal blankness, but eventually the void yielded up a remarkable capacity for emotional experience and creativity. I think the big lorry represents the truly substantial, solid sense of herself that she developed through her analysis. It also seemed strange, though, for this woman to be a lorry driver. Did the lorry stand for something *too* heavy that she had to haul around with her? She kept in contact after her analysis ended, letting me know about projects resulting from her new-found creativity. Her gratitude for the analysis was profound. She was obviously glad to express it to me and I was interested to hear what she was doing. But her occasional letters had a certain intensity about them: there was a degree of detail, and a way of referring back to the analysis, which made me wonder about a wish in her for the analysis to continue, or even a fantasy that it was doing so. Had she, perhaps, had difficulty in working through the separation because of transference issues that were not fully resolved during the analysis? And could my countertransferential involvement, not simply with her, but with the difficult, interesting analytic process we shared, have made it harder for me to help her resolve whatever those issues might have been? I do not know. But for all the success of the analysis, and the satisfaction of letting me know its continuing value for her, would it have been better, although a loss to both of us, if she had felt free enough of the experience not to need to keep in touch with me as she did?

Another patient was lying on the couch telling me the story of an emotionally important episode in his life. As he spoke he gestured with his arm in an expansive, somewhat assertive way, and I had a sense of his wanting to persuade me. In fact it was more controlling than that. I felt presented with a narrative which I was expected to understand in the way that he wanted me to. It came into my mind how I myself use my hands when I talk. Sometimes I am aware of gesturing quite actively when I interpret, even though a patient cannot see me behind the couch. Then I thought, 'Is that what *I'm* like?' meaning, am I, when I do that, trying to control a patient into accepting my interpretation, as I felt this patient was trying to control my mind? This was a disconcerting thought. How important is it to me that my patients should agree with the way I understand them? If I am more invested in that than I am consciously aware, my countertransference to the process might seriously interfere with the analytic quality of my work. I noted that I must monitor my own responses to how patients respond to what I say. Alongside this, the strength of my reaction to the thought about how I use my own hands suggested to me that I could be picking up something about the patient as well. His unconscious need to control me, and the anxiety that lay behind that, might be stronger than I had appreciated so far.

As I reflected further after the session, the word 'narrative' brought back something from my own analysis. Realising once that I was going on, as I sometimes did, in a rather relentless, unstoppable kind of way, I had said, 'Oh! I suppose I've started on another King Mark's Narration', referring to a famous monologue in Wagner's *Tristan und Isolde*. The state of mind out of which I said that—a knowing sort of self-mockery, containing a good deal of intellectual arrogance—is not one I look back on with pleasure. The association warned me that if I am still vulnerable to the wish to be a king in my consulting room, as I had clearly wanted to be king of my analyst's, then this patient might have a particular way of keying into that, provoking me to engage in a kind of intellectual jousting with him for my own satisfaction. Whatever this alerted me to in myself, however, it was also, again, clearly related to the patient. This man's profession involves regular public speaking of a combative nature. Jousting is what he does. He comes from a large family in which he felt submerged, and his own interpretation of why he chose this profession was that it helped him 'find a voice'. It is difficult for him when I interpret the more aggressive aspects of his need to dominate an opponent and control the minds of his audience.

The self-analysis shown here functioned in three ways: on my own account personally; to deepen my relationship with my work as an analyst; and for the better understanding of particular patients. As I have said, it is the way these are bound up with each other that I want to underline. The more disturbed the patient, the more challenging it is for analysts to break the seal of their countertransference to the process, and confront these interrelations. Analysts like Searles and McLaughlin reveal in their writings the courage that this can require.

It is worth noticing that these examples are not about finding an interpretation. Accounts of how analysts made use of their responses to a patient, so as to understand the analytic interaction better, often show something being interpreted that could not be put into words before. My emphasis, however, is on the quality of engagement, with the analytic process as well as with the patient, out of which an analyst's interventions arise. Naturally these are guided by the analyst's theoretical viewpoint. But analytic interventions are not derived abstractly from an analyst's theories. They implicitly express the individual ways in which analysts make use of their theories; that is to say, the role that those theories play in an analyst's own psychic economy. This internal relationship to the analytic process is what Sacha Nacht (1962, 1963) called the analyst's 'deep inner attitude'; and it is an essential element in the quality of the analyst's engagement with a patient.

> As I see it, amid the essential problems involved in a course of treatment lies the importance of a *common denominator* of which the integral value can entirely change the final result: I am speaking now of the person of the analyst in so far as he represents and *embodies* a certain deep

inner attitude in the analytic situation. It is this deep inner attitude which, in my opinion, is a decisive factor, and that is why I have often maintained that it is what the analyst *is* rather than what he *says* that matters ... The basic relationship of the patient to the analyst springs from what his unconscious *perceives* of the unconscious of the doctor, perhaps even more than the interpretations that are given him.

(Nacht, 1962: 207)

Nacht seems to give greater importance to the quality of the analyst's presence than to the interpretations the analyst makes. But the two cannot be separated. How an interpretation is experienced by a patient depends, of course, on the patient's own state of mind, but also on the true quality, at an unconscious level, of the analyst's presence. Nacht emphasises that this is not something the analyst can decide to adopt. It is a matter of the truth of the analyst's being. In Edward Glover's words, 'A prerequisite of the efficiency of interpretation is the *attitude*, the true unconscious attitude, of the analyst to his patients' (Glover, 1937: 131). Notice that Glover says 'to his patients', in the plural. As with Freud's comments on his crisis while analysing Herr E, Glover is referring to the analyst's relationship to being an analyst.

Out of the reciprocal engagement with the patient and with the process, what may often arise is an interpretation, in the sense of a more or less specifically formulated perception of the patient's psychic functioning. But not always. As Catherine Parat vivdly expressed it:

Our best interventions do not rest on knowledge nor even often on an elaboration, but on something perceived or felt, and are expressed in a direct communication which short-circuits consciousness; the psychoanalytic work is then akin to artistic creation. In order to lend oneself to the other's progression by identification, it is often sufficient to give a verbal form to the internal movement which it has aroused, to accompany it ... on the waves which it has set off. The resonance awakened by certain words which spontaneously stand out from their manifest content and which we grasp, or the perception of the double meaning of some expressions, open in us a road or a breach toward our unconscious world; we do not know at once where it leads, for it leads where the other one needs to go.

(Parat, 1976, cited in Dufresne, 1992: 357)

The interventions that really touch patients are ones that arise out of psychic work involving the analyst's unconscious. That is why the analytic process feels at once familiar and a mystery. This psychic work may crystallise in the analyst's conscious mind to a greater or lesser extent. If thoughts articulate themselves distinctly enough, the result appears in the form of an interpretation. If the psychic work only emerges partially into consciousness, analysts may find themselves saying something without fully understanding why, but with a feeling of authenticity and a sense that it needs saying. Bollas (1992: 101–33) describes how analysts can use their own incomplete associations, if these emerge out of a self-enquiring, free-associative listening, to facilitate the same kind of self-enquiry in the patient. If the analyst's psychic work does not reach consciousness at all, there may be no intervention, although the patient may still sense the quality of the analyst's engagement. Or else there may come one of those times when patients tell their analysts that a certain comment—one which the analyst did not consider specially significant, and may hardly even remember making—was profoundly helpful. These are occasions when the analyst really did 'catch the drift of the patient's unconscious with his own unconscious' (Freud, 1923a: 239), without being aware of doing so.

My focus on the analyst's countertransference to the process, and on what happens in the analyst's mind as well as the patient's, at the boundary between conscious and unconscious, is not in order to democratise the analytic situation and put the participants on a more equal footing. The psychoanalytic relationship is not symmetrical. Of course the analyst is a real object to the patient and the analytic dyad is an interpersonal relationship. But it is also a relationship between two internal worlds, and the analyst must remain a symbolic object, available for fantasy and projection. Anything that reduces an analyst's availability as this sort of object reduces the analyst's availability as an analytic object. It would also constrict what it means to say that analysts listen in to their own unconscious minds, if the word 'mind' were taken too narrowly. In Chapter 11 (pp.176ff), the need is stressed for 'mind' and 'heart' to come together in the analyst. In order to be the analytic, potentially transformational objects that their patients need, analysts have to be alive to what the analytic process arouses in themselves at all levels of their being: intellectual, emotional, and also in their bodies (Milner, 1969: xxx; Searles, 1979: 153–4). A function of the inwardly directed, free-associative awareness that I have been emphasising is to help analysts become more open and sensitive to the reverberations in their whole selves of the process in which they are engaged.

This is not to idealise disturbance in the analyst, as something to be desired for its own sake. Neither do analysts have to be working at the deepest levels within themselves for every moment of an analysis. What matters is for the analyst to be sensitive to the level of emotional work that a given moment calls for. In the Chinese martial art of t'ai chi chuan, the practice called 'pushing hands' is an exercise in sensitivity to another person's energy. A couple stand opposite each other. One of them moves forward, pressing with her hands on her partner's arm to shift his centre of gravity. He moves back, yielding to her pressure, but not breaking touch with her hands. He must soften his body so as to give his partner no purchase against him, while keeping just enough contact for him to sense the movement of her energy. He in turn presses forward against her arm, trying to feel her centre and push against it, while she now yields and softens so that he cannot find it. She has to sense where her partner's energy is directed, as he did while she was pushing. He, for his part, must not be drawn off-balance by the movement of her yielding. And so they continue back and forth. This cumbersome description belies how delicate and fluid the interchange in fact feels. The experience can be strikingly reminiscent of the subtle explorations that go on in psychoanalysis. It exemplifies physically the way that analysts try to hold themselves psychically in a state of supple responsiveness so that, at whatever level the patient needs to be met, the analyst is there at that level to meet them. What is crucial is the *emotional availability* of the analyst. At times, this will mean an availability to be disturbed by the process, as Freud was in the case of Herr E. By its nature, the analytic process will stir up, to varying degrees in different situations, conflict and anxiety in the analyst. The quality of their engagement with their own countertransference to this process will determine for analysts the quality of their engagement with a patient. If they discover that engaging with what the process stirs up in themselves refreshes their freedom and flexibility, and enlivens the dynamic flow of their own psyche, there is a good chance that their engagement with the patient also may be therapeutic.

Note

1   See, for example, the quotations from Andy Goldsworthy on pp. 116 and 118.

10

RAIDING THE INARTICULATE

Internal setting, beyond countertransference

Internal and external aspects of psychoanalytic listening have been a central theme of the last two chapters. On a broader front, there are internal and external facets of clinical technique in general.

Take the question, for example, whether analysts should be the same with every patient or whether they need to be different with different patients. There are answers from either perspective. Certain aspects of clinical technique are constant. Analysts always attend to unconscious meaning in a patient's associations, always take note of the transference and always seek to maintain analytic neutrality. Other aspects, such as the balance of emphasis between history and the here and now, how active or how silent the analyst is, and whether interpretations are focused and specific or open-ended and allusive, will vary according to the perception of a particular patient's needs. This is an answer couched in terms of external aspects of clinical technique.

A different kind of response would be that analysts need to be authentically themselves with every patient, but will also need to express their emotional availability, or deploy the qualities of their analytic identity, in different ways with different patients. Such an answer again shows how an analyst is both the same and different with every patient, but this time with reference to internal aspects of the analyst's technique.

External aspects of clinical technique comprise the ways that analysts behave, and what they say, or do not say, in response to what they hear from the patient. By internal aspects of technique, I mean all those elements that contribute to analysts' ways of being with a patient—verbally, non-verbally, emotionally and in their bodily presence—that come about in response to what analysts hear from inside themselves.

It is accepted that an analyst's external listening should be undirected and free of preconceived aims. Monitoring a patient's material for particular themes is not free-floating attention. As regards internal listening, the situation is more problematic. Different understandings of countertransference were referred to in Chapter 8 (p.115). The classical view of it might make analysts watchful lest their own reactions hinder the analysis, while the perception of it as offering clues to the analytic relationship might have them focusing on whether their feelings are their own or emanate from the patient. In either case, the result may be a self-monitoring, inwardly directed listening *for* something by the analyst, as opposed to listening simply *to* whatever there is to be heard (Chodorow, 2003). Analysts would then be treating themselves in just the way that they try not to treat the patient. If analysts can arrive, on the other hand, at an inward listening that is genuinely free-floating in relation to their own internal processes, they may become truly analytic listeners to themselves. Such listening, free of focus, open and willing to be vulnerable to whatever analysts hear emerging from within themselves, needs the containment of a certain kind of internal space.

The notion of the analytic setting is fundamental to psychoanalysis. If we enter a theatre, a children's playground, or a place of worship, we cross a boundary which tells us that the reality we are going to meet on the inside works differently from the reality outside. The analytic dialogue needs a similar enclosure to denote that what happens inside it will have a different status, and be considered from a different viewpoint, from what happens outside. Patients can discover that however overwhelmed they may become by their emotions, or however outrageous, extreme and irrational the things they may say, they do not have to censor or inhibit themselves, because the analytic setting safely separates the experience from the rest of their lives.

The setting also provides a framework for clinical technique. Just as the patient is free within it to be different from normal, so is the analyst. Analysts need not answer questions. They need not speak at all. What they say when they do speak might appear by ordinary standards strange, illogical, perhaps sometimes a bit crazy. An analyst is free to be like this because for the analyst, as well as the patient, the analytic setting delineates a space in which the expectations of everyday reality are suspended.

The external structure of the setting is familiar: consulting room, chair, couch; sessions that begin and end on time; fees and how they are paid; a pattern of holidays. But the analytic setting also exists internally as a structure in the analyst's mind. This concept of the internal analytic setting, or framework, has been central to my thinking for several years. For a long time, though, it was hardly present in the literature. When I was writing the paper on which this chapter is based (Parsons, 2007), I was struck by how little the idea seemed to have been articulated and developed, at least in English, as a specific concept.[1]

The idea of the internal setting took shape in my mind through a seminar for newly qualified analysts, which Jonathan Sklar, a colleague in the British Psychoanalytical Society, and I ran for some ten years during the 1990s (Sklar and Parsons, 2011: 145ff). We aimed to help analysts consider how their analytic identities might develop in the period following qualification. Discussion ranged from practical questions, such as getting referrals and running a practice, to more internal aspects of how one evolves into being a psychoanalyst. We noticed repeatedly how the former were linked to the latter.

Apparently external issues—how to tell senior colleagues that one had an analytic vacancy; whether it was time yet to have one's own consulting room—turned out again and again to depend on, or rather to reflect, where someone had got to internally in the development of their identity as an analyst. A member of the seminar said, for example:

> I have realised that one reason I haven't any patients in full-time psychoanalysis is that I have never asked anyone to refer them to me. I have never really thought of myself as being able to have a psychoanalytic practice. When I realised that, I could begin to see how there might be space in my mind for a psychoanalytic patient.

There is external work in letting it be known that one has a vacancy for analytic patients, and another sort of work in developing that as an internal truth about oneself.

The material reality of the new analyst's consulting room also has a powerful symbolic meaning. The most evocative analytic space one has known so far is the room of the analyst on whose couch one has lain for hundreds of hours. That was shaped by another analytic mind. Now it is time to shape a space of one's own. Large practicalities about finance and property dealings or rearranging the home, apparently minor details about doorbells and couch covers, questions of how to let patients in and who opens the door when they leave: such issues would evoke in group members a recognisable kind of joyful anxiety, because the external event represented a major development in the internal realisation of an analytic identity. Even with an already established consulting room, there was a deepening understanding of how it stood for an internal space that was becoming more available for analytic work.

Just as the external setting defines and protects a spatio-temporal arena in which patient and analyst can conduct the work of analysis, so the internal setting defines and protects an area of the analyst's mind where whatever happens, including what happens to the external setting, can be considered from a psychoanalytic viewpoint. The external setting may be breached from the outside if, for example, the builders next door start hammering or someone accidentally enters the room; or from the inside, by a patient's acting out or if the analyst does something to disrupt it. But provided the analyst's internal setting remains intact, infringements of the external setting can still be thought about in terms of their analytic significance and brought within the analysis.

If a woman in analysis has a baby she will be ready, some time after the birth, to come back to her sessions. She may not be able to arrange childcare, however, or may not want to leave the baby. What about coming to her sessions and bringing the baby with her? In a discussion between French and British analysts in 2005, some French analysts said they could never permit this. The presence of the real baby, they said, would displace the baby's symbolic meaning for the patient and sabotage the reality of her fantasies about it. This would destroy the analytic setting's function of protecting the symbolic realm against intrusion by the real, and the analytic work could not continue.

This view rests on a perception of the analytic framework in external terms only. The real baby has, after all, been coming to the sessions already, inside the mother. The relation between outside and inside is central to psychoanalytic work, as to breathing. When analysts have in their minds the psychic structure that I call an 'internal analytic framework', then whatever the external setting comprises, including a real baby, can still be considered in terms of its unconscious, symbolic meaning. The baby's presence in the session is then full of analytic potential.

A woman began her analysis having not much sense of her individuality as a person or of the boundary between herself and the world around her. A time came when she wanted to bring her dog to her session. It had a chronic health problem which she said meant it should not be left alone for too long, and the person who normally looked after it was away. So could she bring the dog? After all, it was only a little one. I might have got involved in interpreting the dog as a container for the patient's projection of her loneliness and malaise; or have taken the position that this was an attempt to disrupt the analysis, and said she must make other arrangements. In my theory of clinical technique, however, sessions are there for patients to discover how they can use them, and I simply said that whether she brought the dog was up to her. She did bring it, and lay on the couch and settled it down on her tummy. It was easy to see, and to interpret, that this small creature, peacefully asleep in that position, represented our baby inside her: an idea that she would otherwise have found extraordinarily difficult to allow into consciousness. One day the dog did not seem very well, and halfway through the session it was sick on the carpet. To have a dog being sick in the consulting room might seem like a pretty thorough breach of the analytic setting. But the patient and I cleared up the mess together, and I said I thought that at this moment the dog might represent an aspect of herself, usually shut away out of sight, which felt angry and hostile towards me and would be glad to mess up my room.

This piece of work depended on there being in my mind an internal setting secure enough to give me confidence that whatever having the dog in the room might lead to, could still be part of the analysis. The patient might have protested at my interpretation, saying she had not made the dog sick, she did not know it was going to happen, and so on. In fact she did not, but seemed relieved that a way had appeared for us to talk about her aggressive feelings towards me. A primary aim of the work of analysis is to help patients develop their own internal arena for analytic self-understanding, and the fact that this woman did not retreat into the rational defences that were easily available to her indicates that this was beginning to happen.

These examples illustrate how the internal analytic setting operates, and also the strength of the concept in making possible considerable flexibility in the external setting, without any sacrifice of its analytic quality.

156

The significance of the idea appears clearly in historical retrospect. Ferenczi struggled for lack of it. He needed the idea of an internal framework in order to make sense, and keep control, of how he was trying to help his very disturbed patients. If the concept had been available to him he might have been saved a lot of difficulty. In Margaret Little's (1985) account of her analysis with Winnicott she describes Winnicott acting in ways that transgress a conventional perception of the analytic framework. He held her head while she supposedly relived the terror of her own birth experience, and he doubled the length of her sessions without increasing the fee. I have considered elsewhere (Parsons, 2002) why Winnicott may have acted like this, and have suggested that, given the somewhat restricted view of the analytic process that was prevalent at the time, Winnicott may have been pushing at the limits of the external framework in an attempt to expand his internal sense of what a psychoanalytic process could encompass. That is to say, his Ferenczi-like experiments with regard to the external setting may reflect efforts to develop his sense of the internal analytic setting.

The external setting constitutes a space protected against the assumptions, expectations and judgements of ordinary reality. Patient and analyst are free within it to be however they find they need to be, and this sets up a different reality in which analytic understanding can emerge. The internal setting constitutes a *psychic* space which is correspondingly protected, so that within it analysts can maintain their own *psychoanalytic* reality. This depends on analysts finding freedom in this area of their minds, just like the analytic couple in the external setting, to be however they need to be internally.

There is more to this than the analyst's ability to free-associate. That is, in Erich Fromm's (1941) and Isaiah Berlin's (1958) terms, a *freedom to* do something. The internal analytic setting involves *freedom from* considerations that operate elsewhere in the analyst's mind. Absolute inner freedom is an ideal not likely to be achieved, but it is still a radical demand to say that in this area of their minds analysts need to work towards it.

Bion's extension of dreaming into waking life, as well as sleep, was discussed in Chapter 2 (p.25). The dream-work that this involves, asleep or awake, is that of making unconscious linkages between elements of experience, so as to enrich the meaning of the whole experience. Closely related to dreaming is the state, also described by Bion (1962: 36f), of reverie. This is a contemplative openness of the psyche by which a mother with an infant, or an analyst with a patient, takes in the experience of the other and lets it interact with her own inward processes, to form something new that is meaningful both to herself and the baby, or the patient. Reverie, in this sense, is not a state of withdrawn vagueness, just as Bion's dreaming is not detached from reality. Dreaming and reverie both mean being connected more deeply to reality by perceiving it through the lens of one's imagination. This recalls Enid Balint's notion of 'imaginative perception' (1993: 103), which she described as 'what happens when the patient imagines what he perceives and thus creates his own partly imagined, partly perceived, world'. The analyst too links what she perceives outwardly (the patient and his 'material') with how her imagination works on that inwardly, to yield an experience that is both perceived and imagined. Listening in a state of psychoanalytic reverie, with imaginative perception, might in Bion's terms be called 'dreaming' the analysis (as I had to dream the clinical seminar in Chapter 2 [pp.28f]). This is the basis for that kind of inwardly directed listening, which I described earlier as the analyst's being an analytic listener to herself.

Such listening is also the object of the seminar described in Chapter 4, which revolved around the idea that 'we hear more sensitively what is going on in another person by learning to be sensitive to the responses which this person stirs up in ourselves' (p.51). As I mentioned there, the seminar makes use of poems. Reading a poem is another situation where, attending to something outside ourselves, we hear more of it by listening to what it does inside us.

As we try to understand a poem, there comes a point when we cannot get any further by studying the words on the page. We only reach more deeply into the poem by allowing the poem into ourselves and seeing what then happens within us. Seamus Heaney (2002: 33–8) described his encounter with T.S. Eliot's *The Waste Land*. At first, he advanced on it with commentaries and all the resources of his university library, but this did not help much. Then in some of Eliot's own writing about poetry, he saw 'a poet's intelligence exercising itself in the activity of listening'. This freed him. Instead of studying *The Waste Land* for its meaning, he began simply to listen to it, to make himself, as he puts it, 'an echo-chamber for the poem's sounds'.

> I began to construe from its undulant cadences and dissolvings and reinings-in a mimetic principle which matched or perhaps even overwhelmed any possible meaning that might be derived from the story ... In the heft and largesse of the poem's music, I thought I divined an aural equivalent of the larger transcendental reality ... The breath of life was in the body of sound.
>
> (Heaney, 2002: 34f)

This sort of experience led Heaney to distinguish between abstracting meaning and hearing it (Heaney, 2002: 28). Clinically also it is an important distinction whether analysts *abstract meaning from* what their patients tell them, or *hear meaning in* what they say. Interpretations which abstract a patient's meaning run the risk, like academic commentaries on poetry, of appropriating meaning to themselves while the breath of life in the original is lost. Since, in the internal analytic setting, reality is defined by unconscious meaning, this internal setting is where an analyst can best hear meaning without needing to abstract it.

When the paper which is the origin of this chapter was originally presented, the following poem by Heaney (1996: 1) was projected on a screen before I began reading the paper. This allowed the audience time to see the poem, and relate to it, as a text.

The Rain Stick

Upend the rain stick and what happens next
Is a music that you never would have known
To listen for. In a cactus stalk

Downpour, sluice-rush, spillage and backwash
Come flowing through. You stand there like a pipe
Being played by water, you shake it again lightly

And diminuendo runs through all its scales
Like a gutter stopping trickling. And now here comes
A sprinkle of drops out of the freshened leaves,

Then subtle little wets off grass and daisies;
Then glitter-drizzle, almost-breaths of air.
Upend the stick again. What happens next

Is undiminished for having happened once,
Twice, ten, a thousand times before.
Who cares if all the music that transpires

Is the fall of grit or dry seeds through a cactus?
You are like a rich man entering heaven
Through the ear of a raindrop. Listen now again.

When I reached this stage of the paper I spoke the poem aloud, the screen being blank. I wanted the audience to experience the difference between relating to the poem as a text, and being an echo-chamber for its sounds as they let the poem inside themselves. The reader also might find it interesting at this point to speak the poem aloud.

The complicated mating of consonants and vowel sounds in 'Downpour, sluice-rush, spillage and backwash' makes these words wonderfully difficult to say. It is impossible to hurry them. They exercise the mind, even while they move around in the speaking mouth as the seeds do in the rain stick.

This quietens to 'a gutter stopping trickling'. The words create in sound the fading of drips into silence which they describe, the 'aural equivalent' that Heaney first 'divined' in Eliot. The lightness that follows, of 'a sprinkle of drops' and 'almost-breaths of air', is breathtaking. A crucial phrase is: 'You stand there like a pipe/Being played by water ...' At that moment, 'you' become the rain stick: a pipe being played by these amazing sounds running through you—the sounds of the poem, made by the poet listening to the amazing sounds that were running through himself. When we hear inside ourselves the poem which recreates the rain stick, we become the rain stick too.

It is a shock then to stumble over the abrupt, throwaway question: 'Who cares ...?' The poem's delight in the play of sound seems almost aggressively dismissed. Liquidity turns to harshness in 'the fall of grit or dry seeds through a cactus'. The beauty of the surface yields to a deeper meaning. The 'music that transpires' offers a way of '... entering heaven/Through the ear of a raindrop'. The biblical echo is significant. What is reached through the eye of a needle is something supremely valuable, but only to be found by giving up the riches on which one is used to depending. It is with this in mind that we are invited to 'listen now again'. This is a poem about listening which embodies, and makes happen, its own multiplicity of listenings.

What does it involve for an analyst to listen to a patient in this way? Heaney's comments on poetic technique have a lot to say to psychoanalysts. First, though, his idiosyncratic use of the term 'technique' must be noted. Heaney sets 'craft' against 'technique', rather like Klauber (1981: 114) discussing the 'craft' and the 'art' of analysis. 'Craft', in Heaney's terms, is more or less what I have called the external aspect of technique, while 'technique', for him, is closer to what I mean by its internal aspect. With this caution, here is what he says.

> Craft is what you can learn from other verse. Craft is the skill of making ... It can be deployed without reference to the feelings or the self ... Learning the craft is learning to turn the windlass at the well of poetry. Usually you begin by dropping the bucket half way down the shaft and winding up a taking of air. You are miming the real thing until one day the chain draws unexpectedly tight and you have dipped into waters that will continue to entice you back. You'll have broken the skin on the pool of yourself ...
>
> At that point it becomes appropriate to speak of technique rather than craft. Technique, as I would define it, involves not only a poet's way with words, his management of metre, rhythm and verbal texture; it involves also a definition of his stance towards life, a definition of his own reality. It involves a discovery of ways to go out of his normal cognitive bounds and raid the inarticulate: a dynamic alertness that mediates between the origins of feeling in memory and experience and the formal ploys that express these in a work of art.
>
> (Heaney, 2002: 19)

Analysts need a similar psychic availability to themselves, in order to mediate between the origins of feeling in memory and experience and the interpretations that express these in the clinical setting. In the security of an analyst's internal setting this raiding of the inarticulate can become possible.

What might all this mean in the consulting room?

Mr W is in his fifties. At the time of the sessions I shall describe, he had been in analysis five times a week for about a year. He is single and has no children. His sexual relationships have always been with women. In his late teens, however, he fell in love with a young man of similar age. The two were friendly but his love was not reciprocated, and no emotional or physical relationship developed. This remains for Mr W the most powerful and passionate emotional experience of his life. Since then he has had several relationships with women which have lasted for some years. They have been sexual, but without great physical attraction or excitement on his part. He does not get erections easily and sometimes avoids intercourse because of this. What he does enjoy is for a woman to spank him on the bottom; not so hard as to cause pain, but so that he feels humiliated.

A significant childhood recollection, with the character of a screen memory, is of waking his parents in the night. They stood with him between them, and his mother told his father crossly to spank him. His father, who was not angry, did so, but gently so that it did not hurt.

In material terms he has been adequately but not strikingly successful. He has felt rather adrift since selling the business he had built up. He is lonely and unhappy at not finding a sexually and emotionally satisfying relationship. What also brought him to see me was the wish for a sense of direction. He was afraid of his life feeling empty and meaningless.

Here is a week from Mr W's analysis.

Thursday: He said that sitting outside in my waiting room he had noticed the smoke alarm. He thought this was funny, and wondered if I had put it there in case one of my patients might set fire to the place. He would not like to do that. I said the thought seemed to be in his mind that he could.

Later in the session, he said the end of the holiday meant phoning the plumber to mend a leak, and the plumber would certainly not come, so he would want to boil him in the bath, or take a big knife and cut his belly open. 'That would be very pleasurable.' I said that wanting to do such a thing could well go with wanting to set my place on fire. He explained that he had thought of some other patient becoming psychotic and doing that, but not himself.

He described having some toast in a café beneath his flat. It was more the image of it going into his mouth than the taste which pleased him. I asked if he knew what it was about the image that was pleasing. He said it was to do with the toast being partly inside and partly outside him. Then he wondered if he was usurping my job, making his own interpretation to push me off my pedestal. I said I thought he might indeed want to do that.

Friday: He seemed to settle himself not just down on to the couch but into it, and was silent. *Time passed, and I remembered having once broken a silence after about forty minutes. The next day he told me how disappointed he was. It crossed my mind that he might stay silent all through today's session. The silence continued. Dream-like images came to me: someone playing with glove puppets; someone trying to knock down a wall with a hammer. But I did not find myself wanting to break down his silence, nor did I feel manipulated. I wondered if his silence were an attempt to break through to something.*

I knew I must not move suddenly or noisily, in a way that could suggest irritation or frustration. But I also knew that absolute quiet was not called for. Sometimes in a prolonged silence one knows that any movement whatever may disturb the utter stillness that a patient needs (as in the session described on p.131). This was not like that. Mr W shifted on the couch from time to time with natural easy movements. I did the same in my chair. Not by conscious decision; I just let it happen when I felt like it, so that he could know I was comfortable. After a while, it seemed as though our bodies were responding to each other in a kind of slow dialogue. *I had the thought: two men whose bodies are moving together in response to each other? It seemed something homosexual might be happening between us, yet it did not feel erotic. I thought of the* Three Essays, *and how Freud broadened the understanding of what sexuality means. Was I experiencing something with this man that was sexual in a wider sense?*

And so this Friday session ended, without either of us having said a word.

Monday: He said he wanted to talk to me and wanted not to. Friday had felt good. Because I did not say anything, he did not feel he had to give me anything. There is stuff in him, he said, that is horrible, aggressive and smells bad. He wants to put it outside himself but thinks that I will not want it. He pictured himself with something brown and foul-smelling in his hand. He wanted to give it to me but that felt impossible. He mentioned the session where I broke the silence near the end. I recalled how angry and disappointed he had been. He seemed surprised and pleased that I remembered.

The rest of the session was occupied with whether I could accept the horrible stuff inside him. He talked about his shit with a striking lack of embarrassment and no apparent need for any response from me. This could have seemed provocative, but in fact it did not. It felt as though he were talking about something in a way that was real for him. There is an obvious narcissism about Mr W, and while he was saying how disgusting his shit was, the underlying idealisation of it was also clear. But for the most part I felt I existed, not in order to be erased by a monologue, but as somebody with whom he was trying to communicate in whatever way he could.

Tuesday: He begins: 'So I see a big wave coming towards me. There is spray coming off the top of it. And now I see a fish in the wave; a big fish facing forwards with its head just coming out of the wave.' *I do not know if this is a fantasy, an illusion he is conjuring from my window blind and the foliage outside, or whether I am being told a dream. He is expecting that I will listen without needing to have this explained. That is to say, he is trusting me to accept whatever he is giving me.*

He talked about seeing a man come out of the house as he arrived. Was it another patient? Are they in competition with each other for me? Is the spray of the wave my sperm and do they both want it? *This felt stereotyped and artificial. I thought he was escaping from difficult real feelings about the other man into a competition to produce interpretations, as with the toast on Thursday.*

Then he began to wonder if the man could be my son. Mr W was interested in this idea for a while, dropped it, fell silent, and then said he wanted to have the feeling of me coming into him from behind in a way that would be gentle and caressing. With the screen memory about waking his parents in mind, I said I thought he was thinking of the sexual intercourse that had produced my son, and he wanted to stop that by thinking I would have intercourse with him instead.

He showed that he understood this interpretation by explaining it to me. He said, 'So you mean that there is somebody that you have sex with, and I do not want this third person to be there; I want you just for myself. And that is why I want you to come into me from behind.' *He had understood me all right, but as he went on his talk did feel this time like a monologue to which I could only be a passive listener.*

Wednesday: He started by saying there was 'a current' coming from behind him. *A draught of air? A current of feeling? I did not know.* Then he mentioned a dream in which someone in front of him had a rucksack, and there was an enormous rabbit on top of the rucksack. He wanted it to come closer so he could cuddle it.

He thinks that what he wants from me is like the current he felt, to have the caring softness of a man coming into him from behind. This would feel undemanding and accepting. He mentioned the incident I referred to as a screen memory, then began constructing an idea about his being jealous of something between his parents and wanting it for himself. *It felt as though he were trying to recreate my interpretation from yesterday.*

I said I was not sure what he really had in mind when he talked about a man's softness coming into him from behind. He said it was something gentle, caressing, maybe like a massage. It would come into him all over, through the feeling of his skin. It was not a penis coming into his bottom. That would hurt and feel aggressive. This would be like a baker, kneading dough low down on both cheeks of his bottom, and maybe in the middle as well. It might also go in the direction of his being gently spanked. *It was clearly myself that he was imagining doing this to him. Again he was talking noticeably without embarrassment, about something which evidently felt to him uncomplicated and straightforwardly lovely.*

He said he had wanted to have this feeling with Peter (the boy he was in love with in his late teens) and it felt terrible when that relationship did not happen. He has the feeling a bit with his present girlfriend. She is small and frail and he can wrap himself right round her. He likes spanking her. I said I thought that when he is wrapped round her or spanking her, he does not really know whether it is a small frail woman or a boy like Peter that he is doing it with. He agreed, and said his dream would be for me to sit beside him and show him diapositives to illustrate a better alternative. *His background makes it easy for him to use the technical 'diapositives' instead of the everyday 'slides', but the word was still striking.*

163

For this to be his 'dream' reminded me of the dream about the rabbit, and I wondered if he wanted to say more about it. He said the rabbit was frightening because it was so big. He talked about a friend's daughter who keeps a pet rabbit in a cage. He used to tease her saying he liked the taste of rabbit, and he would cook the rabbit and eat it. It emerged that this was ten years ago, when the friend's daughter was seven. She is now seventeen and the rabbit is still alive, and still in the cage. Her brother, the son of Mr W's friend, had just got married. *I found this a very moving association. He wants to get close to the furry animal and stroke it, but it is frighteningly big, so it has to be imprisoned in a cage and threatened in an orally sadistic way. The rabbit seems to be a confused representation of both breast and genitals. Years later, it is still being kept in the cage; but the marriage of the son does seem to show hope for an alternative.*

I commented on the word 'diapositive' in his other 'dream', saying I thought he believed there is something repulsive, very negative, about a woman's body, and especially about putting his penis into whatever is inside there. He wants me to help him see it differently, so that a woman's body could become something positive for him. He responded by recalling the day he got off the couch and sat opposite me. He had thought at one time that I was going to sleep, but then realised I was going inside myself to try and feel more of what he was talking about.

The session ended.

His association about the rabbit and my subsequent intervention illustrate what I take from Heaney about the difference between abstracting meaning and hearing it. If I had made an interpretation beginning 'I think the rabbit stands for …' or 'What you are talking about is …', I would have been *abstracting meaning from* the patient's material in a way that could have distanced me from him. Likewise in the first session, I might have said explicitly that the unreliable plumber, whom he needed at the end of the holiday and would torture for not being there, represented myself. Instead of abstracting his meaning into such interpretations, I preferred to talk about his disgust for a woman's body and his hope that I could help him change that, and to make the comment that torturing the plumber and setting fire to my room belonged together. These interventions were based on meaning that I *heard in* his associations, and I hoped they might keep us more in contact with each other in an interpretative dialogue.

Such choices of clinical strategy go on all the time in an analyst's mind, usually at a preconscious level. Only in retrospect may there be conscious reflection on the options that were available, and the reasons why particular interventions were or were not made. Such reflection is valuable nonetheless, not so as to make these clinical decisions conscious in the moment after all, but to give ever more depth and complexity to the preconscious soil out of which they will continue to grow.

A touchstone of psychoanalytic activity is whether it can be sensed that patient and analyst are generating fresh meaning between them: whether they are engaged, that is, in an analytic conversation, or only a set of intersecting monologues. In this respect, there is an interesting difference between Monday, when Mr W went on about whether I could accept his shit, and Tuesday, when he took up my interpretation about his wish to stop the intercourse that had produced my son.

What he did with my interpretation on Tuesday was to abstract the meaning and appropriate it into a commentary on what I had said. He demonstrated his understanding but nothing fresh transpired between us. The Wednesday session reveals why. Its material was almost totally pre-oedipal, and full of anxiety about contact with an indeterminate kind of genital. My interpretation on Tuesday had been misjudged. It followed his saying he wanted me to come into him from behind, and I thought I was addressing his anxiety about one sort of genital intercourse (parental), and his wish to substitute a different sort (passive homosexual with me as his father). But Mr W had no notion, at that moment, of any sort of genital intercourse. He had not, in fact, been able to hear meaning at all in the interpretation. He deciphered it all right, but deciphering is not hearing: it is abstracting. I intended my interpretation as part of a dialogue between us, but for him it was an empty monologue. He could only respond with a monologue of his own.

His talk about his shit on Monday looked, on the face of it, more like a monologue than what happened on Tuesday. In fact we were in dialogue, even though I was mostly silent. He and I could both hear meaning in what he said, without having to abstract it. I hardly needed to interpret because he made use of my listening presence in a way that let him go on generating fresh meaning for both of us.

The significance of the silent session also becomes clear. I sensed the alternating movement of our bodies and wondered, at first, if I were involved in a homosexual interaction. But it did not feel erotic. I thought of Freud's extension of the meaning of sexuality and, sure enough, in the light of Wednesday's session, we can see that on Friday Mr W was in a state of pregenital and pre-verbal regression. The mutual responsiveness of our bodies was not that of two men, but of mother and infant.

My capacity to handle Friday's session as I did, and think about what might be happening, depended very much on my internal analytic setting. Here was an area of my mind in which I could suppose that I was having intercourse with a man, and expect that I should find that erotic. Despite the rest of my mind not operating by such a reality, it could hold sway in this part. Since I could expect, in my internal analytic setting, to feel homosexually aroused, I was able to be surprised that I was not. This put me on the track of what was actually taking place instead.

Where, topographically, does the internal setting live in the analyst's mind? When the patient I mentioned earlier wanted to bring her dog, my decision to accept as part of the analysis whatever this might lead to was a conscious decision to trust my internal analytic setting. As regards the session just discussed,

I had to realise retrospectively that I had been inhabiting my internal setting. In the session itself, my use of it was preconscious. Like much of an analyst's theoretical repertoire the internal setting moves between preconscious and conscious, operating most of the time preconsciously, but accessible to conscious awareness when this becomes necessary.

At the beginning of this chapter, when I introduced the idea of the internal setting as an area where analysts may be analytic listeners to themselves, I linked this to the concept of countertransference and its evolution. The development from the classical view of countertransference to the post-1950s understanding of it, involves two distinct shifts. One is from seeing countertransference only as an impediment, to seeing it also as potentially useful for the analysis. The other shift concerns its origin. In the earlier view, countertransference derives from unanalysed aspects of the analyst's psychic structure. In the later view, it derives from what is happening in the patient. This second shift in viewpoint, regarding whose psyche it is from which countertransference originates, has had less emphasis than the shift from its being a hindrance to a help. But separating out like this the component elements of the revision allows a new possibility to emerge. If countertransference may originate from the analyst's psyche and hinder the analysis, or from that of the patient and be able to help it, might the analysis also evoke unconscious elements belonging to the analyst's psyche which can benefit the analysis?

This differs from the first two instances in a significant respect. Those both imply that something has to be made conscious, in the analyst or in the patient, so that the analytic work may proceed. The new possibility that I am raising does not involve a demand on analysts, either to become aware of an obstacle in themselves, or to recognise a patient's projective identification, in order to get the analysis back on track. The idea that unconscious aspects of the analyst's psyche stirred up by the analytic encounter may not impede the analysis, but bring fresh creativity into it, takes us beyond the usual conception of countertransference.

Psychoanalytic writing has tended to represent the unconscious as a sort of black box with unknown things inside it. Some of these—wishes, thoughts, anxieties, fantasies—sometimes get out of the box into the light where they become visible, i.e. conscious. Freud's use of spatial metaphor is largely responsible for this picture, so it is important to remember that he spoke of the *system* Ucs (e.g. Freud, 1900: 541; 1915b: 173). Systems are not containers, with objects that are inside or outside them. They are conceptual structures with functions, potentials and limitations. Admittedly we may ask: Is this family system able to contain the disturbance of these children? Can the democratic system contain the demands of fundamentalism? But we know that the functional capacity of a system is what we are talking about. Bion's concept of container and contained is a case in point. He makes explicit use of the metaphor, and makes it equally explicit that a mental function is what the metaphor refers to (Bion, 1962: 90; 1963: 3, 31; 1970: 106ff).

So evoking unconscious aspects of the analyst's psyche does not necessarily mean bringing unconscious mental content into the light of consciousness. The analytic situation may also evoke functions, and capacities, in an analyst's psyche of which he or she was not previously aware. This depends on an availability in the analyst, an openness to the potential for this to happen. Analytic encounters will vary in how evocative they are in this way. But if analysts are internally available to be touched at whatever deep level in themselves a particular analysis can connect with, then their own psychic range may be enlarged, to the benefit of the analysis as well.

My work with Mr W illustrates how an analyst may be moved to listen analytically to himself, beyond the countertransference, in a way that can extend his psychic capacities and enrich the analysis at the same time.

At the time of Mr W's analysis I had been sitting behind the couch for twenty-five years, so I was fairly well along in my working life as an analyst. This patient gave me a sense of how much that is fascinating there is yet for me to discover about psychoanalysis, and how far my analytic capabilities have still to develop. I found myself thinking 'If I could have another twenty-five years, where might I get to then, in understanding all this?' But I was not going to have another twenty-five years. So this analysis forced me to recognise how much I would never understand about psychoanalysis. It was not required countertransferentially, to keep this particular analysis on track, that I should contemplate my inescapable losses, failures and, finally, my death. As Chapters 1 and 2 explored at length, it is a necessary psychic function for all human beings to accept these and find a way to face them. What Mr W's analysis did, in an area beyond countertransference, was to make me more conscious of the need to discover this capacity in myself.

Any analysis must benefit if an analyst is prompted by the work to recognise more fully their own humanity. Alongside the general truth of this, the self-analytic reflections which this analysis stirred up in me relate more specifically to Mr W's condition. The most meaningful emotional experience of his life was some twenty-five years earlier. In heterosexual relationships he has not found anything like the passion and emotional significance of his feelings for Peter, nor could he establish a homosexual identity that might have let him fulfil those feelings with a different man. The emptiness of his sexuality has been tragic, and he has not found a way of realising his individuality in any other area of life. Nothing yet contributes meaning to his life in the way that, for example, psychoanalysis has done to mine for the last twenty-five years. Now here he is, over half his life gone, and wondering how to bear the rest of it. Mr W does express fear of his life feeling empty and pointless, but the sense of loss and curtailment, and the sorrow at not having been able to be who he might have been, do not make their way fully into words. The understanding of these, which I hope can let me help his future be a happier one, comes to me more through the psychic work on my own situation that this analysis provokes in me.

This work with Mr W illustrates my earlier description of the analyst as analytic listener to himself. It also shows that the analyst is not somehow parasitising the analysis for the purpose of his own self-analysis. Self-analysis there certainly is, but because it is grounded in the analyst's internal setting for a particular analysis, what results from it for the analyst works to illuminate the analysis as well. Is it possible, in fact, for an analysis to be really life-enhancing for a patient unless it is life-enhancing for the analyst? The intimations of mortality are my own, and facing them is personal work in an area beyond countertransference. But this personal psychic work folds back into the internal setting that exists in my mind for this analysis. This gives Mr W's life a depth and texture for me that lets me hear more in what he says, and helps me know more about his pain; to which I need to be as alive as I can, in the hope that he may come to be more fully alive.

Note

1 In 2006, a search of the PEP database (www.p-e-p.org; see Chapter 13, endnote 1) yielded a bare handful of examples, none of which set out to develop the concept systematically. Papers by Marie Bridge (1998, 2006/2013) and John Churcher (2005) did address it more thoroughly, and it seemed that the idea might also have been explored more fully in the Spanish literature, especially by Mariam Alizade (2002: 107–20).

PART IV

CLINICAL PRACTICE
TAKING SHAPE

You keep both Rule and Energy in view,
Much power in each, most in the balanced two.
    Thom Gunn, 'To Yvor Winters, 1955', (1993: 70)

11

WHAT DOES INTERPRETATION
PUT INTO WORDS?

This chapter and the following one, like those of Part III, are about how analysts work with their patients. They are also, like the chapters of Part II, about theory. Behind what happens in the consulting room lies a theoretical hinterland which remains, for the most part, invisible.

Above all things, psychoanalysts listen. The nature of psychoanalytic listening is a theme running through this book. When their listening makes them think something needs to be put into words, analysts also make interpretations. But the word 'interpretation' does not only refer to certain kinds of utterance by the analyst. Interpretation is also an activity. It is something analysts do. This chapter investigates the nature of the activity which underlies the interpretations to which an analyst gives voice.

It may be assumed that, behind any given interpretation, there is a pre-existing understanding in the analyst's mind, and that what the interpretation does is to express in words that pre-existing thought. This takes interpretation to be a kind of translation activity, making something available to patients in language they can understand. In his paper 'Remarks on the theory and practice of dream-interpretation' Freud says, according to the *Standard Edition*, that 'The interpretation of a dream falls into two phases: the phase in which it is translated and the phase in which it is judged or has its value assessed' (Freud, 1923c: 111f). What Freud wrote would be better rendered as 'the phase in which it is translated and the phase in which it is evaluated or made use of'.[1] Freud's clear implication is that behind the interpretation which an analyst puts into words there is a previous stage of interpreting which has gone on in the analyst's mind. At this earlier stage, the analyst interprets to himself the meaning of a dream. Then comes the question of how this interpretation is to be transmitted to the patient. In his paper 'On beginning the treatment' Freud says that originally analysts 'took an intellectualist view of the situation' (Freud, 1913: 141). They assumed that the job of interpretation was to communicate to patients what the analyst had discovered about the basis of their problems. Such discovery might derive from a patient's dreams or associations, or sometimes, in those early days of psychoanalysis, from external information which confirmed a patient's repressed history. Freud notes wryly, however, that 'the expected success was not forthcoming ... The patient, who now knew about his traumatic experience, nevertheless still behaved as if he knew no more about it than before' (Freud, 1913: 141). The assumption that the job of interpretation is to communicate the analyst's insight to the patient, so that it can become the patient's insight as well, turned out to be insufficient.

Hanna Segal states explicitly that 'the aim of the analyst is only to acquire and impart knowledge' (Segal, 1962: 212). This seems to correspond to the two-stage process outlined by Freud, with analysts acquiring knowledge by translating for themselves a patient's unconscious communications, then imparting it by translating this knowledge into language the patient can make use of. Segal goes on, though, to say that the knowledge she is referring to is 'psychoanalytic insight: that is, the acquiring of knowledge about one's unconscious through experiencing consciously ... hitherto unconscious processes' (Segal, 1962: 212). Her point is that although insight might appear to be a cognitive process, it can only be therapeutic if it is also experiential. Freud tells of a young woman whose mother had observed the homosexual encounter which underlay her daughter's 'attacks'. The episode was repressed from the patient's memory, and whenever Freud repeated to her what her mother had seen, she responded with a hysterical attack and promptly forgot the story again. Freud comments:

> After this there was no choice but to cease attributing to the fact of knowing, in itself, the importance that had previously been given to it and to place the emphasis on the resistances which had in the past brought about the state of not knowing and which were still ready to defend that state.
>
> (Freud, 1913: 142)

An important theoretical and clinical advance! But of course if Freud had said to the patient that this recurrent amnesia was clear evidence of her resistance, which she must therefore now be able to acknowledge and understand, this would have been no more help to her than previous interpretations. The only interpretation of any use would be one that helped her to experience the actuality of her resistance.

There is a tension between theoretical and experiential understanding which pervades the whole of psychoanalysis. It can be seen at work in clinical debates throughout the history of psychoanalysis and all over the analytic world.

In the late 1940s and early 1950s in the United States, for example, Franz Alexander proposed the idea of psychoanalysis as a 'corrective emotional experience' (Alexander, 1950; Alexander and French, 1946). This aroused great controversy. The idea that analysts should create a corrective experience, by deliberately presenting themselves as being different from a patient's parental figures, contradicted the neutrality of the analytic stance. Alexander seemed at times, moreover, to regard emotional intensity as a substitute for rational understanding, in a turn back towards a more cathartic view of therapeutic work. These deviations from the analytic position were strongly condemned by Kurt Eissler (1953), for whom analysis was a treatment resting solely on resolution of intrapsychic conflict by means of interpretation and working through. All deviations from this exclusively interpretative mode were designated as 'parameters'. Many followed Eissler in dismissing the idea of psychoanalysis as a corrective emotional experience. However, analysts do hope to make a difference for the better, emotion is certainly involved somehow, and the analytic process does need to be experienced. There were also those who welcomed Alexander's approach as antidote to an orthodoxy which seemed to reduce the therapeutic relationship to a matter of impersonal technique, with no place for the analyst's natural humanity. Leo Stone, while clearly opposing Alexander, found Eissler's stance too restrictive. Stone allowed a place for affective aspects of the therapeutic relationship, commenting: 'In his combined "role" as analyst, as physician, as friendly human being, there is a considerable reservoir of attitudes with which the analyst may appropriately and unaffectedly respond' (Stone, 1957: 403).

This led on to Elizabeth Zetzel's (1970 [1956], [1958]) and Ralph Greenson's (1965) concepts of the 'therapeutic alliance' and 'working alliance', which were in turn opposed by others who considered them to be departures from a proper transferential relationship. The evolution of this debate has been well documented by Robert Wallerstein (1990).

In the end, Alexander's approach lost ground and effectively disappeared, but the debates it gave rise to moved psychoanalytic thinking forward in two areas. The more prominent of these at the time was that of the relation between psychoanalysis and psychotherapy. More significant in the long term was the impetus given to debating the purpose of the analyst's clinical interventions, in relation specifically to affective experience in the analytic relationship as compared to intellectual insight resulting from correct interpretations.

At about the same time in Britain, the growing importance of object-relations theory also led to increasing interest in the quality of the analytic relationship, and particularly its emotional aspect. In 1956, Charles Rycroft wrote a paper called 'The nature and function of the analyst's communication to the patient'. His central point was as follows:

> The patient's increasing capacity to be aware of, communicate, and share his mental life cannot be attributed solely to the intellectual content of the analyst's verbal communications to him ... Every 'correct' interpretation, even when ... entirely free of suggestion or reassurance, contains within it a whole number of additional implicit communications.
>
> (Rycroft, 1968 [1956]: 67)

Rycroft explained that as well as its explicit content an interpretation also carried other messages: that the analyst was going on reliably being there for the patient, listening attentively, remembering what the patient said and thinking about it; and that the patient was not someone abhorrent, but a person who could be accepted and understood.

Other analysts were exploring similar ideas. Winnicott (1965: 37) emphasised the need to wait a long time, if necessary, so as to interpret in terms of a patient's own psychic realities; and for Michael Balint (1968: 173–81), unobtrusiveness was a quality essential to the analyst's work. Both of these, along with others, claimed that it was sometimes necessary to allow patients to regress without impinging on this with premature interventions (Balint, 1968; Winnicott, 1975 [1954]).[2] This was contested, however, by analysts who saw regression as an avoidance of reality and believed that accepting it represented a failure to interpret the evasion. Thus analysts in the classical tradition of Anna Freud would tend to view regression as a defensive retreat to a point of developmental fixation and think it needed interpreting as such. Kleinian analysts also, in the words of Elizabeth Spillius:

> … strongly disagree with the idea of encouraging regression and reliving infantile experiences in the consulting-room through non-interpretive activities. Analytic care, in [Klein's] view, should take the form of a stable analytic setting containing within it a correct interpretive process.
>
> (Spillius, 1988: 6)

Every analyst would agree about the importance of the setting and of interpretation, but the emphasis is significant. Though Spillius would no doubt accept the need for patience and receptivity in the analyst, what really matter for her about the setting and interpretation are stability and correctness. Compare this with, for instance, Harold Stewart's (1992: 127–40) paper, deliberately entitled 'Interpretation *and other agents* for psychic change' (author's emphasis).

So on either side of the Atlantic there were analysts who stressed the subjective, experiential quality of the analytic relationship, with an accent on its affective elements, while there were others who stressed the role of intellectual understanding, expressed through accurate interpretations. In terms of content these British and American debates have their overlaps and differences. In Britain, the former group stayed fundamentally within an analytic framework of transference and neutrality, and their work did not fade away as Alexander's did. Indeed, it has contributed significantly to the development of British psychoanalysis, especially its Independent tradition which is discussed in the next chapter. What strikes me, though, about these debates is a similarity in their form. Each side tends to regard the other as a threat to be warded off. There are admittedly statements on both sides of the need to balance one aspect of analysis with the other. Segal, for example, whose declaration I quoted earlier that 'the aim of the analyst is only to acquire and impart knowledge', says elsewhere that 'purely intellectual insight produces no changes' (Segal, 1990: 409). Stewart (1992: 101–26), on the other hand, writes in sympathy with Winnicott's and Balint's views on regression, but is still at pains to underline the importance of interpretation. Generally speaking, however, the quality of these debates is oppositional. Advocates of the primacy of interpretation tend to treat with caution those who highlight emotional aspects of analysis, as though a bid to subvert the role of analytic understanding needs to be resisted. And those who underline these emotional aspects tend to do so as if protecting them against a dogmatic attitude which doubts their authenticity. Amid this tendency to regard intellectual understanding and emotional experience as rivals for pole position in psychoanalysis, the nature of the connection between them is not so often considered. This is what I am interested in exploring: not the tension between them that pulls in opposite directions, but the link that binds them together.

Despite the title of this chapter, not all interpretation does put something into words. I quoted earlier Rycroft's comment about interpretations containing within them 'a whole number of additional implicit communications'. Ronald Baker suggested that unspoken aspects of the analytic setting and relationship could be regarded as 'implicit transference interpretations'. The fact of the analyst's survival, he says, is crucial. 'He may be the first such survivor in the patient's life: this is what is therapeutic. But it is therapeutic because *the survival is itself an implicit transference interpretation*' (Baker, 1993: 1229). The connection with Winnicott's (1971b) 'Use of an Object' paper is evident, where the subject relates to the object, destroys the object, the object survives destruction, and the subject can then make use of the object. Similarly, the analyst's provision of a safe and reliable framework is an implicit interpretation that the patient is not in the original traumatic situation (Eagle, 1984, cited in Baker, 1993: 1229). These implicit interpretations cannot be simply replaced by verbal interpretations. If the analyst tries to tell the patient that the analyst is surviving, or draws the patient's attention to the safety and reliability of the setting, the patient still has to decide whether what the analyst is saying, or the motivation behind it, can be trusted. The implicit interpretations that Baker indicates can only be registered if patients themselves notice the analyst's survival, or if they in fact experience the setting as being safe and reliable.

I remember an incident in my own analysis when I said something—I do not now recall what—and I heard behind me a rather ironic-sounding laugh. There was a pause, and my analyst said, 'I hope you realise that that laugh was an interpretation'. Aside from the laugh, the remark itself implied an interpretation about a propensity on my part to dismiss things too easily without giving them proper attention. There was no way, at that moment, for my analyst to verbalise such an interpretation. We were not talking about anything of the sort. But that my analyst should find it necessary to say what she did about her ironic laugh made an impact on me. Of the laugh itself, we might want to ask: what then was the interpretation behind it that my analyst was pointing to? What did she mean? But that would be like asking what an artist or composer means by a painting or a piece of music. There is no pre-existing meaning behind the work which the work aims to express. The meaning is in the painting or the composition and has no existence other than in the work itself (see pp.117ff). Similarly my analyst's spontaneous laugh, with its ironic tone, was itself the interpretation. It served the purpose of stopping me in my mental tracks, and making me ask what it was in me that had provoked this clearly benign, but at the same time gently mocking, response. All this would evaporate if the laugh were laboriously translated using some analytic phrase book, while the essence of it disappeared.[3]

These examples of interpretations which do not operate by the use of words are very different. The first is mediated by the patient's recognition of unspoken qualities in the analytic environment, while the second involves a patient hearing himself laughed at. But this difference underlines, as a common factor, that their impact consists of bringing about an experience in the patient. I want to extrapolate from this back to the more familiar sorts of verbal interpretation, to say that they too operate as *generators of experience*. Understanding is not the acquisition of knowledge; it is the occurrence of an event. This event is what all interpretation, whether explicit or implicit, seeks to generate in the mind of a patient.

I say 'in the mind' of a patient. The phrase does not seem quite right. It leaves something out (see also pp.119ff). The mind is the seat of the intellect and, as I have indicated, my central concern is the way interpretation makes something happen by bringing intellect and emotion together. Metaphorically speaking, the seat of emotion is the heart, and we might try saying that interpretation seeks to make something happen in the heart of a patient. Again this seems one-sided, this time for the way it leaves out intellectual understanding. It is interesting how rarely psychoanalysts talk about the heart. In ordinary speech we might say, 'That touched my heart' and we know perfectly well what we mean. But while psychoanalysts are happy to talk about the mind, they seem to steer clear of the heart. Perhaps the idea seems too romantic, or too folksy, to be allowed into the analytic lexicon. There may indeed be a risk of its being sentimentalised so as to avoid the nitty-gritty of emotional reality. However, to let the mind displace the heart would be to neglect an essential aspect of human existence.

Psychoanalysis has found it useful to adopt the word 'psyche' from Greek, via German, to signify the matrix of a person's mental and emotional life as a whole. Interpretation operates at the point in the psyche where mind and heart come together. Curiously, though, the English language does not seem to have a specific word for this. Perhaps the lack of such a concept explains the tendency to see intellect and feeling as being at odds with each other, instead of connected. 'Spirit' means something different. 'Soul' has, at least in English, an inevitably religious meaning (but see Kennedy (2013) for its wider connotations). Not necessarily, it seems, in German. Bruno Bettelheim's (1983) book *Freud and Man's Soul* describes how subtleties in Freud's use of German have been lost in the English translations of the *Standard Edition*. Bettelheim pays particular attention to the German '*Seele*' and '*Seelisch*' (pp.70ff). These are almost always rendered in the *Standard Edition* as 'mind' and 'mental', but Bettelheim points out that German has exact equivalents for those in '*Geist*' and '*Geistig*', which Freud chose not to use. Bettelheim writes:

> [Freud's] greatest concern was with man's innermost being, to which he most frequently referred through the use of a metaphor—man's soul—because the word 'soul' evokes so many emotional connotations. It is the greatest shortcoming of the current English versions of his works that they give no hint of this.
>
> By evoking the image of the soul and all its associations, Freud is emphasising our common humanity. Unfortunately, even in these crucial passages the translations make us believe he is talking about our mind, our intellect. This is particularly misleading because we often view our intellectual life as set apart from—and even opposed to—our emotional life ... The goal of psychoanalysis, of course, is to integrate the emotional life into the intellectual life.
>
> (Bettelheim, 1983: xi, 71)

There is a word which does refer specifically to the bringing together of emotion and intellect to generate a particular kind of understanding. This is the Greek word '*nous*' (νοῦς), which I have discussed in an essay on the relation between psychoanalysis and spiritual traditions (Parsons, 2006: 127). '*Nous*' is usually translated as 'mind' and it is the word used generally in Greek for the intellectual function. In a particular context, however, it has a more specific meaning. The Eastern Orthodox spiritual tradition speaks of 'bringing the mind into the heart'. This phrase describes a method of contemplation which unites the intellectual and emotional aspects of a person in the service of spiritual understanding. In this vocabulary, '*nous*' refers to the capacity for inward perception that is produced by this bringing together of heart and mind. The knowledge that *nous*, in this sense, yields is said to be immediately and unmistakably recognisable as true. This seems very similar to the response to certain interpretations, when patients know without doubt that they have heard something profoundly true and important, from the analyst and by resonance from within themselves. If the concept of '*nous*' can extend beyond this religious context, it might apply well to the capacity in the psyche to combine intellect and emotion, through which interpretation seeks to produce an internal event.

The idea of the 'mutative interpretation' (Strachey, 1934) has become a standard psychoanalytic concept. It is not the interpretation, however, that is mutative. What brings about change is an experience that happens in the patient when intellect and emotion come together. To speak of a 'mutative interpretation' is shorthand for an interpretation that brings about such a mutative experience. Does the interpretation convey this experience to the patient? That cannot be right. It is in the patient that the experience must take place. It has to be the patient's experience, and an interpretation cannot, so to speak, parachute an experience into somebody from outside. The only experience that an analyst's interpretation can convey is an experience of the analyst's. So how can an experience taking place in one person bring about change in another person? Of course we know in everyday life that it does. In close relationships of all sorts, if one person undergoes a significant change this can also produce a change in the other. It is not so surprising to think that an event occurring in the analyst's psyche could lead to something happening in the patient's. We cannot point to any given intervention by an analyst and say categorically: 'That is an example of a mutative interpretation'. We can say something, though, about what is needed for an intervention to have the potential for being mutative. As an analyst listens and attends to a patient with psychoanalytic awareness, something may happen to bring the analyst's intellect and feeling into conjunction. An intervention which carries the quality of this experience that has happened in the analyst may have the potential to trigger a corresponding experience in the patient.

A patient in analysis with me had reached the point of grasping quite clearly the intrapsychic conflicts and character patterns that were holding him back from developing his life as he wished. The kinds of internal shift he would need to make in order to live more creatively were becoming evident to him. At a certain moment, he said something along the lines of: 'Yes, I realise I probably could make some moves in that direction. But I know that I'm also perfectly capable of seeing that well enough, and then just deciding to stay where I am'. This was said apparently casually, as though it did not matter either way, and I was irritated. Then I found I was more than irritated. I felt a fierce anger and heard myself thinking: 'Over my dead body will you do that!' I was not going to utter this thought to the patient, but I was taken aback by my fury, and by reacting in a manner so contrary to how I like to believe I think about patients' freedom of choice. This was not analytic neutrality. Then the interpretation appeared from somewhere in me: 'You are free to commit suicide like that if you want to, but if you do, you will be intending, and trying, to kill me off as well'. Without going into details I can say that this intervention had a significant effect, not just *on* the patient but *in* him. This was someone for whom pleasantness was an important part of his way of being. He did genuinely value his analysis, but he was also keen to make sure I knew that. When I presented him to himself as a potential murderer, it negated the image he nourished of himself and shocked him into a different awareness.

Given what this patient had said, it would have been straightforward to formulate an interpretation about an attack on the analysis, or on the analyst. That would have been correct, and might have made the patient pause and think again about what he was doing. Whether anything would have actually happened *in* him is not certain. I think my intervention conveyed the quality of something that had happened *in me*, both at an intellectual and an emotional level. And this gave it, I believe, the capacity to arouse in the patient a recognition which happened *in him*, in the same way, both intellectually and emotionally at once.

Here is another example, from a case reported in a clinical seminar. The patient was a man in his late thirties and the analyst, a woman, was seeing him three times a week. His childhood had been dominated by trying to support his mother and not upset her. She used to complain regularly that she had almost died giving birth to him, and told him she would have preferred a daughter. He had been coming for about six years when, during a holiday period, he phoned his analyst in the middle of the night and left a message to say his mother had just died, and asking if he could have a session. The analyst arranged to see him a few days later, still in the holiday break.

The patient's mother had died suddenly of a heart attack, following a heart condition which she had concealed from him. He swung between being tormented with grief on the one hand—going to church for Mass (he was Catholic) and wanting to believe in an afterlife where he hoped his mother could be happy—and an empty feeling, on the other hand, that nothing mattered; his mother did not exist anymore and he was bound to forget her.

She had been cremated. He said it had been a depressing occasion. The place was ugly and he was not even sure of the location where her ashes had been deposited. He did not know whether it was more painful to love a dead person or to feel no love for anything or anyone.

The analyst commented to him that, in talking about his mother no longer existing in the world outside, he was also trying to talk about how he felt on the inside. This led to a rather consciously painful story from the patient about his mother's end. She had visited him and went home on her own because he was too busy to take her back himself. Shortly afterwards he got the news that she had collapsed. He rushed to the hospital but was too late to see her alive. He said that when he was feeling depressed recently his mother had brought him food she knew he liked. She had made some kebabs, and now he was trying to eat them before the meat went bad. With everything that had happened, he lamented, all he could think about was eating these kebabs!

Then came the following, as written up by the analyst:

A: Perhaps because you wanted your mother's nourishment to be inside you, as a way to transform her flesh into your flesh.

P: It is as if my mother is everything to me, my whole world. Perhaps it's not right for me to say that I don't deserve to go on living but it's what I feel. I feel a huge hole, as if someone reached inside and ripped everything out. I feel horror at being alive.

A: Feeling your pain reminds me of what used to happen in a Hindu marriage. When the husband died, his body was burnt on a pyre and his living wife was expected to burn with him. 'You will accompany me even in death', that was the promise that was extracted at the wedding. Her body ceased to belong to her. She was obliged by this pact to burn alive in the fire, something she would not naturally want.

The patient begins to cry, sobbing loudly. Suddenly he stops. Then more crying – sobbing – choking – silence – then crying again – sobbing –

P: And that is exactly what I feel![4]

This is a remarkable exchange. The patient had been narrating his emotions as genuinely as he could, but displaying them somewhat at a distance. He could not bring his pain to the analyst in a way that let him experience it directly. Suddenly, this changes and he can know, and feel, that he is with a woman who is not requiring him to support her image of herself, but who wants to help him be more in touch with his own self. There is no occasion at the moment to interpret how this relates to his mother, but the transferential impact is there nonetheless.

In the first intervention the phrase 'transform her flesh into your flesh' is highly charged in two ways. There is an implicit allusion to marriage, where husband and wife become 'one flesh'. So the phrase carries a silent interpretation about the patient's oedipal bond to his mother. There is also an unmistakable echo of the Christian Eucharist in the idea of internalising nourishment from someone so that their transformed flesh becomes one's own flesh. (The patient, it will be remembered, had gone to the Catholic Mass to seek consolation.)

Then comes the unexpected reference to Hindu marriage and funeral customs. The analyst introduces an astonishing association of her own, apparently out of the blue. The first thing to note is that this was a well-established analysis. The patient had been coming three times a week for six years. He and the analyst knew each other well, and the analyst had had time to develop trust in her unconscious perceptions of him. This is not an episode one can imagine happening early on in an analysis. The analyst's opening words, 'Feeling your pain reminds me ...', show (and let the patient know) that she is listening at the level of feeling, as well as thinking. Then comes the association, which is an extraordinary condensation of themes: cremation; the religious context; the patient's relationship to his mother as a marriage; his identification with her in death, so that instead of her flesh being transformed into his, his body now belongs to her and must suffer the same fate—a fate which the alive part of him does not want. All these are interwoven in the analyst's association. It would not be possible to make an equivalent act of interpretation by spelling these themes out piecemeal. It is their allusive condensation into a single expressive structure—the image of the Hindu funeral —which gives them their evocative power.

The analyst said she had been disturbed and bewildered by the association when it appeared, and was uncertain whether she should voice it, but in the end did so because it felt somehow true to the patient's situation. The patient's response shows how right she was to trust what was happening in her at a level where her intellectual and her emotional understanding could interact.

The key idea I am proposing is this: *interpretation puts into words the analyst's experience of bringing mind and heart together in trying to understand a patient, in the hope of bringing mind and heart together in the patient so as to facilitate a corresponding experience of self-understanding.*

The context of this example, with its bereavement and emergency session during a holiday break, was an unusual and rather special one. Does what this gave rise to stand outside regular analytic practice? What about the ordinary, continuing routine of everyday analysis?

Not all interpretations can be mutative. Strachey himself was clear about this, pointing out that a cake cannot be made of nothing but currants (Strachey, 1934: 158). He likens the patient's acceptance of a transference interpretation to the capture in battle of a key position. Extra-transference interpretations correspond to the general advance and consolidation made possible by this. Eventually, though, another key position will need to be captured by another mutative transference interpretation. Strachey is somewhat ambiguous about the value and purpose of the interim, non-mutative interpretations. The implication is that currants remain the best part of a cake. If significant change is thought to come only from so-called 'mutative' interpretations, there is a risk of seeing the in-between interventions simply as ways of working up to the next opportunity to be mutative. This would be a wrong view, to my mind, of the analytic dialogue. It does not allow for the continual, gradually shifting exchange between patient and analyst, where small interventions turn out, later on, to have been important; where nothing may seem to happen, but the capacity to tolerate nothing happening makes a difference; where the couple persevere through frustration and difficulty, working to maintain belief in what they are doing. The 'over my dead body' episode did occur during ordinary run-of-the-mill analysis, so perhaps the unusual context of the second example spotlights something that does, after all, belong to the nature of the analytic situation. Do these ideas about interpretation show themselves in the week-to-week, month-by-month ebb and flow of analytic work?

Not long after I had qualified as an analyst, a patient asked me, 'What is the place of effort in this work?' He had discovered something about the power of his unconscious conflicts and resistances, and was saying that if all of that went on in him unconsciously he had no way to influence it. So, 'What is the place of effort?' I thought it was a good question that needed answering, as well as interpreting. Eventually, I said I thought one could make an effort to remember, an effort not to let go of the things we come to understand about ourselves. There might certainly be an impulse to repress them again, but I thought that an effort to remember did make sense.

It is not a bad answer and I still think it is true. But since then, I have found another answer to my patient's question. There are times in an analysis when a patient's resistance to progress noticeably increases. This can take all sorts of forms: acting out, blocking free association, moods of despair that feel somehow purposeful, rationalisations for not taking practical steps. The list could go on and examples would be easy to find. At such times, the increased resistance is being provoked because the patient's constructive, progressive impulses are becoming stronger. The pull backwards is a sign that something in the patient is trying to press forwards. It is the psychological equivalent of Newton's Third Law of Motion: to every force there is an equal and opposite reaction. The closer patients come to liberating themselves psychically, the more powerfully their conflictual, anxiety based or perverse psychic structures fight to preserve the status quo.

At this point we may remember how important in psychoanalysis is the idea of triangularity. Its significance extends far beyond the Oedipus complex. The intervention of the third element is fundamental to the evolution of all psychic structure (Parsons, 2000: 109–15). In a world of two points only, there can be no shape or structure, but only degrees of closeness or separation. For something to take shape a third element is required, in a new dimension off the line between the first two points. Developmentally progressive impulses, and the forces of resistance, pull against each other in opposite directions. As the tension along the line between them grows, there is an increasing sense of emotional discomfort. In one-person terms this is an increase in what Freud called '*unlust*', or 'unpleasure', which the pleasure principle operating in the patient would seek to reduce. The analytic situation, however, involves a relationship. The analyst is another human being, a witness to the increasing struggle between progressive and retrogressive forces in the patient. Empathy with this growing tension has an effect on the analyst, producing at a given moment the sense that intervention is required to release the stasis. The quiet urgency of this awareness may generate in the analyst an experience in which intellect and feeling come into conjunction. The resulting act of interpretation, originating from outside the patient's intrapsychic tug of war, is a third element which may generate a corresponding experience in the patient of bringing heart and mind together. (My 'over my dead body' reaction, and the intervention that arose from it, is a case in point.) In this way, patients may be helped to open up their own new dimensions in which new structures become possible.[5]

The function of the patient's effort is, paradoxically, to stimulate an increase in the patient's own resistance. The greater the tension thus provoked between progressive and retrogressive forces, the greater will be the call for the intervention of a third element. Analysts may then find themselves mobilising the connection between their intellectual understanding and their feelings, to help the patient open up what Ken Wright (2006) has called 'an experiential space in which we glimpse something more than what is actually said'. I think this is how, in the ordinary routine of analysis, those acts of interpretation that can most hope to generate mutative experience in a patient are drawn into being.

Notes

1   Freud's German reads: '*Die Deutung eines Traumes zerfällt in zwei Phasen, die Übersetzung und die Beurteilung oder Verwertung desselben*' (Freud, 1998 [1922]: 304). The description of the two phases refers to the interpretation's '*Übersetzung*' (translation) and its '*Beurteilung*' (evaluation) or '*Verwertung*'. '*Verwertung*' is translated in the Standard Edition as the interpretation's 'having its value assessed'. But this is not what '*Verwertung*' means. The translator seems to have read the word as '*Wertung*', a noun that does mean judgement or assessment, which would repeat the meaning of '*Beurteilung*' as the Standard Edition does. But '*Verwertung*', the word Freud used, means not 'assessment' but 'utilisation'. I am grateful to Dr med. Christine Gerstenfeld for drawing my attention to this.

2   The ideas of Rycroft, Winnicott and Balint are described in more detail, and their context is elaborated, in the following chapter.

3   Compare Seamus Heaney's comments on academic analysis of T.S. Eliot's *The Waste Land*, cited in Chapter 10 (p.158).

4   I am grateful for the analyst's permission to quote this clinical example.

5   Compare these two paragraphs with a story told by G.I. Gurdjieff (1963: 94f), whose writing carries meaning at many levels. Gurdjieff was on a journey of particular importance to him, when he was set upon by a pack of vicious sheepdogs. He found the only way of pacifying them was to sit down and remain motionless. As long as he showed no interest in proceeding further the dogs sat around him in a peaceful and even friendly manner. When he made to resume his progress, however, they threatened to attack and tear him to pieces. The intervention of a third party was needed, in the form of the shepherds. Standing away from the line of direct opposition between Gurdjieff's intention and the dogs' resistance to it, they were able to call off the dogs and allow Gurdjieff to continue on his way.

12

AN INDEPENDENT THEORY OF
CLINICAL TECHNIQUE

The theoretical hinterland to the clinical practice of psychoanalysis, mentioned at the beginning of the last chapter, sometimes goes by the name of 'theory of technique'. There is no single, unified theory by which every analyst understands the therapeutic process of psychoanalysis. Different analysts base their work on a variety of theories of technique, and their clinical viewpoints reflect these different theoretical understandings.

Analysts do not simply consider what theories they subscribe to and then derive a clinical approach from them. The connection is more complex, because the theories an analyst espouses are inevitably to some degree an expression of the analyst's own self (Parsons, 2000: 52–4). This is true most of all about the theoretical foundations that analysts elaborate for their clinical work. Analysts form their identities in different ways, and for all of them there is a trajectory by which they have become the individual analysts that they are. Their particular way of working with patients is the outcome of that trajectory. Widely divergent models of psychoanalytic training are discussed in Chapter 13. Even within a single system, like that of the British Psychoanalytical Society, a remarkable variety of training experiences may be found (Anderson, 2009; Johns, 2009; Laufer, 2009; Parsons, 2009; Perelberg, 2009; Rayner, 2009; Spillius, 2009). This chapter is about the orientation in which my own identity as an analyst has taken shape: the Independent tradition of the British Society. As we shall see, this is an approach which by its nature resists being standardised. Portraying it as faithfully as I can therefore involves me, of necessity, in exploring my own perception of it.

The word 'Independent' with a capital 'I' entered the psychoanalytic vocabulary around 1950, when certain members of the British Psychoanalytical Society agreed to constitute themselves formally as the Group of Independent Psychoanalysts. In the late 1920s, Melanie Klein had settled in London and become an influential member of the British Society. A polarisation developed between her views and those of Anna Freud about early psychic development and child analysis. So long as Anna Freud was at a safe distance with her father in Vienna, these debates had remained at the level of theoretical and technical discussion. The flight of the Freud family to Britain in 1939, however, brought

Anna Freud to settle in London, and from then on the arguments between Klein's adherents and hers took on an acrimonious personal quality. The essential points of theoretical disagreement were about Klein's emphasis on early infantile phantasies, which Anna Freud did not believe in; Klein's stress on innate destructiveness as the main factor around which development was organised, which Anna Freud thought devalued the importance of infantile sexuality; and Klein's early dating of the Oedipus complex. The Controversial Discussions in the early 1940s clarified these differences, but did not resolve them (King and Steiner, 1991).

The British Society was in danger of splitting, and the solution was to work out a scheme involving two parallel streams of training. One was for students who would follow the views of Anna Freud. This was known as the 'B Group'. The other training was run jointly by those analysts who identified themselves specifically with Melanie Klein's ideas, and by those who did not subscribe to either of the two factions. This 'A Group' thus comprised both Kleinian and non-aligned analysts. Whichever stream of training, 'A' or 'B', a student followed, the second training case had to be supervised by one of the A group's non-aligned analysts. However, the polarisation in the Society continued and this requirement for a non-aligned supervision was dropped. The 'A Group' was replaced by a specifically Kleinian group, while those analysts who still did not want to align themselves with either Anna Freud's B group or the Kleinians were known informally as the 'Middle Group'.

For some years, they resisted the idea of being considered as a group at all. It was their independence from any particular psychoanalytic doctrine that mattered most to them, and the fact that there might be quite striking differences amongst them was all part of that. But the pressure to become a third group within the Society was eventually too great, and so they became what is usually called the 'Independent Group'. This is the moment at which the word 'Independent' arrived on the scene. It is worth noting however that, as was mentioned earlier, the proper name of the group is not the 'Independent Group' but the 'Group of Independent Psychoanalysts': an important nicety which still shows the original unwillingness to sacrifice individuality.

When I qualified as an analyst in the British Society I was invited to join the Independent Group. My analyst was an Independent, and Group membership in the Society operated, so to speak, on the hereditary principle. Analysts might occasionally decide, as their sense of their analytic identities developed, to cross the floor from one group to another, but the default position on qualifying was that the Group to which your analyst belonged became your own Group. For some years, I took it for granted that what made me an Independent analyst was being a member of the Independent Group.

There was an ambiguity, however, about what it meant to be an Independent which it took me some time, first of all to register, and then to disentangle. This is linked to the way the Group came into being. The sketch just given of the historical background is not simply a matter of information, in case a reader might not be familiar with it. For Independent thinking, it is important always to locate situations, like patients, in their historical context. No analytic orientation, Independent or otherwise, can be made sense of without a grasp of its origins. The genesis of the group structure of the British Society meant that all three Groups—Independent, Kleinian and 'Contemporary Freudian', as the B Group came to be called—had their lineages of important writers and teachers. The writings of Michael Balint, Marion Milner and Donald Winnicott, to take just three examples, were valued by various analysts, but for me, as an Independent, they were primary influences in a way that was not the same for members of the other Groups. Being an Independent meant one was connected to a certain theoretical and clinical orientation. But belonging to a Group also had administrative significance. The so-called 'Gentlemen's Agreement' governed the rotation between the Groups of important positions in the Society, such as the Presidency and the Chairmanship of the Education Committee (King and Steiner, 1991: 907f, 929f). This was a political arrangement to preserve the balance of influence among the Groups. You might have to wait three or six years to apply for a post you were interested in because it was not the turn of your Group. If you became a Training Analyst you were obliged to declare formally your Group affiliation. So which Group one belonged to had two quite different sorts of implication, one clinical and theoretical; the other administrative and political (see Parsons, 2009: 244f, for comments on the abolition of the Gentlemen's Agreement in 2005).

To equate being an Independent analyst with belonging to the Independent Group was clearly not the whole story. Thinking my way through this issue, I realised that the Independent Group's history means there have always been two aspects to its identity. One is to have been defined by a negative. Its members were the residue of the Society, who would not align themselves with either of the other two groups. But it was not just a buffer zone whose inhabitants selected themselves by default. Its members also constituted, by and large, the original structure of the British Society, like the original part of a building with a new wing added on either side. This original structure had its own characteristics, and these are the roots of what may be called the Independent tradition. It is noteworthy that of three books devoted to surveying Independent psychoanalysis—Gregorio Kohon's (1986) and Eric Rayner's (1991) books, *The British School of Psychoanalysis: The Independent Tradition* and *The Independent Mind in British Psychoanalysis*, and the more recent *Independent Psychoanalysis Today* (Williams, Keene and Dermen, 2012)—none makes reference in their titles to the idea of a Group. The Independent Group was faced with a continuing question, over the years, about what kind of group it was to be. It had the options, either of emphasising its negative identity as a home for those who wanted not to align themselves with any other viewpoint, or of seeking positively to represent and develop the Independent tradition. The Group implicitly but clearly chose the former direction.

This means that the Independent tradition does not coincide with the Independent Group. There is a large overlap, in that the majority of analysts who have exemplified and developed the tradition have been part of the Group. However, there are members of the Independent Group that do not stand within the Independent tradition. Conversely, the Independent tradition is not limited to the Group, or even to the British Society. There are analysts who have no connection with either, yet whose work places them clearly in that tradition (see, for example, Chodorow, 2004). Being an Independent analyst was not, after all, linked intrinsically to membership of the Independent Group. What being Independent meant for me, I discovered, was to stand within the Independent tradition.

Articulating this position is not a matter of enunciating a specific theoretical viewpoint. Independent analysts have tended not to organise their analytic identities around particular analytic doctrines, but around underlying intellectual and human values. More precisely, the desire for freedom to do that is what makes Independents unwilling to organise their identities around a doctrine. This is not simply a historical reluctance to sign up to Melanie Klein's or Anna Freud's specific viewpoints. There is a deeper sense that any theoretical position that claims overarching, universal validity should be treated with suspicion. Freud's theory of instincts, for example, evolved through various stages, but what did not change was his fundamental view of human beings as the products of a system of biologically determined drives. For all Klein's differences from Freud, she also saw development in terms of an innate schema; one that was, in her view, determined at root by the need to deal with the death instinct. The two new wings were at opposite ends of the original building, but they shared a certain universalising approach, seeing particular human beings in terms of the way they exemplified a general theory. Analysts of the Independent tradition represent another cast of mind; a non–universalising attitude whose emphasis is on what differentiates human beings and makes them unique, rather than on how they typify general principles.

The logic of this attitude is that there can be no 'standard' Independent position. While Spillius, for example, sees Melanie Klein as having 'left us a very important legacy: a general theory that was not watertight or rigid, but that allowed her colleagues to work on particular ideas within it without interfering with the whole' (Spillius, 2009: 215); and while Ralph Greenson could set out to write what he called 'a textbook on psychoanalytic technique' (Greenson, 1967: 1), nothing comparable obtains where Independent analysis is concerned. It is not a 'general theory' to be seen as a 'whole', and Independent clinical technique cannot be systematised in textbook fashion. There is no norm to refer back to, or against which to measure variations. Independent analysts can only articulate what they have done with a tradition, creating from it a way of thinking and working that will both express the tradition and be individually their own. As a Japanese ceramics master expressed it: 'Tradition is to receive past knowledge, break it down and use

it in a creative way, and to hand down that knowledge again as a true history'
(Ohi, 1997: 1).[1]

This book embodies one outcome of such an encounter between the
tradition and an individual. It is not a representative account of Independent
psychoanalysis. The last paragraph indicates why such an idea, in any case,
would not make sense. But it was in the Independent tradition that I was
trained and developed my identity as an analyst, and it might be said that the
book as a whole cannot avoid being, in some sense, an expression of Independent
analysis. Why, then, this one chapter carrying the Independent label? No doubt
the clinical examples in the book give some impression of how this particular
Independent analyst works. What is the basis in theory, however, for the
clinical approach which the Independent tradition has helped me develop?
That theoretical foundation is the theme of this chapter.

One of the most passionately individual of psychoanalysts was Sándor
Ferenczi. It is through him that the Independent tradition derives ultimately
from Freud. Ferenczi saw psychoanalysis as grounded in experience rather than
dogma and, above all, as a matter of the unique experience of the individual
patient. His influence on the Independent tradition came most directly through
Michael Balint, but there is a widespread resonance between Ferenczi's thought
and the ideas of many Independent thinkers.

In his paper, 'The Elasticity of Psycho-Analytic Technique', Ferenczi
(1955 [1928]) introduced the idea of 'tact', as an essential quality in the
analyst's relation to the patient. This came under fire from Freud and
Fenichel, who thought it relied on subjective intuition instead of systematic
theory (Falzeder and Brabant, 2000: 332; Fenichel, 1941: 5, both quoted on
p.222). Ferenczi, trying to clarify his concept, responded that 'the tact which
we are called upon to exercise' (Ferenczi, 1955 [1928]: 90) exemplified the
moral obligation not to do to others what in the same circumstances we
should not desire to have done to ourselves. All analysts would agree, of
course, that it is important to understand things from the patient's point of
view, but different preconscious assumptions about what this means can
produce distinctly different therapeutic climates. I am not simply observing
that Ferenczi believed in an obligation of care and concern from one human
being to another. What I am emphasising is that an ethical principle like this,
and not a metapsychological or theoretical belief, is what he takes as the
starting point for his theory of clinical technique.

As a result of this humanistic rather than scientific starting point, Ferenczi
has been criticised as though he did not have any theory of clinical technique.
However, his papers on technique and his *Clinical Diary* (Ferenczi, 1988) show
him to be thoroughly aware of the need for it, and struggling to develop the
clinical theory he required. His struggle was frustrated because concepts he
needed, such as the internal setting, were not available in his time (see p.157).
After being dismissed for years, Ferenczi's work is appreciated nowadays by
analysts of various orientations. But it is the Independent tradition in particular

that has developed concepts which make it possible to articulate the kind of clinical theory for which Ferenczi was searching.

Ferenczi placed particular emphasis on the quality of the patient's experience in the analytic relationship. Sometimes, he says, conventional technique may have been thoroughly deployed, and the developmental basis of a patient's condition worked through, but the 'throb of experience' is still lacking (Ferenczi, 1950: 220). He knew that without this, analytic work would not bring about structural change. Here he points towards a central feature of Independent psychoanalysis: that what patients experience as their own living discovery in the analytic encounter matters more than anything that comes from the analyst. Such a moment is described in Chapter 2 (p.30), when a patient discovered that the person she habitually presented to the world was, in fact, a bit of stage scenery. What comes from the analyst is crucial, of course, but only for the way it facilitates patients' own experience of themselves.[2] Once spelled out, this may not sound controversial. What characterises the Independent tradition is the way it takes this as a primary focus in its theory of clinical technique. Winnicott, for example, referring to therapeutic consultations with children, says that 'the significant moment is that at which *the child surprises himself or herself*. It is not the moment of my clever interpretation that is significant' (Winnicott, 1971a: 51). Likewise for Christopher Bollas, the essence of psychoanalysis is that it 'supplies a relationship that allows the analysand to hear from his or her own unconscious life' (Bollas, 2002: 10). The fundamental question for an Independent analyst then becomes how best to facilitate this self-discovery in patients, and help them take themselves by surprise.

One approach to an answer comes from inverting Ferenczi's 'moral obligation not to do to others what … we should not desire to have done to ourselves' (see above). The positive implication of Ferenczi's negative is that we *should* do to others what we *do* desire for ourselves: analysts need to bring to bear on themselves the kind of attention and understanding that they give to the patient. Since almost the beginning of psychoanalysis the need has been recognised for analysts to be alert to the dangers of their countertransference reactions, and through the second half of the last century, views of countertransference expanded so as to give it a more positive function as well (see p.115). Countertransference awareness is both necessary and helpful. As Chapters 9 and 10 indicate, however, it is not just a safeguard and a useful adjunct to help the analyst understand the patient. The psychoanalytic attention of analysts to their own state of mind is itself the vehicle of their analytic activity. If analysts do not listen to themselves in the same way that they listen to their patients, nothing psychoanalytic will happen.

Near the end of 'The Elasticity of Psycho-Analytic Technique', Ferenczi writes: 'The ideal result of a completed analysis is precisely that elasticity which analytic technique demands of the mental therapist' (Ferenczi, 1955 [1928]: 99). The aim of psychoanalysis is thus to foster in the patient a quality which, for that development to happen, needs also to be present in the analyst. Analysts do not want their patients to identify with them in a compliant or mimetic sort of way, and to speak of the patient's introjecting the analyst would not be typically Independent language. More characteristically Independent would be the idea of patients internalising a capacity, to use a Winnicottian word (Hopkins, 1997), which they find in the analyst. But the essentially Independent idea prefigured in Ferenczi's formulation is that patients are enabled to discover something in themselves, because they are in a particular kind of relationship with someone who is open to that same sort of discovery in his or her own self.

This theme is notably explored in Neville Symington's (1983) paper 'The analyst's act of freedom as agent of therapeutic change'. Symington's examples include a patient, originally seen in a reduced-fee clinic, whom he was continuing to charge a low fee, on the assumption that she could not pay more. References in the patient's material to a patronising employer led Symington to realise that he had become 'the prisoner of an illusion about the patient's capacities' (Symington, 1983: 283). When he brought up the question of her fee she said, 'If I *had* to pay more, then I know I would'. He did raise her fee, at which 'she cried rather pitifully but then became resolved that she would meet the challenge'. Striking changes followed in the direction of self-sufficiency and independence, both in her work and her emotional life. Another patient regularly expressed a fear that the analyst would think him pathetic, inducing Symington each time to make an interpretation that tacitly implied he would not. The patient, says Symington, 'would then obligingly tell me the thought in his mind'. At a certain point Symington happened across a passage by Bion, which led him to realise how his analytic freedom of thought was constrained by the predetermined response that the patient was extracting from him.

> I had been a prisoner of this patient's controlling impulses and at the moment of reading this … I had a new understanding in which I felt freed inwardly … The next time he expressed his apprehension that I would think him pathetic I said to him quietly, 'But I am quite free to think that'. He was much taken aback. It was then possible to see how much he operated by controlling my thoughts and the thoughts of others.
>
> (Symington, 1983: 284)

There is a reciprocity between the analyst's and the patient's ability to free themselves from outdated ways of being.

> The patient is there to see further into the things that really matter about himself and his life. But for this to happen he has to sacrifice the arrangement which, until now, it has mattered very much to preserve.

The analyst needs to see further into what really matters about the analysis. But to do that he must be prepared to let go of the way he has seen things so far. The two situations reflect each other, and the analyst's being open to his version helps the patient to experience his.

(Parsons, 2000: 43f)

Such an emphasis on the relation between the patient's self-discovery and that of the analyst runs through Independent writing. At the end of both Chapter 9 and Chapter 10, it was emphasised that the therapeutic quality of an analyst's engagement with a patient is linked to the capacity of the analyst to be enlivened himself or herself by the analytic process. Unless analysts find personal meaning in their work, there is not likely to be personal meaning in it for their patients either.

What distinguishes such a mutual effort at self-discovery as being psychoanalytic? Independent analysis tends not to wear its theory on its sleeve. When the British analyst Martin James (1980) discussed what concepts might be essential to Independent analysis, his first point was that Independents tend towards a vernacular style, using everyday language in speaking and writing about analysis. Ferenczi's comment too, that the ideal result of analysis is a kind of elasticity, is not a metapsychological statement. It refers to a quality of psychic life. Ferenczi tends not to invoke such terms as the resolution of intrapsychic conflict, adoption of less primitive defence mechanisms, giving up infantile fixations, or progression from one developmental stage to another. No doubt he would have agreed with these if they were put to him, but his natural way of thinking is in terms of psychic qualities, such as elasticity and flexibility. If these were put to non–Independent analysts they would probably agree in turn, like Ferenczi faced with a metapsychological formulation. For analysts in the Independent tradition, though, it is a natural habit of mind to think primarily in terms of the quality of psychic life, using ideas such as elasticity and flexibility, intellectual freedom, emotional availability, openness to relationships, tolerance and enjoyment of complexity, and the sense of being real.

In the clinical situation, all analysts would probably favour the simple, non-technical language described by James; this is especially important for Independent analysts because of the stress they place on not saying things that might get in the way of a patient's self-discovery. Nor is it just for talking with patients that Independents value an ordinary, conversational style. In their own thinking and writing as well, they tend to avoid language that carries pre-packed theoretical baggage. James emphasised what he called an 'existential point'; that for an Independent analyst, every clinical observation exists in its own right, and not as an example of something. One of the functions of theory in Independent psychoanalysis is to imbue our use of everyday language with psychoanalytic understanding.

This raises a general question about the role of interpretation. Ferenczi (1955 [1928]: 95f) advises: 'the analyst must wait patiently', and 'above all, one must be sparing with interpretations'. As before, his emphasis corresponds to later

Independent developments. Compare Pearl King's comment that 'we have to *wait* without any preconceptions for whatever our patients communicate to us' (King, 1978: 334), followed by her emphatic quotation from T.S. Eliot that 'the faith and the hope and the love are all in the waiting'. Winnicott stressed the need to interpret in terms of patients' own psychic realities, and said: 'The analyst is prepared to wait a long time to be in a position to do exactly this kind of work' (Winnicott, 1965: 37). Enid Balint highlights the tension between necessary waiting and the temptation to activity.

> The analyst must not be intrusive or lead the way, but he must be there, listening alertly; and he must sometimes ... point out obstacles, which prevent the patient from finding what he is looking for but which have been put there by the patient himself so as to avoid having to undertake this painful task. The analyst ... may sometimes be tempted to follow an easier path without realising it ... Usually, however, the analyst has to wait.
>
> (Balint, E., 1993: 122)

> Imagination is a precondition of the creative life. It can be safely used only if the structure and training are there; but the structure and training are useless if the analyst's imagination, or the patient's, is imprisoned. In order to release himself and the patient from prison, the analyst must exercise the ability to wait.
>
> (Ibid: 129)

What is the purpose of all this waiting? What is the analyst waiting *for*? One answer is that the question should not be asked. The point is exactly *not* to be waiting *for* anything. In Pearl King's phrase quoted above, we have to wait 'without preconceptions'. Nancy Chodorow's (2003) distinction between 'listening for' and 'listening to' was mentioned in Chapter 10 (p.154). When patients are silent, analysts need to listen to the silence itself, and not for what it may mean or what may come out of it. Bion's (1994 [1967]) caution against memory and desire, against clutching at either past or future, is something most analysts understand and appreciate. In the discussion in Chapter 8 of Monet's painting of his studio boat (Figure 8.4), I described the artist as 'fishing quietly in the waters of his mind, alert to see what may rise and break the surface' (p.129). This is the 'alertness' of reverie, which is not an effortful striving to perceive, but rather an availability for whatever may reveal itself (see pp.157f). In Chapter 8 I also described a busy session where the patient had a lot to say (pp.131ff). I commented (p.133) that if the analyst wants to help the patient apprehend his state of being rather than his state of mind,

> ... the complex unconscious counterpoint of the material has to reveal itself gradually. This is not just because the session takes time to evolve,

but because the listening itself needs to be slow. Time is required both for the unconscious structuring of the material to develop, and for the analyst to observe the effect of this on his own internal silence.

This does begin to suggest, after all, a sense of purpose in the waiting. It takes time for unconscious structures in a patient's mind to express themselves in what the patient is saying. That has to be waited for. It also takes time for the impact on the analyst's mind of what a patient says, or of the patient's silence, to become clear. This applies both to the microcosm of an individual session and the macrocosm of the analysis in the longer term. On both time scales the analyst has to wait for recognition of the patient's self-expression to evolve in the analyst's mind.

Ludwig Wittgenstein (1980: 80) said that a proper greeting between philosophers would be '*Laß dir Zeit!*' ('Give yourself time!').[3] It would be a good greeting between psychoanalysts too, and even more so between analysts and patients; in both directions. As an analyst I want to help my patients not to feel rushed. If ever I become a patient again, I want an analyst who will give my unconscious mind time to reveal itself, and give their own unconscious mind time to absorb the impact of mine, and time to reflect to me what happens inside them in response to that impact. This is why the listening has to be slow.

In Bion's 'Notes on memory and desire', he writes that 'psychoanalytic "observation" is concerned neither with what has happened nor what is going to happen but with what is happening' (Bion, 1994 [1967]: 380). There may be another clue here to what the waiting is for. As an analyst Bion knows that history, and the trajectory of a life, are important: 'what is ordinarily called forgetting is as bad as remembering' (Bion, 1977 [1970]: 41). He does not eschew past and future in themselves, but only the wish to have recourse to them for understanding, as a retreat from being in the moment with a patient. Attending to 'what is happening' in the present is not, either, a matter of referring everything to the here–and–now transference. Bion is pointing to what was explored in Part I of this book: the awareness that past and future are contained in the present moment, and that the analyst's business is not to look for them outside it. However, it takes time for past and future to reveal themselves as 'a lifetime burning in every moment' (see p.57), which includes the moment in the analytic session. For a patient's past and possible future to become audible in the now, may call for a lot of unobtrusive waiting.

In the latter of the two paragraphs by Enid Balint quoted above, there are two things to note besides the emphasis on waiting. Firstly, the need for the analyst, as well as the patient, to be freed, which is so clear in Symington's clinical examples, demonstrates the typically Independent parallelism between the analyst's and the patient's internal processes. Secondly, there is Balint's view of theoretical structure and technical discipline as serving to mediate the analyst's creative imagination. This also is a characteristically Independent way of thinking.

In the sessions with Mr W described in Chapter 10, there is an example of what happens when, instead of allowing theory to help free his imagination, an analyst uses it as something to fall back on. I made an oedipal transference interpretation in response to Mr W's thoughts about a man he saw coming out of my house. After this, the session became lifeless. The next day's session, full of pre-oedipal content, showed that my apparently plausible oedipal interpretation had been misjudged. I was using theory intellectually, to decode the patient's material, rather than creatively, to liberate my responsiveness (pp.162f, 165).

Ferenczi's emphasis on restraint in interpretation recurs in Michael Balint's work, notably in the chapter in *The Basic Fault* entitled 'The Unobtrusive Analyst' (Balint, M., 1968: 173–81). Enid and Michael Balint shared and developed their ideas closely together, and Enid expressed her own view of the analytic stance as follows.

> If I am asked ... what I think is essential to analytic work, I may answer, after I have stressed the need for a basic and thorough training in psychoanalytic theory and practice, that it is important for the analyst not to be too intrusive.
>
> (Balint, E., 1993: 121)

This unobtrusiveness applies especially with patients in a state of regression, whom the Balints thought did not need interpretation so much as a particular kind of environment. It may be assumed that when analysts discuss regression they have in mind occasions when it dominates the analysis unmistakably and persistently. Extended episodes of profound regression do occur—Marion Milner's (1969) book *The Hands of the Living God* is a classic account of such a case—but the regressive episodes that occur commonly in analysis are on a smaller scale. 'Regressive periods may be very brief, but they must be observed and respected' (Balint, E., 1993: 122). Ferenczi and Michael and Enid Balint, along with Winnicott (1954), Stewart (1992: 101–26) and others, exemplify the interweaving in Independent clinical theory of the following themes: that regression subtly pervades the whole analytic experience; that this needs to be accepted as a purposeful unconscious communication; and that such acceptance of regression may imply great restraint in interpretation, however true the unmade interpretations might have been.

Nevertheless, the subtle pervasiveness of regression is not the only reason why Independent analysts make a point of not being intrusive. Their way of interpreting is as much to do with creating a therapeutic environment as with conveying particular bits of insight.

> In addition therefore to their symbolic functioning of communicating ideas, interpretations also have the sign-function of conveying to the patient the analyst's emotional attitude towards him. They combine

with the material setting provided by the analyst to form the analyst's affective contribution to the formation of a trial relationship, within which the patient can recapture the ability to make contact and communication with external objects.

(Rycroft, 1968 [1956]: 68)

At the time Rycroft wrote this, it was controversial to value interpretations for conveying to patients that their analyst had a benign emotional attitude towards them. For some, this seemed too close to Franz Alexander's (1950) 'corrective emotional experience', arousing fears of seduction and collusion that needed guarding against by the austerity of pure understanding (see the discussion in Chapter 11, especially pp.174f). Hanna Segal's (1962) paper, 'The curative factors in psychoanalysis', exemplifies this anxiety, and even today, one may hear the careworn assumption that Independent analysts 'soft-pedal' their patients, neglect the negative transference, and so on. Yet as far back as 1928, Ferenczi himself, who most of all, perhaps, has been caricatured as collusively indulging his patients, wrote that 'the analyst must accept for weeks on end the role of an Aunt Sally on whom the patient tries out all his aggressiveness and resentment' (Ferenczi, 1955 [1928]: 93).

The mistake of the 'soft-pedalling' criticism comes from a failure to grasp the theory behind an Independent clinical stance. In their early papers, Rycroft, Michael Balint and Winnicott were developing the idea that the function of the analytic setting is to provide for a particular quality of object relating. To speak of the object relationship between patient and analyst might seem obviously to refer to the transference, with the interest being in how the transferential object relationship is affected unconsciously by the patient's repetitions and projections. All analysts think continually in those terms. This is part of what Enid Balint meant by 'a basic and thorough training in psychoanalytic theory and practice'. The analytic relationship, however, is not simply a substrate for transference. What Rycroft, Winnicott, the Balints, and others since them in the Independent tradition, have progressively articulated is a quality of object relating that needs to be a fundamental bedrock of the analytic setting, whatever the vicissitudes of the transference. Some analysts, in discussing the importance of the setting, will stress, on the one hand, keeping practical boundaries about session times and so on, and on the other, a firmness about not being drawn into non-analytic responses when interpretation is what is called for. Again, this is common analytic currency. The emphasis on the framework which characterises Independent thinking has an extra dimension. Ferenczi knew that the exchange between analyst and patient needed to be at the level of ordinary human interaction. What he searched for with such difficulty, and what Independent analysts have worked to articulate, is a framework that can infuse ordinary human interaction with psychoanalytic awareness, and that can maintain this conjunction, so that the exchange does not stop being either human or analytic.

Two aspects of Independent analysis in particular characterise this way of relating. One is an appreciation of the importance of a patient's external reality. I have mentioned the analyst's provision of an 'environment'. Joan Rivière said, in a symposium on child analysis:

> Psycho-analysis is Freud's discovery of what goes on in the imagination of a child ... Analysis has no concern with anything else: it is not concerned with the real world, nor with the child's or the adult's adaptation to the real world, nor with sickness or health, nor virtue or vice. It is concerned simply and solely with the imaginings of the childish mind, the phantasied pleasures and the dreaded retributions.
>
> (Rivière, 1927: 376)

In 1927, Rivière was fighting the Kleinian corner against Anna Freud, and I do not know how many analysts would still take such an extreme view. But it is against this background that Winnicott, who understood that human beings grow psychically only within a relationship, made his statement that there is no such thing as a baby, only a *baby and someone* (Winnicott, 1964: 88), and chose to call his book *The Maturational Processes and the Facilitating Environment* (1965). One source of the difficulty between Freud and Ferenczi was Ferenczi's insistence that the analytic environment should not replicate the traumatic quality of patients' earlier relationships. Rycroft's comment has already been noted, that the analyst contributes to a relationship 'within which the patient can recapture the ability to make contact and communication with external objects'. And for Enid Balint (1993: 121), 'the core of psychoanalysis is, in brief, the understanding of intrapsychic processes and states, and their relationship, or lack of it, with external reality'. This emphasis on the interrelation of intrapsychic and external reality makes it important to locate the experience of the analysis in the historical context of the patient's life as a whole.

The second aspect of this analytic climate has more to do with how analysts listen than with the things they say. Independent clinical technique can be considered, in fact, more as a way of listening than of interpreting. When Enid Balint writes about the analyst's need to wait, she says: 'In my experience this seems more and more necessary, not less so, as the analyst becomes more experienced and more able to listen for variations and contradictions' (Balint, E., 1993: 122). This is striking. One might think that the experienced analyst, understanding more quickly, would not have to wait so long before interpreting. But no, it is the listening and the waiting themselves that matter.

So much emphasis on waiting and unobtrusive restraint might give the impression of a passive sort of analyst who sits there doing not very much. Independent analysts do interpret, and there is plenty of active interpretation in this book. The crucial point lies in the title of Part III: The *Activity* of Listening. If analysands are to hear from their unconscious lives (see above, p.189), they have to learn to listen out for them. What helps analysands discover how to do this is the unconscious recognition of being in a relationship with, and being listened to by, an analyst who knows how important it is to hear from their own unconscious life, and who is open to their own internal surprises.

What is the purpose of the analyst's free-floating attention? It might seem obvious that, as described by Freud, it is to decipher the patient's unconscious communications. It also facilitates free association in the patient, which helps the patient produce 'material' with unconscious content, ripe for interpretation. All this is only part of the story. The analyst's free-floating attention is really a free-associative listening, and the free-association that the analyst's listening facilitates in patients becomes for them, in turn, the activity of a free-associative listening to themselves. Free association is an imaginative activity in its own right, and to help somebody become less anxious about controlling the movement of their thoughts and feelings, is itself to facilitate their psychic growth and development.

In this connection Bollas lays stress on the *use* that the patient makes of the analyst. 'The patient's idiom is able to use the analyst's analytic personality as a complex field of mental objects through which to elaborate itself' (Bollas, 1989: 86; see also 25–31, 101–13). That the analyst, as well as understanding and interpreting, is there to be made use of psychically by the patient, is a key Independent concept. Bollas mentions times when an analyst may find, while making a comment, that the patient appears to have drifted off.

> The analyst discovers that his or her interpretation is not used for its apparent accuracy, but as a kind of evocative form: because the analyst is talking, curiously the patient is free not to listen! But in not listening, the patient seems intrapsychically directed towards another interpretation. To the analyst's observation 'You are thinking of something else?', the patient replies that as the analyst was speaking the patient was thinking of *x*, where *x* is an interpretation from the analysand's unconscious that will be different from the analyst's; but *x* will not have been possible without the analyst's interpretation constituting difference in that moment.
>
> (Bollas, 2002: 42)

What Bollas articulates so strikingly about interpretations applies also to silence. When a patient is not speaking, perhaps for a long time, there may seem nothing to listen to, and nothing for the analyst to do except wait. But the silently waiting analyst is not doing nothing. Just as when the analyst listens to a patient speaking, the way an analyst listens to silence is an 'evocative form' for the patient to make use of. The quality of an analyst's attentiveness to silence, in fact, may reveal more clearly than anything what it means to call listening an activity.

In silences that go on for some time, it is possible for analysts not to pay much attention to the silence itself, but just to be waiting in a desultory way for the patient to say something. When I notice myself in this state, I think the quality of my own silence is poor, and I try to listen more attentively to the silence that is happening. This does not mean listening harder: it means listening in a different way. In Chapter 8 (pp.130f), a session is described in which very little was said. The patient felt like crying, and I said he might want me just to be with him while he did that. There were only half a dozen utterances, by either of us, in the rest of the session. These were, as I put it, 'punctuation points in an extended moment of stillness'. This called for a quality of listening that required me 'to let myself feel the silence inside me. As I become part of the stillness myself, time is suspended and the immediacy of the moment can extend itself as I think this person needs'. I tried to convey the same thing with the description in Chapter 4, of standing outdoors at night, 'listening' to the smells of the wood around me. 'The longer I stood, letting an inner silence occupy me as I breathed in the night air, the more fascinated I became by the subtle variety, the richness and texture in the tapestry of scent that slowly unfolded' (p.53). The move in the analyst's mind, from a rather empty awareness that the patient is not saying anything, to being occupied by the silence and becoming part of the stillness, is definite and unmistakable. It can be tangible to patients as well. When I have felt this shift in myself, patients have often clearly experienced a change in the quality of the shared silence. This kind of listening, both to patients' silences and their speech, is the continuous activity by which analysts make themselves available to be utilised.

The silent session with Mr W described in Chapter 10 (pp.161f) is an especially clear example of the analyst's listening as a way of making himself available, and not as a way of trying to reach an interpretation. There is another point as well. In the passage just quoted, Bollas shows the patient doing something different with an analyst's intervention from what the analyst had in mind. Following the silent session, it took me three sessions to realise how differently Mr W had been making use of my silence from how I had imagined at the time. It is characteristic of Independent analysts that they try to be available to be made use of in ways that they were not necessarily expecting.

I have mentioned that, in my theory of clinical technique, sessions are there for patients to discover how they can use them (p.156). This is an example of a seemingly straightforward statement in everyday language, which is in fact imbued with theory. However much a patient's acting-out, or acting-in, constitutes an attempt to disrupt the analysis, for someone to be in analysis at all indicates an underlying impulse towards psychic growth, and it is important to try, actively and persistently, to keep contact with that area of the patient's being. It may be necessary to interpret the negative transference, but the Independent approach is always to come at this through the anxiety or conflict that makes patients feel the need to be the way they are. In Bion's words, it is a question of talking the language of achievement, not the language of blame (see Brenman, 2006: 33; Grotstein, 2007: 109–13).

My comment about patients discovering how to use the session was prompted by the patient who wanted to bring her dog (p.156). I was interested to see what her unconscious was getting at, and specifically, how she might be wanting to experiment with the analytic setting, and with me as an analytic object. Two classic texts in particular lie behind my clinical handling of this episode. One is Winnicott's (1971b) paper 'The use of an object and relating through identifications', which also underlies Bollas' discussion of the patient's use of the analyst (see above, p.197). Winnicott discusses the shift from object-relating to object-use, and he emphasises the role of aggression in making this possible. A patient's aggressive attacks on the analyst are not axiomatically a matter of anxiety driven resistance, or hostile attempts to destroy the analysis, but may rather be attempts to establish the analyst as an object that can reliably be made use of. If my patient bringing her dog contains an element of aggression against the setting, this is how I would understand it.

The other text is Milner's paper on 'The Role of Illusion in Symbol Formation' (Milner, 1987 [1952]), where she describes her work with an eleven-year-old boy whose play could be alarmingly destructive. He devised a game which involved setting fire to the analytic toys and once burnt a whole stack of matchboxes. Milner comments: 'He makes me stand back from the blaze, and shows great pleasure' (Milner, 1987 [1952]: 89). The important thing, according to Milner, was that, because he could do what he liked with the toys, and yet they were outside him and had qualities of their own, they offered him a new way of relating to external reality. The boy regularly began sessions by treating the analyst aggressively but, says Milner:

> ... as soon as he had settled down to using the toys as a pliable medium, external to himself, but not insisting on their own separate objective existence, then apparently he could treat me with friendliness and consideration, and even accept real frustration from me.
>
> (Milner, 1987 [1952]: 92)

He became able to use both Milner herself and the playroom equipment as what she calls an 'intervening pliable substance'. She likens this to paint for an artist or words for a poet. Artist and poet can do what they want with their materials, but not just anything they want, because paint and words, like the playroom toys, have their own existence and qualities, which have to be understood and respected. This is what lets artists and poets make use of them to create and express 'an appetitive interest in external reality' (Milner, 1987 [1952]: 99). Milner accepted this boy's aggression and survived it in a way that freed him to discover in safety how to make imaginative and creative use of her.

Central to Milner's method, as with Winnicott and Bollas, is her aim to allow patients to discover their own way of using her. Different clinical traditions, which do not work by this concept, may misunderstand or mistrust it. I have heard Milner criticised as though, because she did not interpret this boy's violence against herself and the analysis as being destructive, she could not be taking it seriously. Herbert Rosenfeld in his last book, *Impasse and Interpretation* (1987), emphasised the need to attend fully to the subjective experience of patients, and not inflict on them an interpretative stance that might feel like an attack on their sense of themselves. This rather Ferenczian position drew an adverse response from Kleinian colleagues who had admired Rosenfeld's previous work (Segal and Steiner, R., 1987; Steiner, J., 1989). When Enid Balint presented a paper at the British Society her discussant felt the need to say: 'Enid's example warns us against premature intervention; there is also in my view the danger of prolonged non-intervention, however thoughtful' (Brenman, 1994: 10). Of course it is possible to go too long without intervening, but if Independent technique does provoke this anxiety among some analysts, it may be reassuring to remember that Enid Balint also wrote:

> In my view the analyst has to be just as observant, perhaps even more so, about what he does not do as about what he does. What the analyst does not say must be remembered by him more carefully than what he does say, because the decision to leave it to the patient, or to wait for the right time, is a very important one.
>
> (Balint, E., 1993: 126)

I have stressed that the analyst's restraint and unobtrusiveness are not passive, that analytic listening is an activity, and that patients may be extremely sensitive to the quality of listening that they encounter. But this is still only one side of a coin. In Chapter 1 (pp.6f), I referred to a dimension along which analysts need to be able to shift their clinical stance, according to the analytic need of the moment. Activity emanating from one vantage point, where the analyst's main concern is not to get in the way of the unfolding process, will be largely receptive, with an emphasis on listening, restraint in interpretation, acceptance of regression, and non-intrusiveness in various forms. From a vantage point elsewhere on the dimension, analytic work will be more focused and purposeful, with interpretations aimed at conveying specific insights to the patient, and a greater readiness in general to intervene. Independent analysts, like those of any other persuasion, must be able to move about on this dimension freely and flexibly.

Clinical examples have shown the variety of intervention that this may involve. In a session reported in Chapter 2 (p.29), I remained silent for half an hour despite obvious transference references. I had a sense of dialogue between the patient's speaking and my listening, and between her speaking and her own listening to herself. Waiting for the patient to make her own connection to the imminent holiday break allowed an interpretation to grow at a given moment out of these two parallel dialogues. The silent session described in Chapter 10 (pp.161f), likewise exemplifies the value of restraint. It was only because I allowed myself to go on saying nothing, and listening to my inner responses to the patient's silence, that I arrived at a crucial thought about the wider aspects of sexuality. I have already discussed the mistake I then made by shifting, with a specific oedipal interpretation, to a different vantage point on the dimension. I was having recourse, at that moment, to theory instead of letting it mediate my creative imagination. I made a similarly specific interpretation when I told the woman with the dog on her tummy that it represented our baby inside her. This time, by contrast, it was not a mistake. Given this woman's uncertain sense of identity, I thought an open-ended invitation to reflect on herself might only confuse her, and that a more structured interpretation would give her a better base for self-exploration. When I spoke of the dog representing 'our baby inside her' I meant it on the one hand quasi-literally, but the phrase also described whatever the analysis between us might unpredictably give birth to. My decision to accept the dog as part of the analysis was based in theory, but in this instance, theory was being used to open the imaginative boundaries of the setting.

Different individual analysts, as I mentioned in Chapter 1 (p.6), will feel more naturally comfortable in different locations on this dimension. Analytic orientations also may be characterised by whereabouts on it they situate themselves, with a tendency to favour one kind of interpretation or another. While it is true that all analysts need to be mobile along this dimension, Independent clinical technique emphasises typically a position towards its more receptive end. In the British Psychoanalytical Society, this attitude developed in counterpoint to the Kleinian and classical Freudian orientations, both of which, in their different ways, tended to see the analyst, in the language of Lacan, as the one who was 'supposed to know' (Lacan, 1977: 230ff). The therapeutic task, in that case, is to transmit the analyst's understanding to the patient. The Independent tradition by contrast developed the view that transformative awareness grows in the space between analyst and patient, fed in qualitatively different ways from both sides. Ogden's (1994) influential paper on the 'analytic third' is a notable contribution to this understanding, squarely in the Independent tradition and showing how that extends beyond the British Society. This standpoint, of seeing growth as originating *between* analyst and analysand, functions for the Independent analyst as a kind of elastic anchorage.

Transference is a theme that pervades every analysis, and the following two examples show an Independent analyst addressing it flexibly, as the need of the moment seemed to require, from different points along the dimension.

A patient coming four times a week rolled over on the couch near the end of a session to lie on his side. The next day, he said he thought I had not realised that this was because he was feeling uncomfortable. I picked up how important it was for him that I should understand what he felt in his body. He said he did not much like talking about physical feelings, and there was a silence. After several minutes, he said he had been thinking about how uncomfortable he used to be as a child. He would feel too hot or too cold, or restless and fidgety, but he would try to keep still and not complain, so as not to challenge his parents.

The word 'challenge' struck me. It carried a resonance, like an element in a dream that catches the attention without one's being quite sure why. There was something in it about how he thought his parents would experience what he might say about his bodily feelings. But I did not take this up. I simply noted my reaction and continued listening.

Later in the session, this man talked about his hopes for a close relationship, and went on at length in a painfully self-critical way. He did not think there was anything about him that could be attractive or interesting to a partner. Then he said he thought that now he had made me depressed as well; I must be, listening to him regurgitate all this stuff. I remarked to him what a physical word 'regurgitate' was. We were back with his body again. I said he was telling me horrible feelings about himself—that he is worthless, unattractive, self-destructive—and I thought he was afraid I would be repelled by what he was vomiting up from inside himself. He said it was not just me who would find it repulsive. He did not want to know about these feelings either. He seemed to think, I said, that he should try and keep them to himself, and not challenge me with them. After a slight pause, he said that what he remembered most, from being a child and trying to convey something to other people, was a sense of emptiness.

In using the word 'challenge' here I am doing various things. I am letting the patient know that I registered his earlier use of the word to tell me something significant (although neither of us may yet know what) about him and his parents. I am also implying that there may be a link between what he feels as he tells me these repulsive perceptions of himself, and what talking to his parents about his body used to feel like. And I am offering him this idea to do whatever he wants with, or to ignore. I am not adding anything of my own about what kind of challenge he thinks he might be to me, or the nature of the connection with his parents. Interestingly, he responded by going back to his childhood and telling me something new about it.

Contrast that with the following. A patient in five-times-a-week analysis, who was well known in the entertainment world, came to a session shortly after giving a newspaper interview. Before it, she said, she went over in her mind the subjects she was prepared to talk about and those she was not. Her life was currently in some turmoil. She had difficult personal decisions to make, and she was uncertain about the future direction of her work. She decided she would discuss her past work, and her current activity that the media were interested in, but she would definitely not talk about future plans, nor mention any of the problems she was struggling with. She told the interviewer what she was willing to talk about, and added that she thought her work might be about to take new directions, but this was very unclear to her and she did not want to go into it. The interviewer replied that this was just what he was interested in, and pressed her to tell him about exactly those things she had decided not to discuss. She found herself doing so, despite her resolutions, and went into a lot more personal detail than she had intended. Afterwards, she was shocked at what she had done, and she agonised in the session about how she had stepped so easily beyond the boundaries she had set herself.

This patient had erotic feelings towards me which she let me know about. There were also, however, deeper conflicts about her sexuality than she was yet conscious of. Her erotic transference was, to some extent, available, but I thought it had more power to disturb her than she realised, and that this needed interpreting. So I said she was telling me about herself and a man, and about boundaries that were supposed to set limits on how intimate they would be together. Then she oversteps those limits to become more personal and intimate with the man than she had told herself she meant to, and the man takes advantage of her. I said I thought the man she wanted to overstep boundaries with was myself. She was greatly taken aback at my words, but then recognised that I had indeed been much in her mind, both before the interview and during it.

This is different from the previous example. It is a classic, head-on, 'it's me you're really talking about' transference interpretation, of the sort Freud described in 'The Dynamics of Transference' as 'an assurance that [the patient] is being dominated at the moment by an association which is concerned with the doctor himself' (Freud, 1912a: 101). Freud thought such interpretations were needed when a patient's resistance manifested itself in the transference. He pointed out in the same paper, however, that resistance and communication go hand in hand; and overcoming resistance was not the primary aim of my interpretation. Even if the patient's feelings and fantasies about me are a substitute for exploring the place of sexuality in her life, and even if she displaces her transference on to the interviewer and enacts it, rather than reflecting on its meaning with me, she is also, and more importantly, beginning to make room for questions. Why did she point out the forbidden area to the interviewer in the first place? If he stood for me, does her story imply she thinks I too must wish for greater intimacy between us? Does her intense response to my interpretation stem not only from whatever truth it may contain, but also from an unconscious desire to be stirred up by me? These are tender topics which are unconscious because, for the moment, they need to be, and I shall not hurry to put them into words. My intervention is not simply because I think she is resisting such thoughts. The directness with which she tells me about this episode is a step, intentional although unconsciously so, towards making it possible for us to explore, in her relationship with me, sexual conflicts that stretch back to her early childhood. The directness of my interpretation is a response to the directness of this move on her part. This contrasts with my deliberate obliqueness in the previous example. Both instances, though, derived from my sense of the analytic process in the immediate moment.

No analyst, as I have emphasised, should be confined to a single region on this dimension. If the explicit end feels *unheimlich* to Independent analysts it is all the more important for them not to shirk it (see p.7). Necessary as it may be, however, to range freely along the dimension when active and specific interventions are called for, the natural condition of an Independent analyst is one of unobtrusive restraint. The anchorage is elastic but it remains an anchorage.

The theory behind this approach is unobtrusive. Trying to grasp the theory of technique from an Independent perspective seems to me rather like trying to see an animal in a forest, whose colouring makes it melt into the background. You stare, and there doesn't seem to be anything there. All you can see are trees and shadows. And then suddenly the visual pattern clicks, and the shape of the animal is so clear that you can't imagine why you couldn't see it before. It is itself part of Independent theory, that theory should be unobtrusive in this way. I mentioned earlier Ferenczi's concern that ordinary human interaction should be able to accommodate psychoanalytic awareness (p.195). Whatever an analyst's orientation, it is the essential *humanity* of the *psychoanalytic* process that helps the human being on the couch think it might be possible to change. And the specifically *psychoanalytic* quality of the *human* process that the analyst offers is what provides patients with the means to change. What typifies Independent psychoanalysis is an aspiration to keep both of these continually in view, not losing sight of either.

Notes

1 Toshio Ohi is the eleventh-generation Master of the Ohi Chozaemon family. His work is exhibited in the Ohi Museum, Kanazawa, Japan.
2 Compare the idea put forward in Chapter 11 (p.176) that the function of interpretation is not to convey knowledge, but to generate an experience in the patient.
3 Thanks to Rowan Williams for this reference.

13

FORMING AN IDENTITY

Reflections on psychoanalytic training

Implicit in this book, perhaps coming into focus as it proceeds, is a certain vision of psychoanalysis and what it means to be an analyst. This, in turn, raises questions about what is involved in becoming one, and this final chapter is an extended consideration of the nature of psychoanalytic training.

I

The apparently straightforward idea, that to be a psychoanalyst one must become one, carries more implications, and is more debatable than may appear at first sight. Becoming something that, to begin with, one is not, amounts to a change in who one is: a development in one's identity. Not everyone, however, would view psychoanalytic training from this perspective. It can also be seen as a matter of learning to do something; to understand and make use of a particular conceptual framework, and to carry out a particular kind of practice. This lends a different quality, and different sort of energy to the training situation. In fact, both attitudes are necessary, and they exist in a necessary tension with each other.

This chapter ranges widely over many topics. What gives direction to its apparent meandering is the idea that the specifically and essentially psychoanalytic quality of analytic training resides in the developmental, not the didactic, aspect of it. Of course, those wanting to be analysts have a lot of learning to do, as growing children have much to learn about the world and how to live in it. Candidates have to learn how analytic concepts are used, and what good analytic practice consists of. But you cannot teach a child to grow up, and you cannot teach someone to be a psychoanalyst: it is a question of helping them to become one.

In the early days of psychoanalysis, training was not systematised. Indeed, the concept of training barely existed. In 1910, Freud's answer to the question of how to become a psychoanalyst was: 'By studying one's own dreams' (Freud, 1910a: 33). A significant milestone was the idea of a 'training analysis'. Two years after the remark just quoted, Freud said he now believed 'that everyone who wishes to carry out analyses on other people [should] first himself undergo an analysis by someone with expert knowledge' (Freud, 1912b: 116). This was proposed formally by Herman Nunberg (1962) at the 1918 International Psychoanalytic Congress, and in 1923, Max Eitingon, the Director of the Berlin Psycho-Analytic Policlinic, reported:

> We are all firmly convinced, with only too good reason, that henceforth no one who has not been analysed must aspire to the rank of a practising analyst. It follows that the analysis of the student himself is an essential part of the curriculum … In order to enable these analyses of our students to be carried out by an analyst whom we regard as competent, we have appointed Dr [Hanns] Sachs to the Policlinic.
>
> (Eitingon, 1923: 266f)

Eitingon was a pioneer of psychoanalytic training. The tripartite training structure which he instituted at the Berlin Policlinic, consisting of theoretical studies, personal analysis and analyses conducted by candidates under supervision, was accepted in 1925 by the International Psychoanalytical Association (IPA) as a standard format, and has remained the basis of analytic training ever since. Patrizio Campanile (2012) gives an excellent account of the development of Eitingon's training model and of his contributions in general to psychoanalysis.

Two phrases in the passages quoted are especially worth noting. Freud states that aspiring analysts should be analysed 'by someone with expert knowledge' and Eitingon appoints Sachs so that students at the Policlinic shall be analysed 'by an analyst whom we regard as competent'. These remarks foreshadow a lasting debate about who should and should not be entitled to analyse candidates. Campanile's paper surveys the views of Freud, Ferenczi, Eitingon himself, Anna Freud, and others in the early psychoanalytic community about this vexed question which continues to bedevil analytic training.

The Eitingon model of training, in the form adopted by the IPA, obliges those who would conduct the analyses of candidates to undergo a selection process, in order to be accredited as 'training analysts'. This was universal throughout the IPA until 2007. In that year, discussions which had begun in 2002 resulted in the recognition of two further training systems: the so-called 'French' and 'Uruguayan' models. The Uruguayan is less prominent internationally than the French and Eitingon models, but has one particularly interesting feature to be mentioned in due course. The Uruguayan model retains an assessment procedure for training analysts, but the French model makes no distinction between analysts who are and are not entitled to analyse candidates. There are local variations to the French model—as there are to the Eitingon model—but, broadly speaking, it allows a candidate's analysis to be conducted by any analyst.

The question 'What is a training analyst?' was the subject of a conference held in December 2011, by the Forum on Training of the European Psychoanalytic Federation. An invitation to speak at it may perhaps have come because I happen to belong to two psychoanalytic organisations which operate different training models. On the one hand, I am a training analyst of the British Psychoanalytical Society, which follows the Eitingon model. From this position, my answer to the question: 'What is a training analyst?' could be to describe the procedure of applying to become one, and the process of evaluation, including presentation of a clinical case to a group of senior colleagues, following which the application will be accepted or rejected. A training analyst is someone who has passed this evaluation process successfully, and has been duly accredited. I am also, on the other hand, a member of the French Psychoanalytic Association, which follows the French model. From this position, I might say: 'What is a training analyst? What indeed? There is no such thing'.

II

My solution at the conference was to transpose the question and ask instead: 'What is essential to the analysis of a future psychoanalyst?'

In any analysis there must be a sense of need on the part of the patient. It may take time for patients to discover what are the deepest needs that have brought them into analysis, but without some real sense of need in the first place, the analysis can have no traction. The analysis of a candidate is complicated in this regard by being an obligation; a prerequisite for becoming an analyst. This different, procedural kind of necessity risks obscuring the question of whether the analysis is motivated by a true sense of emotional need.

Why does this matter? In the analysis of a future psychoanalyst, what is at stake is not only the well-being of one individual, but also the transmission of psychoanalysis itself. If learning to be an analyst meant simply the acquisition of a clinical technique to be applied to patients so as to remedy their suffering, analysts would indeed be like the surgeon to whom Freud compared them (1912b: 115). There is truth in Freud's image, for an analyst does have to carry out a technical procedure correctly, but an analytic patient is not just a person with an ailment or with symptoms requiring correct treatment. The essence of psychoanalysis is to address what interferes unconsciously with a person's capacity to be fully alive. To enter analysis is to embark on exploring oneself from this perspective.

What interferes with someone's aliveness cannot be explained to them. It has to be discovered. This comes about to varying degrees with different patients. But since this discovery is the therapeutic core of psychoanalysis, for future psychoanalysts the experience of it is essential. If there is no sense of needing such liberation, there is no way to internalise the nature and meaning of psychoanalysis.

To be capable of offering an analysis that can transmit this, analysts need to have internalised the experience into their own analytic identity. Concern to make sure that this is so prompts institutes that follow the Eitingon model to insist on evaluating it in prospective training analysts. The contrary view of the French model is that this cannot be evaluated and accredited externally. Lacan, in particular, maintained that the quality of a psychoanalyst's analytic identity could only be authenticated by the analyst himself, out of his own self-experience and awareness (e.g. Lacan, 1977: viii). In either view, what analysts-to-be need is the same: to encounter in their own analyst a deeply internalised sense of what psychoanalysis is.

III

What psychoanalysis is ... Different systems of analytic training are not conjured up by accidents of history or geography. They are the expression of different responses to this fundamental question. Claire Marine François-Poncet (2009) discusses the view of what psychoanalysis is, that is implicit to the French training model. When the IPA was considering whether to recognise the French model, its Education Committee prepared a report for the Board of the IPA. This report, as quoted by François-Poncet, states that in the Eitingon model the psychoanalyst is regarded as a professional, 'and training [is] geared to enable him to become as good a professional as possible ... A professional development implies an acquired expertise and the readiness to act in accordance with it; e.g. the medical profession'. By contrast the French model, says the report, conceives 'the entire educational process in psychoanalytic terms and not along ordinary "professional" training lines' (François-Poncet, 2009: 1420f). François-Poncet comments that 'this opposition is based on different conceptions of psychoanalysis', and quotes this question from the Education Committee's report:

> To what extent is psychoanalysis a professional development subject to general professional ethics, or a unique human endeavour, which may or may not require professional training, but consists mainly in personal sensitisation to unconscious processes?
>
> (François-Poncet, 2009: 1421)

The French model inclines in the latter direction. In François-Poncet's words, it takes 'the analytic experience as the principal mode of transmission', so that 'the ethic of transmission in the French model would consist above all in the ethic of treatment' (François-Poncet, 2009: 1422). This does not simply mean that the experience of personal analysis is given pride of place. It means that supervision and seminars, the other two constituent elements of training, are also conducted experientially as far as possible, so that instead of being didactic, they too become contexts for candidates to internalise the nature of psychoanalysis.

When the Education Committee's report considers the idea of psychoanalysis as 'a unique human endeavour, *which may or may not require professional training*' (author's emphasis), it floats the implication that the French model might not aspire to be any form of professional training at all. Here the connotations of the word 'professional' are important. A criterion of professionalism 'in its Anglo-Saxon sense', says François-Poncet:

> ... is the quality of education according to the university model: the more a training is academic or university-based, the more professional it will be. The French training model fears this form of professionalism in so far as training through experience is favoured over any kind of training along academic or university lines.
>
> (François-Poncet, 2009: 1421)

There may be different views of what 'professional' means, but followers of the French model would certainly insist that the training it provides is rigorously specific to the practice of psychoanalysis.

The question at issue is: How can analytic training be organised in such a way as to reflect the nature of psychoanalysis? The problem for the IPA's Education Committee was that psychoanalysis is *both* 'a professional development subject to general professional ethics' *and* 'a unique human endeavour', involving 'personal sensitisation to unconscious processes'. The Eitingon model of training seems to reflect the former more than the latter, while the French model does the reverse. Both can become one-sided, and François-Poncet, having set out the position of the French model very clearly, goes on to discuss some of its possible drawbacks. In this chapter, at the same time as expressing my own standpoint, I try to give as balanced a view as I can of the two perspectives.

IV

Because of the insistence in the French model on the purely personal nature of a candidate's analysis, and on its total separation from any institutional requirements, decisions about when to terminate it are made solely according to the dynamic of the analysis, without regard to the training situation. Candidates are free to end their analysis according to its internal evolution, regardless of external timetables. The result is that in institutes using the French model candidates may, and frequently do, terminate their analyses well before they finish their training and qualify. According to François-Poncet, the main purpose of a candidate's analysis is to analyse their motivation for becoming a psychoanalyst. This means that candidates may be expected to have completed their analyses even *before* they apply for training. 'The admission interview assesses the quality and nature of the psychoanalytic process the candidate underwent' (François-Poncet, 2009: 1420). It might be argued that any analysis will transmit to the patient what psychoanalysis is, simply by the patient's experience of the analytic process, so that whatever analysis, at whatever time, a prospective candidate has had should be acceptable for training purposes. The issue is more complicated, however, and a major difference between the French and Eitingon models is that the latter requires candidates to remain in analysis until they complete their training.

To embark on becoming a psychoanalyst is an enormous decision. It has roots deep in a person's history and character, with conscious and unconscious ramifications into many areas of their life. Such issues do have to be analysed, and work on them will no doubt be under way by the time of approaching an analytic institute. It is hard, though, to imagine them being fully resolved in isolation from the reality of training. The application process, with all the hopes and anxieties it arouses, will bring into sharp focus questions about why applicants are doing this, what significance psychoanalysis holds for them and whether, in the end, this is a path they truly want to follow. Then comes the experience of the training with its excitements and frustrations, relationships both rewarding and difficult, times of progress and of stagnation. Finally, there is qualification: a milestone charged with known and unknown meanings and with questions about what lies ahead. All of this needs to be explored at conscious and unconscious levels. As a training analyst in the British Society I know well how fruitful, how painful sometimes, and certainly how necessary, this internal work is for candidates. Candidates need to unpack these concerns and contend with them all through their training. In the first instance, this is for their own psychic well-being. In addition, however, it is by dealing analytically with such issues that these future psychoanalysts will internalise the nature and significance of psychoanalysis itself.

The stipulation that candidates remain in analysis throughout their training ensures that the experience of becoming an analyst, right through until qualification, can always be brought back into a candidate's personal analysis. This requirement, however, is a general demand imposed from outside the analysis, not an individual decision arising organically from within it. This may well appear theoretically unacceptable, and proponents of the French model would certainly deem it an interference. When the dynamic of an analysis brings it to a conclusion, they would say that this is the analytic truth, regardless of the stage of training, and the analysis should terminate. The drawback to such theoretical correctness is that the later stages of training, which include working with one's own analytic cases and the approach to final qualification as an analyst, may provoke all sorts of inner turmoil. A candidate whose analysis has already ended lacks a setting for the psychic work that this may entail.

Nor does this work stop with the end of training. Pearl King (1983: 184) remarks that 'many young analysts wisely continue their personal analysis' even after qualifying, because the situation of being no longer a candidate provokes its own anxieties and conflicts. The group for newly qualified analysts described by Sklar and Parsons (2011: 145ff; see Chapter 10, pp.154f) was set up in response to just this need.

V

The difference about whether candidates have to continue analysis until qualification gives supervision a different character in the two approaches. In the French model of training, the supervision of training cases is considered to play a much more important role than in the Eitingon model. The reasons for this, however, are not always clearly articulated.

Supervisors in an institute using the Eitingon model tend not to lay deliberate emphasis on a candidate's countertransference. Of course they do not ignore it, for it is an essential aspect of any analysis. If a candidate's emotional reactions affect the analysis, or reveal something about the analytic relationship, the supervisor will take this up. But supervisors know that candidates have an analytic setting where they can think about the personal impact on them of their cases. Supervision is not the sole opportunity for candidates to talk about what their work stirs up in them, so the countertransference does not have to be spotlighted for the candidate's sake; it can play as large or small a part in the supervision as the analysis being supervised calls for. In a system where candidates may no longer be in analysis while analysing their training cases, the supervisor is in a different position. The difference is not with regard to countertransference provoked specifically by the analysis under supervision. This will be taken up by a supervisor in the same way whether or not the candidate is in analysis. However, when candidates have nowhere except the supervision to bring the totality of reactions and responses that the analytic work arouses in them, their countertransference takes centre stage for different reasons. The concept of countertransference to the psychoanalytic process is relevant here (see Chapter 9). In both the Eitingon and French training models, supervision will address a candidate's countertransference to the particular patient. But understanding their countertransference to the process of psychoanalysis itself is also crucial for candidates, as they discover the nature of the work to which they are committing themselves. Here is where the difference lies. When candidates are still in analysis, as the Eitingon model guarantees, their countertransference to the analytic process can be explored and worked with analytically in their own personal analyses. When a personal analysis is not in place for candidates alongside their training cases, as often happens with the French model, supervision has to accommodate their countertransference to the psychoanalytic process, as well as to the individual patient.

Supervision in the French model has to fulfil both these different functions. It has more work to do than in the Eitingon model. This makes it more complicated, and perhaps more challenging, for both candidate and supervisor. The complexity may be interesting, but the line between supervision and a quasi-analysis of the candidate may also be a fine one. François-Poncet goes as far as to state that 'some supervisors will ... stimulate an analytic process within the supervision frame' (François-Poncet, 2009: 1420). To an Eitingon-trained analyst this would be an unacceptable confusion of roles.

VI

Not only candidates and supervisors, but also the analysts of candidates, are faced with issues which compel them to contemplate the nature of psychoanalysis and what becoming an analyst means. For the most part these are implicit, but even when not overt, they are not absent from the analysis. These issues centre around the notion of analytic neutrality. Precise definitions of this concept are elusive, but it is recognised nonetheless as fundamental to any analysis. Certain features particular to the training situation, however, colour the setting and impinge on the analytic relationship so as to pose specific challenges to a training analyst's neutrality.

The training analyst—in the sense of one who analyses a candidate, whatever the model—and the candidate belong to the same analytic community. Candidates may bring to their analyses powerful feelings, positive and negative, about people the analyst knows and is involved with professionally. These include other candidates whom the analyst teaches, supervises or is analysing as well, and other analysts who have important significance for the training analyst. Candidates in analysis are subject to decisions by the analyst's colleagues in the training organisation; decisions about which the analyst may have strong views. It makes unusual demands on the analytic neutrality of training analysts to be able to put their personal responses to such material on one side, without denying or suppressing them, and treat it only in terms of its psychic meaning for their patient. Candidates will realise, moreover, that their comments on these other figures, and on the training organisation, can have an impact on their analysts. This lends itself to all sorts of possible manoeuvrings in the transference, and training analysts need to be especially watchful over their countertransference responses. It can be all too easy for them to get drawn into inappropriate enactment of transference scenarios, either in what is said or does not get said, both in sessions and sometimes outside the analytic setting.

This is complicated further by the fact that training analysis has a double function, and the training analyst a double responsibility. A training analysis is a personal analysis, needed for the analysand's psychic development. In this respect the candidate is a patient. It is also the experiential transmission of what psychoanalysis consists of. In this respect the candidate is a student. Both elements are essential and they are linked. I have already mentioned that without personal meaning to the analysis arising from the *patient's* emotional need, there is no possibility of transmitting to the *student*, or for the student to discover, the meaning of psychoanalysis. The training analyst is responsible to candidates as patients for safeguarding the framework of their personal analyses. The training analyst is also responsible to the training institute, to possible future patients, and to psychoanalysis itself, not to acquiesce with the qualification of someone who should not, or not yet, become an analyst.

There is a contradiction between these two responsibilities. The analyst's commitment to a candidate as patient, and to the analysis as the patient's personal analysis, implies that there should be no impingement of any sort on the analytic situation by considerations external to the analysis. But the second kind of responsibility constitutes exactly such an impingement. Psychoanalytic training institutes deal with this contradiction in one of two ways. They may accept it and define within their procedures what are, in fact, breaches of the normal analytic setting, such as the externally imposed obligation to continue analysis until qualifying. By codifying them, they make these exceptions explicit for the analyst and the candidate, and see to it that they are controlled clearly and transparently. In the British Society, for example, the training analyst used historically to be involved at various points in the training, such as reporting to the Education Committee that a candidate's analysis was continuing, recommending commencement of the first training case, and agreeing that a candidate was ready to qualify. Over the years, these impingements on the training have been reduced almost, but not quite, to vanishing. The only regular contact left between the analyst and the training institute is that the analyst recommends when the candidate is ready to start attending lectures and seminars. (This remains true as of January 2014). Other institutes, especially those using the French model, would regard all such occasions, even the single one left in the British Society, as unacceptable infractions of the setting. They place an absolute priority on total separation between the theoretical and clinical training and a candidate's personal analysis. Under no circumstances may there be any interaction between the analytic and the training situations of a candidate.

Neither the pragmatism of the first solution nor the purity of the second removes the contradiction.

In an institute which takes the first route, such as the British and others operating the Eitingon model, the personal aspect of the analysis is sustained by analysts not breaching the setting in any way except that required by the training procedures, of which the patient is aware. The training function is sustained by analysts being prepared, within the agreed procedures and bringing it into the analysis, to operate in ways that a normal analytic framework might preclude.

Both elements in this strategy, the personal responsibility to the candidate as a patient, and the training responsibility, can involve strain. For example, an institute may become concerned if a candidate is struggling in seminars or has a pattern of disturbed relationships with peers or teachers. In such cases it may be especially hard for analysts, with their unique knowledge of the candidate, if they disagree with how the situation is being handled by the institution. Training analysts may sometimes feel under pressure to breach the framework by stepping outside normal procedures and becoming involved in issues of this sort. This would mean, however, that the candidate is no longer being treated analytically as a patient. It can be painful to address real difficulties in a candidate's training only in terms of their analytic meaning, protecting candidates as patients by leaving their evaluation as students to the training organisation.

On occasions when a training analyst does have a decision to make about a candidate as a student, the analyst may be apprehensive about how this will impact on the candidate as a patient. A training analyst in the British Society might think it is not yet right to recommend that a candidate should commence lectures and seminars. When it comes to taking training cases or to qualifying, for which the analyst's agreement is not required, a candidate's analyst might still want to question, within the analysis, whether the candidate is ready. However, there may be anxiety that delaying recommendation, or expressing doubts about a step forward for the candidate as a student, will disturb the analytic relationship and impair the personal analysis of the candidate as a patient. Such fears on the part of the analyst could lead to inappropriate progression through the training and the qualification of candidates who are not ready to be analysts. Training analysts need a clear sense that whatever they do as part of their training responsibilities is also analytic material within the personal analysis of their patients. Candidates' reactions to being held back, or having their progress queried, may be challenging and disturbing. For analysts to be able to deal with this analytically, as part of the personal analysis, depends on the depth and security of their identity as a psychoanalyst.

In this kind of system, therefore, the setting of a training analysis may be compromised in two ways, according to its double aspect: its framework as a personal analysis is broken if an analyst becomes involved in irregular communications with the training organisation; and its training function may be sacrificed if analysts are inhibited by misplaced anxieties about their role as personal analyst.

Such occasions of conflict and uncertainty stem from a failure to discriminate the double responsibility, for the personal analysis of candidates and for their progress as psychoanalysts in training. To incorporate into training procedures what amount to breaches of the analytic framework might seem only to increase the likelihood of such confusion. Is it not obviously better to insist on absolute separation between a candidate's personal analysis and the training programme? To believe, however, that this second approach releases a training analyst from the contradiction simply fudges the issue in a different way.

If an institute takes the second route, as in the French model, so that there is no contact between analyst and training institute, and the analyst plays no part in a candidate's progress as a student, it might seem that the personal analysis remains uncontaminated. A candidate's analyst, however, may teach and supervise fellow candidates, or sit on committees which are responsible for organising the training. Candidate and analyst may not meet each other physically in these contexts, but the candidate will nonetheless be aware of them. They amount to situations, outside the analysis, in which the analyst impinges, albeit indirectly, on the candidate's training experience. More importantly, the analyst, simply by going on being a candidate's analyst, consents implicitly but actively to the candidate's continuing in training, and qualifying, under the analyst's auspices. Suppose that the analysis reveals a candidate to have a deeply perverse or psychopathic character structure. The analyst might think it would be dangerous for this person to progress, at least at the moment, towards qualifying as an analyst. In such a case, analysts are not powerless, even in this model. They may offer to go on with the analysis provided that the candidate withdraws, temporarily or permanently, from the training. If the candidate refuses to accept this, the option is always there of refusing to continue the analysis. All this would be within the personal analysis, with no reference to the training institute. In such training schemes this may be the only avenue available to the analyst, and however infrequent the need for such extreme action, it remains a possibility.

Considerations of this sort may only rarely take concrete form in particular instances. But whatever the training model, when a candidate qualifies as a psychoanalyst the analyst must accept responsibility for having allowed the personal analysis to be made use of for training purposes.

A candidate's analyst needs a grasp of this double responsibility so as to handle its conflicting demands. Candidates also need to be somehow aware of it: not in the same way, or as explicitly, as the analyst; but to have no sense at all of tension between the personal and training aspects of their analyses would imply some disavowal of reality. The need for analysts to stay preconsciously alert to the potential for ambiguity in their analytic relationship with a candidate helps them keep sharp their awareness of what their role as analyst means. This helps candidates in turn to develop, unconsciously as much as consciously, an awareness of what they are training to become.

VII

In fact, the distinction between training models is not always as cut and dried as may appear. Even Lacan had to modify his absolute insistence that the choice to be an analyst, and in particular an analyst of candidates, could be validated by no one other than the analyst. He was driven, against his inclinations, to institute the role of 'passers' ('*passeurs*'), who would monitor whether an individual's self-authentication appeared genuine or not (Parsons, 2000: 73). The Eitingon model, by contrast, takes for granted this need for validation. Here the corresponding necessity is to see validation not merely as something bestowed from outside, but as the necessary confirmation of an analyst's own sense of being ready to become a training analyst. However structured the procedures of training may be, the structure is not there for its own sake. A psychoanalytic session also is structured by its framework, but the analytic frame does not make psychoanalysis happen of itself. It creates a space in which analytic exploration is possible. In the same way, the framework of a training is there, not because it automatically turns candidates into analysts, but to maintain a safe and reliable space for the potential development of analytic identities.

This will be facilitated if all the various facets of an analytic training exemplify a psychoanalytic spirit. In their own analyses, and in the supervision of the analyses they conduct, candidates are exposed to an analytic attitude. Other aspects of a training system should, ideally, demonstrate a similar quality of psychoanalytic awareness. Laurence Kahn (2012: 116) comments that the words 'administration' and 'psychoanalysis' rub shoulders uneasily, and committees are not expected, of course, to operate by free association. But despite being made up of analysts they may administer training with a surface rationality, appropriate enough in a bureaucratic context, which lacks psychoanalytic sensibility. Psychoanalytic knowledge can be organised and taught in ways that do not embody an analytic attitude. Such a training environment risks producing analysts who see psychoanalysis more as an instrumental procedure than as a creative exploration of the unknown.

The experience of applying to join the French Psychoanalytic Association affected me by the way it revealed an organisation which did operate with psychoanalytic awareness. I approached the president of the Association to ask if an analyst trained in a different IPA Society would be eligible to apply for membership. The answer came that the statutes did allow this. My candidature could be considered on the basis of published works rather than a clinical presentation, but in all other respects I would have to go through the same procedure as any candidate completing the Association's training. This would include three separate interviews with senior analysts (*analystes titulaires*), who would report on the interviews and present their assessment of me to all the *analystes titulaires* of the Association, who would then vote on my candidature.

I asked whether I should provide a statement of how I saw my life as an analyst so far and of what led me to apply to join the Association.

'No', replied the president. 'In the French Association what matters to us is the spoken word in a personal encounter'.

When I talked about this with friends in the British Society one of them was surprised that I should 'be willing to submit to all that'. On the contrary, I did not want to bypass whatever the French Association's entry procedures might be. I was interested to learn, later on, that leading members of the Association had debated how to deal with my application, and had also decided that, whatever status I might already have as an analyst, my acceptance as a member could only be authentic if I passed genuinely through the standard evaluation procedure, including the possibility of my not being accepted. There was a truthfulness about this, and a respect for the Association's structures, which were important to me. The procedure depended on what I would put into words in a living dialogue, and on how that would be listened to. This was not to be short-circuited by a written statement prepared in advance. The respect for administrative procedure was in the service of a specifically psychoanalytic attitude.

VIII

The institutional embodiment of a psychoanalytic attitude also matters where teaching is concerned. Even though the content is psychoanalytic, the style and manner of teaching may or may not exemplify an analytic stance. In many psychoanalytic institutes, for example, there is a standard method of conducting clinical seminars. The seminar leader asks a member of the seminar beforehand to present a case. This means giving a brief account of the patient's background and history, followed by an explanation of how the patient came into analysis, and a description of one or two sessions in as much detail as the analyst can remember. After this presentation, the seminar considers what factors in the history may be relevant, the clinical material is discussed and its unconscious meanings elucidated, and the presenter is helped to reflect on their clinical technique. All this is valuable. It is genuine teaching of psychoanalysis and the members of such a seminar will learn from it. As an experience for the participants, however, it is not very psychoanalytic.

An essential aspect of clinical psychoanalysis is the unpredictability of free association. At the beginning of an analytic session neither patient nor analyst knows what form the next fifty minutes will take. Within certain practical limits anything may happen. The format of the kind of seminar just described, however, is predetermined. Everybody knows what is going to happen. The details of the case are not known in advance, except to the presenter, but all the participants know what form the seminar will take and more or less, therefore, what kind of experience to expect. It has become common practice, and is sometimes required by seminar leaders, for presenters to type up and print their account of the sessions to be described, and copies of this are handed around the seminar so that participants can follow the material as the presenter reads it out. This removes the associative freedom for presenters to say what comes to mind in the moment, as they have to keep to the track they have laid out already, so as not to derail the listeners. I have even heard of seminar leaders who ask a presenter to send them the write-up before the seminar, so that they can prepare how they are going to comment on it. This means that both presenter and seminar leader have decided in advance what is going to be put into words. No doubt this system produces well thought out presentations which give rise to well thought out, instructive teaching. There seems something problematic, however, about a setting for clinical teaching which so negates the quality of the clinical setting itself. From an experiential viewpoint, these developments take the clinical seminar further and further away from the situation the participants are trying to learn about.

Clinical seminars, whether they are for candidates in training or for qualified analysts, can be conducted in a different way which links the work of the seminar more closely to the clinical situation. The first essential is for the seminar leader to know, and to emphasise to its members, that the seminar is not supervision. Candidates will be having supervision on their cases, qualified analysts should be consulting with colleagues if they need to: this is not the purpose of the seminar. The purpose is rather for the participants, leader included, to extend and deepen their vision of the potential inherent in the analytic encounter, and thus to enlarge the analytic identities they are in the process of developing. Discussing individual cases may be the substrate for this, and perhaps the work will help those analyses, but that is not what the seminar is about.

At the beginning of a new seminar, I explain why I have not requested anyone to prepare a case in advance, and ask whether anyone has a patient they want to talk about. At first the group may assume I am asking for someone to come up with the usual kind of presentation, but on the spur of the moment. The operative word, however, is 'want'. I am not requesting someone to provide the seminar with material. I am asking whether anyone has a case which for some reason, understood or not, makes them feel a need, or desire, to see what happens if they talk about it. This means feeling free to talk about it in any way whatsoever. If people do not know how they want to talk about a case, that is fine. They can see what happens anyway, and discover by doing it. A group that is not used to this may feel disconcerted. It can be hard for them to believe that 'presenting a case' is the last thing they are being asked to do, and that there really are no assumptions about the way a patient should be brought to the group. Yet all I am saying is what an analyst tries to convey to a patient in a session: 'You are free to say whatever you want, however you want to. You can make use of this situation in any way that interests you'. The only difference is that I am saying this in the context of a clinical seminar. As in a session, so in the seminar: whatever happens is what happens. The job of the seminar leader is to foster an atmosphere where someone may risk talking about a patient without knowing where it will lead, and to help the seminar group think psychoanalytically about what transpires.

There are no judgements about how well or badly someone performs in such a seminar. This is not a question of refraining from judgement: the idea has no meaning. In the traditional clinical seminar, where everyone is expected to make a similar kind of presentation, comparisons may seem inevitable. With no preconceptions about what should happen, however, and the very idea of 'presenting' being out of place, there is nothing against which to be measured. The seminar group may have the same problem in grasping this, to begin with, as patients may in grasping that analytic sessions are not about trying hard and making a good showing. Members of a clinical seminar may feel the same relief that patients do when they can give up the idea of turning in a good performance. Like an analyst in the clinical situation, the seminar leader has to trust the process and be genuinely willing not to know what is going to happen next. The seminar can then begin to function, as its members come to trust the leader, and themselves, to provide a containing framework within which it feels safe to be spontaneous.

A candidate once found herself talking about a patient differently from how she intended to when she began. What mattered then was not so much what was being described about the patient, but what was happening in the analyst's mind. She thought she knew what she wanted to say, but in fact found she was not sure how to start or where to go next. Quite a lot of information about the patient came through, but in rather random fashion. When I invited the group to reflect on their experience of listening, they turned out to feel puzzled and frustrated. The candidate was disappointed in herself, but she felt safe enough to free-associate about why she wanted to talk about this patient and what seemed to happen in her when she did. She discovered that she was more confused in her thinking about the case than she had been aware of. Her effort at an organised presentation was an attempt to ward this off. She found it a relief to be able to let herself know about her confusion which, it was now plain to see, reflected how the patient was trying to make sense of his own experience against an aura of confusion in himself. In a different kind of seminar, where the candidate would have prepared her presentation in advance and seen to it that she did get it organised successfully, the defence against confusion, shifting between patient and analyst, might perhaps have been recognised and addressed theoretically. The truly psychoanalytic experience, however, for both group and analyst, of being subjected to something baffling, discovering what it was, and finding a way through it, would not have been possible.

Another time someone was eager to speak about a patient but found he could not do so. Every time he tried to say something about the case he got stuck. Again, it was important not to see this as a failure in presenting. On the contrary, as details of the case began to emerge and the group helped the candidate think about what was happening, it turned out that there was a theme in this analysis of active desire being continually blocked and frustrated. The candidate had not been consciously aware how important an issue this was, but the freedom of the seminar made possible his unconscious communication of it.

One candidate did talk about his patient in a very organised way, giving lots of information, very clearly, item after item. As the story went on it became more and more noticeable that the one aspect we were hearing nothing at all about was the patient's family. Then the analyst said, 'And he has a brother … should I stop? I mean, I could go on telling you about him more or less indefinitely'. The group laughed. It was so clear that we had been waiting for the missing bit of the picture. And now here it was, flashed in front of our eyes and immediately taken away again. The group in question was used to this way of working and saw that this peculiar occurrence must be full of meaning.

Someone once commented on how clearly divided the discussion was: half the group was focusing on the patient's neediness and dependence, while the other half was insisting on her hidden aggression and sadism. There seemed to be two different discussions going on at the same time. This participant had heard the case presented in other clinical seminars, but what was happening in this group, she said, enabled her to experience, as she had not done before, the nature of the splitting that made it so hard to keep both aspects of the patient in focus, and bring them together.

These examples may recall the parallel process that sometimes appears in individual supervision, when what is happening in an analysis is reflected not just in the content, but in the tone and feel of the discussion between supervisee and supervisor. What distinguishes this way of conducting clinical seminars is the seminar leader's deliberate facilitating of a free-associative atmosphere, without expectations or judgements, where regardless of what happens, the group will accept it and try to think about it psychoanalytically. This brings the seminar closer to the clinical situation and gives the group a more vivid, lived experience of how analytic understanding works.

Such an approach demands, from participants and seminar leader, what an analytic session demands of both patient and analyst: being open to the unknown and unpredictable. The leader, as well as the group, needs to be like the analyst described by Enid Balint, 'who can tolerate the absence of a consistent story ... and use the muddle' (Balint, E., 1993: 166). In the first two examples in particular, the analysts needed courage to risk themselves, trusting the framework of the group to look after them. In a series of clinical seminars, not only do I not ask anyone to prepare for the first meeting, but I suggest that members always arrive having given as little thought as possible to what they may talk about. Seminar groups vary, unsurprisingly, in how they respond. After initial perplexity, some take to the idea and can play with the freedom it offers. Others find this more difficult. One group could not bear it, and had to decide privately among themselves who was going to present each week. But they seemed, at the same time, to regret what they were doing, as though they sensed they were missing out on something.

Leaders also may find their trust in the process challenged. A candidate in one seminar gave a lively account of his patient. The family background and life history were interesting and a spirited discussion developed. More questions kept being asked and new aspects of the story kept appearing. After some time, I asked the analyst if he had any sessions he wanted to describe. Yes, he did. But the discussion continued. Time was passing and I raised the same question. Yes, there was clinical material. But on went the discussion. I tried again and the same thing happened. The discussion was certainly fascinating, but it was also stopping the analyst describing the sessions he wanted to. Why, though, was he not taking up the opportunities I provided? This was in the early days of my developing this method, and as we neared the end of the seminar time I became anxious. Could one possibly have a valid clinical seminar, especially for candidates in training, with no clinical work described? If we got to the end and I had still not helped the candidate introduce it, what kind of seminar would that be? I commented on the repeated pattern and asked the candidate, not to present his material, but to imagine what would happen if he did. He immediately replied, 'Chaos'. This was the word that came into his mind. All of us, including the analyst himself, were startled. We had been enjoying a fruitful and productive discussion. Now suddenly chaos? Then we saw that the genuine interest of the patient's story must be being used unconsciously to fend off something that both group and analyst were afraid of not being able to deal with. This helped the candidate with regard to his case, but more generally, it was a remarkable psychoanalytic lesson in how positive elements may be made use of for defensive purposes.

The French Psychoanalytic Association's emphasis, in evaluating a possible new member, on the spoken word in a personal encounter, and its refusal of a statement prepared in advance, brought home to me that the aim of psychoanalytic training is the internal development of an analytic identity. It is worth noting, in fact, that what in English is called 'training' is referred to in French as '*formation*'; a word which carries the connotation not of teaching or learning, but of something taking shape. The aim of this method for conducting clinical seminars is not to teach clinical technique as such but, as I said earlier, to encourage participants in the evolution of their identities as analysts.

IX

In the 'Forum on Training' conference, referred to near the beginning of this chapter, I discovered that the concept of analytic identity may be controversial. A speaker in the discussion after my presentation challenged the idea, saying it should be replaced by that of analytic 'competence'. I recognised this as belonging to a viewpoint which takes psychoanalytic practice to be the exercise of a certain set of skills. Analytic training is then seen in terms of teaching candidates the necessary competences for being a psychoanalyst, and qualifying as an analyst becomes the certification of a candidate as having acquired these.

Of course analysts have to be competent and skilful. However, as I mentioned in reference to Freud's analogy of the surgeon, analytic patients do not simply need a correct 'curative' technique to be knowledgeably applied. Clinical psychoanalysis requires technical competence in such things as maintaining the analytic setting, identifying expressions of transference and unconscious connections in a patient's material, and formulating well-timed, appropriate interpretations. But consider, for example, the need for an analyst to let the internal world of a patient impinge on the analyst's internal world. This is not just so that the analyst's countertransference can be observed safely and instructively. The analyst has to allow it to happen in a way that does *not* feel safe. Patients are helped to change by knowing, consciously or unconsciously, that they are with someone who is open unconditionally to whatever impact the patient may have on them. Analysts must be willing to be profoundly and unpredictably affected in relation to issues of their own that their patients stir up in them. In fact, more than willing; grateful to be thus disturbed because this is how their work enlivens them. If a patient has a conviction—and again, I stress that this need not be conscious—that the analysis matters developmentally to the analyst, there is a greater chance that it can matter developmentally to the patient (Parsons, 2000: 35–51). For analysts to make themselves psychically available in this way requires the courage to be vulnerable. Are we to call this a 'competence', as though it were a skill that could be taught? Rather it depends on a deep level of inward awareness, which is not acquired from outside but grows from the inside. The vulnerability can be risked because it is located in a securely founded analytic identity.

Ferenczi (1928) found a quality of emotional sensitivity especially important on the analyst's part, to which he gave the name of 'tact' (see p.188). Freud responded:

> What we undertake in reality is a weighing out, which remains mostly preconscious, of the various reactions that we expect from our interventions, in the process of which it is first and foremost a matter of the quantitative assessment of the dynamic factors in the situation … One should thus divest 'tact' of its mystical character.
>
> (Falzeder and Brabant, 2000: 332)

Fenichel's response was similar:

> The so-called 'tact', which determines when and how a given matter is to be revealed to the patient, seems to me … quite determinable in a systematic way and therefore teachable in a proper degree through comprehension of the definite dynamic changes which take place in the patient during the analysis.
>
> (Fenichel, 1941: 5)

Freud and Fenichel insist on psychoanalysis as an objective discipline, operating quantitatively with empirically validated concepts, so as to exclude subjectivity and intuition. Such a positivist agenda may lead ultimately to the reduction of psychoanalysis to a formalised protocol: 'Manualising psychoanalytic treatments, though challenging, is, we believe, necessary to facilitate research on psychotherapy outcomes and to insure that psychoanalytic approaches survive and flourish in this brave new world of evidence-based treatments' (Diamond, 2010). The idea that psychoanalytic therapy can be reduced to following a set of instructions in a manual, so as to tailor it to the criteria of non–analytic forms of treatment, is the negation of psychoanalysis. On the contrary, as was said in Chapter 12 (pp.195, 204), an analyst seeks to create:

> … a framework that can infuse ordinary human interaction with psychoanalytic awareness, and that can maintain this conjunction, so that the exchange does not stop being either human or analytic.
>
> Whatever an analyst's orientation, it is the essential *humanity* of the *psychoanalytic* process that helps the human being on the couch think it might be possible to change. And the specifically *psychoanalytic* quality of the *human* process that the analyst offers is what provides patients with the means to change.

The challenge is to arrive at systems of training that will help candidates develop this conjunction between the universally human and the specifically psychoanalytic in the form of a professional identity.

X

Psychoanalytic attention to the concept of identity stems from the work of Erik Erikson. In 1956, he published 'The problem of ego identity' (Erikson, 1956), the first of several contributions centred on the idea. A search of the PEP database for articles with titles containing the word 'identity' gives only two results prior to 1956. In the decade after Erikson's article appeared, there were 60, in the following three decades, 70, 73 and 98; with the number rising to 116, in the decade 1996–2005.[1] Not all analysts found the concept theoretically useful (e.g. Thomä, 1983), but it made a powerful and lasting impact.

Erikson's book *Identity: Youth and Crisis* (Erikson, 1968) was a collection, with revisions, of articles he had published since the mid-1950s. In the book's prologue Erikson invokes William James and Sigmund Freud, as figures on whom the concept of identity is founded. He writes:

> As a *subjective sense* of an *invigorating sameness* and *continuity*, what I would call a sense of identity seems to me best described by William James (1920: 199) in a letter to his wife:
> > A man's character is discernible in the mental or moral attitude in which, when it came upon him, he felt himself most deeply active and alive. At such moments there is a voice inside which speaks and says: '*This* is the real me!'
> > (Erikson, 1968: 19)

These words recall the question with which this book began: 'What does it mean to be fully and creatively alive?' Between them, James and Erikson suggest that it means inhabiting one's identity in as full a way as possible. Erikson also quotes from Freud's address in 1926 to the Society of B'nai Brith. Freud said his Jewishness did not include religious or national sentiments.

> But plenty of other things remained over to make the attraction of Jewry and Jews irresistible—many obscure emotional forces, which were the more powerful the less they could be expressed in words, as well as a clear consciousness of inner identity, the safe privacy of a common mental construction.
> (Freud, 1926b: 273f)

Erikson (1968: 21) remarks how hard it is to capture in translation the subtlety of Freud's German. 'The safe privacy of a common mental construction' is a rendering of '*die Heimlichkeit der inneren Konstruktion*'. Again we are taken back to Part I of this book. Identity is linked not only to being fully alive, but also to what is '*heimlich*'. We are 'at home' in our identities. But this *Heimlichkeit* cannot be expressed in words. It is also *unheimlich*. There is something hidden and mysterious about the way we just *know*, deep down inside ourselves, that this is who we really are (see the quotations from Augustine at the foot of p.37).

Where psychoanalytic identity is concerned these passages from James and Freud imply two things. Firstly, to have an analytic identity means that being an analyst makes the analyst feel *alive*. This corresponds to references in this and previous chapters (pp.152, 168), to the need for analysts to find themselves enlivened by the analyses they conduct. Secondly, it means that being an analyst is in harmony with an analyst's inner sense of who they really are. As the passage quoted above from Chapter 12 emphasises, the essentially human quality, and the specifically psychoanalytic quality, of what an analyst does are not separate things which have to be managed in tandem. They need to be absorbed into each other so that the psychoanalytic work and the expression of the analyst's humanity become one and the same thing (Parsons, 2000: 11f).

Erikson (1968: 208) described the sense of identity as 'a conscious sense of individual uniqueness' and 'an unconscious striving for a continuity of experience'. These are what might be called internal connotations of the term, and Erikson's citations of both James and Freud emphasise this subjective, inward aspect of identity. In addition, Freud stressed his awareness of belonging to a social and cultural community. This corresponds to another description of identity by Erikson (1968: 208), in more objective, external terms, as 'solidarity with a group's ideals'. Both these external and internal aspects of identity are relevant when it comes to an analyst's psychoanalytic identity. In 1976, a conference was organised by the IPA on 'The Identity of the Psychoanalyst'. The potential conflict between objective and subjective views of analytic identity revealed itself in the opening contributions by Edward Joseph and Daniel Widlöcher, and went on to permeate the conference. The proceedings were edited into book form by Joseph and Widlöcher (1983), and this volume remains a valuable reference point that is worth discussing in some detail.

For Joseph (1983: 1–21) the identity of the psychoanalyst is that of an objective scientist. It is defined by the acceptance of specific concepts such as unconscious mental processes, resistance, transference and continuity of psychic life, concepts which the analyst puts to use in recognised ways in a specific therapeutic situation. A psychoanalytic identity can be described systematically and explicitly by reference to these theoretical foundations and clinical methods. Being defined objectively in this way allows it, if necessary, to be externally validated.

For Widlöcher (1983: 23–39), on the other hand, an analyst's identity is founded in the subjective experience of the psychoanalytic encounter. Widlöcher places 'the psychoanalytic experience', as he calls it, at the heart both of an analyst's identity and of analytic training. He stresses, as I have done, the need to ensure 'the psychoanalytic candidate's discovery of this experience'. At the same time, he says that 'despite all efforts to conceptualise this experience, by and large it eludes systematisation' (Widlöcher, 1983: 25). It can happen only in the context of the analytic encounter, which therefore becomes fundamental to Widlöcher's thinking about analytic identity. John Klauber picked this up, saying that although there is:

... a technical necessity in enabling analysts to know what to do when confronted with a patient, Widlöcher rightly, in my opinion, stresses the centrality of the encounter. This is where the mystery takes place, in which one human understands another, and where the sense of wonder at the persistence of unconscious patterns is engendered, without which no psychoanalyst can feel at home in his profession.

(Klauber, 1983: 42)

Again, it seems that to be 'at home' as an analyst implies the acceptance of an *unheimlich* mystery.

Klauber observed that this is an 'endopsychic' definition of identity (Klauber, 1983: 43). The word is apt, capturing as it does the interiority of this view of the analyst's identity. However there is also, as Erikson observed, the question of identity in relation to a group of which one is part. This applies to analysts in two distinct ways. Psychoanalysis occupies a position, firstly, in society at large. How analysts identify themselves, and are identified by others, in relation to the social and cultural environment they belong to, are important questions which certain speakers at the conference addressed. Less broadly, analysts belong to the psychoanalytic community, and it was much debated how to conceptualise the identity that analysts share in this respect. The relation of candidates to their training analysts, and the necessity for this to be worked through satisfactorily, figured largely in the discussion. There was agreement that to arrive at an analytic identity of their own, candidates need to identify with their analyst in the first place, but then to relinquish the identification.

We aim, in *all* analyses, to establish lasting identifications, not with the analyst as a transference object, but with his function. To develop an analytic identity, a patient who is also a candidate requires, in fact, an ability to achieve relative freedom from identification with the analyst as object.

(Orgel, 1983: 226)

Erikson had written likewise about identity in general: '*Identity formation*, finally, begins where the usefulness of identification ends. It arises from the selective repudiation and mutual assimilation of childhood identifications and their absorption in a new configuration ...' (Erikson, 1968: 159). Again, this has a familiar ring. The theme of Chapter 6 is the 'selective repudiation' of childhood identifications, with specific regard to the Oedipus complex, and that chapter begins with the same need that Orgel underlined, for analysts to liberate themselves from an identification with their own analysts. But despite agreement about this, the nature of the identity to be arrived at by an analyst was viewed in this conference from very different perspectives.

Widlöcher and Klauber pose an existential question: What does it mean to know, deep down inside myself, that a psychoanalyst is what I am? No systematic answer may be articulated, but going on asking the question brings me closer to an answer I can experience. Joseph might say that I know I am an analyst because I use the concepts that characterise psychoanalysis, and I can say what these are; and because I practise by definite methods that analysts have derived from these concepts. J.-B. Pontalis, in his overview of the conference, found the identity of the psychoanalyst to lie in 'the acceptance of contradictions', and in 'the irreconcilable element that [Freud] himself always recognised as being a specific characteristic of unconscious ideas'. He responded to Joseph's approach by asking: if we require 'a logical and psychological definition of identity, how could we have any idea of the paradox of the psychoanalyst?' (Pontalis, 1983: 281f).

This difference persists, I think, in the contemporary debate couched in terms of 'analytic identity' and 'analytic competences'. If the purpose of psychoanalytic training is to help candidates develop an identity of the sort Joseph has in mind, then what matters will be the acquisition of specifically defined and verifiable competences. If the purpose, on the other hand, is for candidates to develop the kind of identity Widlöcher and Klauber write about, competences of that sort will be less crucial. The fundamental objective will be the interior sense of an analytic identity.

Part III of this book emphasises a distinction between external and internal aspects of psychoanalytic listening and, in Chapter 10, of clinical technique in general. The same distinction shows itself in the contrast between externally objective and 'endopsychic' views of psychoanalytic identity. Discussion of identity and competences should perhaps be reframed in terms of internal and external aspects of a psychoanalyst's identity. The concepts and procedures of psychoanalysis are specific to it in the sense that they are distinct from those of other disciplines. To be rooted in an identity which, by definition, operates at the level of unconscious inner experience, is specifically psychoanalytic in a more fundamental way.

Two sides of a single coin have to be kept in view. How an analyst works clinically is an expression of the person that the analyst is. As Freud put it:

> Psychoanalytic activity is arduous and exacting: it cannot well be handled like a pair of glasses that one puts on for reading and takes off when one goes for a walk. As a rule psychoanalysis possesses a doctor entirely or not at all.
>
> (Freud, 1933: 152f)

Human individuality must not be lost by making technique, or competences, the measure of a psychoanalyst. Nevertheless, this expression of the person operates through the medium of psychoanalytic technique. A sense of existential commitment to being an analyst does not offset the need for long, hard study of theory and clinical method.

XI

Corresponding to the two sides of this coin are certain anxieties to which analytic institutes are liable, and which can lead to either aspect of training being overemphasised. Otto Kernberg's (1996) article, 'Thirty methods to destroy the creativity of psychoanalytic candidates', satirises a tendency towards excessive control of what candidates learn and how they learn it. This dampens candidates' excitement about their training and inhibits a spirit of independent enquiry and exploration. Kernberg offers a fiercely ironic set of recommendations for 'achieving' this. Candidates, for example, should study Freud's writings for the purpose of agreeing with them, but at all costs they must avoid dangerous identification with the originality of Freud's thinking. The article also stresses that the more hierarchical an organisation is, either in its formal structure or in less formal aspects of its culture, the harder it will be for candidates and recently qualified analysts to feel confidence in their own ideas and contributions.

Excessive systematisation of training was also criticised by Siegfried Bernfeld. Born in 1892, Bernfeld was educated in Vienna and became a student of Freud's. He moved to Berlin, emigrated in 1932, and settled eventually in San Francisco. He was esteemed as an outstanding teacher of psychoanalysis, and in November 1952 he presented to the San Francisco Society and Institute a paper entitled 'On psychoanalytic training'. Less than six months later he died, so the paper became, in a sense, his testament. It was highly critical of accepted methods of training, and following Bernfeld's death, it was not rescued for publication until a decade later (Bernfeld, 1962).

Bernfeld compares the current practice of his time with what happened in the early days of psychoanalysis, shedding fascinating light as he does so on the historical evolution of analytic training. He makes the same point as was emphasised earlier in this chapter, that psychoanalysis can only have meaning if there is some awareness of need for it on the part of the analysand. Bernfeld claims that obliging candidates to undergo analysis as a matter of routine, regardless of their emotional state or where they are in the development of their lives, runs counter to psychoanalytic principles. He therefore questions the requirement for every candidate to have a training analysis. The problem is a real one. If there is truly no feeling of personal need there is no point in undergoing an analysis. However, this means there is then no chance to experience the meaning of psychoanalysis. If assessment of an applicant really does not reveal any sense of needing what psychoanalysis has to offer, the applicant should perhaps not be considered suitable for analytic training.

Another focus of Bernfeld's critique was the curriculum that candidates are required to study. Students of any subject, he says, may be taught by a variety of different methods and arrive at the same end point in terms of what they know. How creatively they can then make use of their knowledge, however, depends very much on what kind of experience went into gaining it. Bernfeld contends that for candidates to become analysts who enjoy their work and contribute to their field, what he calls a student-centred learning approach, as opposed to a teacher-centred teaching approach, is essential. This implies a curriculum that encourages exploration and intellectual experiment on the part of candidates, not one that prescribes what they have to learn so as to conform to institutional requirements.

Behind the tendencies criticised by Kernberg and Bernfeld lies a fear, as it is typically expressed, of not 'maintaining standards'. Standards do have to be maintained, of course, but the question is what this means psychoanalytically. From an analytic perspective, what matters is to promote not just the acquisition of knowledge but the development of a candidate's internal autonomy. Marion Milner describes how, during her training, she kept a 'diary of misgivings' about the theory she was trying to learn. When she came to give seminars herself she encouraged candidates to do the same (Milner, 1987: 9). If a curriculum presents candidates with a sequence of requirements like a university syllabus, this reduces the freedom of their learning, and turns qualification into a warranty that they have met the requirements and achieved a requisite level of knowledge. The standards being maintained in this case are not psychoanalytic standards.

In a different training model, which did emphasise individual autonomy rather than organised structure and hierarchies, there might be a corresponding distortion in the opposite direction. Fear of over-controlling candidates, so that they were being 'trained' rather than helped with their 'formation', could lead to 'wild' training, so to speak, which lacked the containing structure to provide a framework for the development of analytic identities. As with the clinical framework, so with training there is a path to tread between rigidity that crushes creativity and a lack of containment that dissipates it.

XII

In this chapter I have tried to give balanced consideration to the advantages and drawbacks of different models of psychoanalytic training. Winston Churchill (1947) famously said of democracy that it is the least bad political system available. Likewise for analytic training, we can only hope for a model that is less unsatisfactory than the alternatives. It may be worthwhile to give some idea, after all this discussion, of what I think such a training might look like.

As regards the question 'What is a training analyst?' I do not believe that any and every analyst, even with a proviso of time spent since qualification, is automatically capable of providing the kind of analytic experience that a candidate needs. I think there does need to be some kind of assessment of analysts who are to be responsible for the transmission of psychoanalysis.

Being a training analyst is more than happening to have a patient who is a candidate. Taking on responsibility for analysts of the next generation is a decision about the evolution of one's identity as an analyst. There are parallels between qualifying as an analyst in the first place, and setting out to analyse prospective analysts. Just as qualifying at the end of training requires assessment of whether a candidate is ready to become a psychoanalyst, so it seems right for there to be an assessment of whether an analyst is ready to become an analyst of future psychoanalysts. The new analyst has analytic patients for the first time; the new training analyst has candidates for the first time. The new analyst must be able to sustain an ethical, professionally appropriate, psychoanalytic framework—admittedly at a basic level—but if that cannot be achieved the candidate should not qualify. The new training analyst is undertaking to transmit psychoanalysis to the next generation. An analyst may be effective therapeutically, but if their clinical work does not embody, as a lived and living experience, a profound sense of what psychoanalysis is, then it does not have what is needed to help candidates develop their own analytic identities.

It is important to see being a training analyst in terms of its function, and not as a designation of superior status. As with qualification, the point is not to identify a cadre of elite individuals but to recognise who is ready, or may not be ready, to take on a certain task. This aspect of the training analyst's role is addressed specifically and interestingly in the Uruguayan model of training (Bernardi, 2008). Around 1974, the Uruguayan Psychoanalytic Association reformed its structures so as to avoid excessive concentration of power in the hands of training analysts. The category of 'training analyst' was replaced by 'member of a group with training functions'. Since then, responsibility for the Association's training has belonged to three groups: those who analyse candidates; those who supervise; and those who teach. In order to carry out any of these functions, a member of the Association has to become part of the relevant group. The groups operate independently of each other. Members wishing to perform one of the training functions are evaluated by the group in question, according to criteria established by the group, and the group decides whether to admit them. Members may belong to just one group, and act only as teachers, supervisors or analysts of candidates. To act in more than one of these capacities, members have to apply separately to the relevant groups. It is also worth noting that membership of a group is not granted for life. It has to be renewed periodically.

If training analysts are regarded as the top of a hierarchy this implicitly devalues the vital contribution of others. For several years, in an institute that followed the Eitingon model, I led a clinical workshop in which training analysts, members who were not training analysts, and candidates, participated together. They all presented clinical cases and the group discussed them. It was refreshing and impressive that candidates could discuss their work with analysts who were much more experienced, without there being any trace of a supervisory atmosphere; and that training analysts could present cases to a group that included candidates, accepting everyone as equal partners in the discussion. Discovering how fruitful for its participants this group could be was among the experiences which gave rise to the method for clinical seminars that I described earlier. Hierarchies scupper such opportunities, and the Uruguayan system seems a creative attempt at retaining the validation of those who are to analyse future psychoanalysts, while avoiding the pitfalls of elitism.

I have outlined the arguments for and against obliging candidates to continue their training analyses until qualification. To my mind such a requirement's advantages, of providing an analytic experience throughout the training and of easing pressure on the supervisory relationship, outweigh its drawbacks. The impingement on the analytic situation must not be disavowed. It needs to be acknowledged within the analysis and dealt with analytically, but given this, I would favour such a regulation.

This position about training analysts and the training analysis reflects the practice of the British Society and other trainings which follow the Eitingon model. It is certainly open to theoretical criticism, and it may give rise to difficult institutional issues. Despite this it seems to me the least unsatisfactory option where the interests of candidates are concerned.

With regard to the curriculum, on the other hand, I am much more in sympathy with the French model.

As a candidate in the British Society I encountered a curriculum typical of trainings that follow the Eitingon model. It consists of a series of seminars, organised by the Curriculum Committee and taught by senior members of the Society. Some are compulsory, such as clinical seminars and the study of Freud's writings, while elsewhere in the curriculum candidates have options from which to choose. Seminars are taught weekly in sets of five or ten, with occasional weekend workshops. To be eligible for qualification a candidate must complete a specified number of these units satisfactorily, which usually takes three or four years. Seminar leaders write reports on the performance of participants, and these are taken into account when a candidate's qualification comes to be considered. In theory, qualified analysts of the Society may also attend these seminars, but this seldom happens in practice. Historically, the pendulum has swung widely between greater and lesser freedom for candidates in their choice of seminars, but broadly speaking, this same structure has existed since the training began.

In the French Psychoanalytic Association, I found something very different. Instead of a designated curriculum, there is a multiplicity of occasions for learning. There are introductory seminars for new candidates, clinical seminars, Freud reading groups, and seminars where authors of the candidates' choice are invited to discuss their work. Members of the Association also lead a number of 'clinical and conceptual research workshops' for candidates, some of which are open to, and are attended by, members as well. These come in all shapes and sizes: weekly; monthly; one weekend a month; four weekends a year … whatever format seems best to the member, or group of members, offering the workshop. Candidates themselves also organise workshops of this sort. These events are under the aegis of the Training Committee, but they are very much the initiative of the individual members or candidates who decide to offer them. In addition, the Association organises several weekend and one-day conferences during the year; some closed, others open to the public. All of the above are regarded as learning opportunities which can form part of a candidate's training.

Candidates have free choice about which of these events to attend, and seminar or workshop leaders do not write reports. There is no notion of progression from one seminar to another, and in the Association's prospectus, the model of a university syllabus is explicitly rejected. The prospectus states simply that it is 'fundamental' that candidates should make 'responsible, sustained and creative' use of the learning opportunities available to them.

Evaluation of this comes at the point of 'ratification' of a candidate's training. Candidates have to analyse two cases under supervision; when both of these have been validated, the candidate is eligible for an extended interview with a senior member which will cover all aspects of the candidate's training and professional life. In the course of this, there will be consideration of whatever seminars, workshops, conferences and other events the candidate has chosen to make part of their psychoanalytic development, and also, no doubt, of what the candidate has chosen not to participate in. Written reports have no place in this. It is, again, the spoken word in a personal encounter. The interviewer reports on the interview to the *Collège des Titulaires*; the body of senior analysts of the Association. If ratification is agreed, the candidate can proceed to a clinical presentation, which leads to election as a member of the Association.

Candidates following a typical Eitingon-based curriculum may learn a lot along the way, and they may find satisfactory avenues of development for themselves, but their learning is structured didactically. There is a delineated channel which candidates have to navigate skilfully enough to come out with a set of good reports at the other end, having conformed to the obligations laid on them. The prescriptive requirements of such a curriculum are not geared to the development of internal responsibility and autonomy. A 'curriculum' of the French type recognises the learning that needs to be done, but gives candidates responsibility for this as part of their developmental experience of being a psychoanalyst in the making.

So, if I am a British conservative where training analysts and the training analysis are concerned, with regard to the curriculum I am a French radical. I would envisage a training where training analysts are those who have wished to take the step of making the analysis of candidates a significant part of their working life, and have been assessed by their peers as having the capacity to do this, and where the training analysis continues until a candidate qualifies. In this training, there would be no set curriculum. It would be the responsibility of candidates to undertake a variety of learning experiences that would contribute to their development as psychoanalysts. The responsibility of the institute would be to provide a sufficient cornucopia of possibilities for this. Candidates might also take advantage of events outside their institute. Public lectures, academic seminars, events organised by other psychoanalytic bodies, conferences in related fields of interest, might all be recognised by the institute as contributing to a candidate's training experience. It would be useful for each candidate to have a senior analyst as consultant and advisor, with whom to discuss strategy in putting together this learning experience: what could be the value of this or that event, which to choose out of various available options, what gaps needed filling, and so on. This would be an important and responsible role. In the French Association, validation of a candidate's training case involves both the candidate and the supervisor being interviewed separately by a panel of senior analysts. At the end of training, in this imagined model, it might be similarly valuable for advisors, as well as candidates, to be interviewed, and to give an account of how candidates had been helped to shape their experience.

In this hypothetical training, ratification of the 'curriculum' that candidates had generated for themselves would take the form of an extended, detailed personal discussion. This would not simply catalogue candidates' activities, but consider all aspects of their training, positive and negative: how they had made use of it, and what, in the end, it had meant to them. The ratification interview should be a powerful learning experience in itself, and how candidates were able to respond to such a discussion would reveal much about the adequacy of their training experience.

XIII

Regardless of particular training models, the important thing in the end is what analysts do with their experience as candidates in the rest of their analytic lives. In this respect, psychoanalytic training resembles the experience of analysis itself. In Klauber's words, already quoted in Chapter 9 (p.144), 'psychoanalysis is a long process in which what happens after the patient has left the psychoanalyst's consulting room for the last time is more important than what happens during the analysis' (Klauber, 1981: xvi). More striking still in its specificity is César Botella's comment on the end of an analysis.

> [The patient] had acquired that permanent ongoing process constituted by every well resolved analytic termination, giving access to the structural incompletion characteristic of so-called normal psychic life which, dominated by the binding force of Eros, tends constantly towards the creation of wider psychic networks.
>
> (Botella, 2011)

What is desirable for any patient becomes crucial when the patient is a psychoanalyst in the making.

> We hope and believe that the stimuli received in the candidate's own analysis will not cease to act upon him when that analysis ends, that the processes of ego-transformation will go on of their own accord and that he will bring his new insight to bear upon all his subsequent

experience. This does indeed happen and, just in so far as it happens, it qualifies the candidate who has been analysed to become an analyst.

(Freud, 1937b: 402)[2]

Formation of an analytic identity is not completed by the end of training, and the training experience as a whole needs to go on growing inside an analyst after it is over.

> The day that one qualifies as an analyst, the analyst that one is *going to be* is a mystery. Ten years later, we may just about be able to look back and discern the shape of the rough beast—ourselves as analysts in embryo—as it slouches along under the months and years until, its hour come round at last, there is some clearer sense of ourselves as analysts. The process of doing analysis has slowly given birth to an identity which we now more or less recognise as an analyst, or at least the identity which we have become, and are still becoming, which for us approximates to the notion of 'being an analyst'. This may be very different from that which we long ago had visualised or hoped for.
>
> (Coltart, 1992: 2f)[3]

A clearer sense but, as Nina Coltart indicates, not a finished one, even after ten years. Most analysts would hope that the individual quality of their identity as an analyst will go on evolving and developing to the end of their working lives.

When I emphasised earlier the necessity for analysts in the making to be aware of really needing their analyses, I said that this should be met by the future analyst's analyst having a deeply internalised living awareness of what psychoanalysis is. Another expression of this would be that an analyst in formation—that is to say, someone whose analytic identity is taking shape—needs to have as an analyst someone whose own analytic identity is well-formed and established, but remains continually alive and evolving. A touchstone of good training, to my mind, is that it should help candidates to become analysts of whom this will be true.

Notes

1 The PEP database (The Psychoanalytic Electronic Publishing Digital Archive; www.p-e-p.org) is a comprehensive digital archive containing virtually all significant psychoanalytic journals from their origins up to the present, the *Standard Edition* of Freud, his Collected Works in German, and many other psychoanalytic books.

2 I have quoted the translation published originally in the *International Journal of Psychoanalysis*, which captures better than the *Standard Edition* the meaning that I want to bring out.

3 Coltart's paper where this passage occurs was based on W.B. Yeats' poem 'The Second Coming' (Yeats, 1950: 210f); hence her allusion to the rough, slouching beast, whose hour comes round at last.

BIBLIOGRAPHY

Abraham, K. (1973) *A Short Study of the Development of the Libido, Viewed in the Light of Mental Disorders* [1924], in *Selected Papers on Psycho-Analysis*, London: Hogarth, pp. 418–501.

Abrams, S. (1987) 'The psychoanalytic process: a schematic model', *International Journal of Psychoanalysis*, 68: 441–52.

Ahlskog, G. (1983) 'Review of Spence, D. (1982) *Narrative Truth and Historical Truth: Meaning and Interpretation in Psychoanalysis*, New York and London: Norton', *Psychoanalytic Review*, 70: 290–93.

Albano, C. (2008) 'The uncanny: A dimension of contemporary art', *ESSE Arts and Opinions*, 62, Fear II: 5–13.

Alexander, F. (1950) 'Analysis of the therapeutic factors in psychoanalytic treatment', *Psychoanalytic Quarterly*, 19: 482–500.

Alexander, F. and French, T.M. (1946) *Psychoanalytic Therapy: Principles and Applications*, New York: Ronald.

Alizade, A.M. (2002) *Lo Positivo en Psicoanálisis: Implicancias Teórico-Técnicas*, Chapter 7. Buenos Aires: Lumen.

Allende, I. (1995) *Paula*, London: Harper Collins.

Anderson, R. (2009) 'Moving on from the suburbs', *Psychoanalytic Inquiry*, 29: 264–76.

Anzieu, D. (1986) *Freud's Self-Analysis*, London: Hogarth.

Archer, J. and Lloyd, B. (2002) *Sex and Gender*, 2nd edition, Cambridge University Press.

Ariès, P. (1962) *Centuries of Childhood*, London: Cape.

Arlow, J. (1986) 'Discussion of papers by Dr McDougall and Dr Glasser'. Panel on identification in the perversions, *International Journal of Psychoanalysis*, 67: 245–50.

Arlow, J. and Brenner, C. (1990) 'The psychoanalytic process', *Psychoanalytic Quarterly*, 59: 678–92.

Bacal, H. (1997) 'The analyst's subjectivity—how it can illuminate the analysand's experience: commentary on Susan H. Sands' paper', *Psychoanalytic Dialogues*, 7: 669–81.

——(1998) *Optimal Responsiveness: How Therapists Heal their Patients*, Northvale: Aronson.

Bach, S. (1994) *The Language of Perversion and the Language of Love*, Northvale: Aronson.

Bacon, F. (1863) *Novum Organum* [1620], Spedding, J., Ellis, R.L. and Heath, D.D. (trans.), Boston: Taggard and Thompson.

Baker, R. (1993) 'The patient's discovery of the psychoanalyst as a new object', *International Journal of Psychoanalysis*, 74: 1223–33.

Baldwin, J. (1895) *Mental Development in the Child and the Race: Methods and Processes*, New York: MacMillan.

Balint, E. (1993) *Before I was I: Psychoanalysis and the Imagination*, Mitchell, J. and Parsons, M. (eds), London and New York: Free Association and Guilford.

Balint, M. (1968) *The Basic Fault: Therapeutic Aspects of Regression*, London: Tavistock.

Barrett, M. (2001) *Crossing: Reclaiming the Landscape of our Lives*, London: Darton, Longman and Todd.

Berger, P.L. and Luckmann, T. (1971) *The Social Construction of Reality: A Treatise in the Sociology of Knowledge*, London: Allen Lane.

Berlin, I. (1958) *Two Concepts of Liberty*, Oxford University Press.

Bernardi, R. (1989) 'The role of paradigmatic determinants in psychoanalytic understanding', *International Journal of Psychoanalysis*, 70: 341–57.

——(2008) 'Letter from Uruguay', *International Journal of Psychoanalysis*, 89: 233–240.

Bernfeld, S. (1962) 'On psychoanalytic training', *Psychoanalytic Quarterly*, 31: 453–82.

Bettelheim, B. (1983) *Freud and Man's Soul*, London: Chatto and Windus, Hogarth.

Bion, W. [1962] *Learning from Experience*, in *Seven Servants*.

——[1963] *Elements of Psychoanalysis*, in *Seven Servants*.

——[1967] 'Notes on memory and desire', reprinted in *Cogitations*, pp. 380–85.

——[1970] *Attention and Interpretation: A Scientific Approach to Insight in Psycho-Analysis and Groups*, in *Seven Servants*.

——(1977) *Seven Servants*, New York: Aronson.

——(1994), Bion, F. (ed.), *Cogitations*, London: Karnac.

Blanchot, M. (1982) 'Orpheus' gaze', in Josipovici, J. (ed.), Rabinovitch, S. (trans.), *The Sirens' Song: Selected Essays by Maurice Blanchot*, Brighton: Harvester, pp. 177–81.

Bluck, S., Alea, N., Haberman, T. and Rubin, D.C. (2005) 'A tale of three functions: The self-reported uses of autobiographical memory', *Social Cognition*, 23: 91–117.

Boghossian, P. (2006) *Fear of Knowledge: Against Relativism and Constructivism*, Oxford University Press.

Bollas, C. (1987) *The Shadow of the Object: Psychoanalysis of the Unthought Known*, London: Free Association.

——(1989) *Forces of Destiny: Psychoanalysis and Human Idiom*, London: Free Association.

——(1992) *Being a Character: Psychoanalysis and Self Experience*, New York: Hill and Wang.

——(1999) *The Mystery of Things*, London: Routledge.

——(2002) *Free Association*, Cambridge: Icon.

Botella, C. (2011) 'Analysis of an early trauma', unpublished paper presented to the British Psychoanalytical Society, 27th October, 2011.

Botella, C. and Botella, S. (2005) *The Work of Psychic Figurability*, trans. Andrew Weller. London: Brunner-Routledge.

Bowie, M. (1979) 'Jacques Lacan', in *Structuralism and Since*, Sturrock, J. (ed.), Oxford University Press, pp. 116–53.

Boyden, J. (1990) 'Childhood and the policy makers: a comparative perspective on the globalisation of childhood', in James, A. and Prout, A. (eds) *Constructing and Reconstructing Childhood: Contemporary Issues in the Sociological Study of Childhood*, London: Falmer, pp. 190–229.

Brenman, E. (1994) 'Discussion of paper by Enid Balint Edmonds', *Bulletin of the British Psychoanalytical Society*, 2: 9f.

——(2006) *Recovery of the Lost Good Object*, London: Routledge.

Brenman Pick, I. (1985) 'Working through in the countertransference', *International Journal of Psychoanalysis*, 66: 157–66.

Breuer, J. and Freud S. [1893–1895] *Studies on Hysteria*, in Strachey, J. (ed.) (1950–1974), *The Standard Edition of the Complete Psychological Works of Sigmund Freud*, London: Hogarth, vol. 2.

Bridge, M. (1998) 'Why five times a week? A defence of the British model', paper presented at the German Psychoanalytic Association Candidates Day (Psa-Info, vol. 50).

——(2006) 'Moving out: Disruption and repair to the internal setting', published in 2013, *British Journal of Psychotherapy*, 29, 4: 481–93.

Britton, R. (2003) *Sex, Death and the Superego*, London: Karnac.

Buber, M. (1956) *The Legend of the Baal-Shem,* London: East and West Library.

Campanile, P. (2012), 'On the origins of the "Eitingon Model" of psychoanalytic training', Carmody, C. (trans.), *Italian Psychoanalytic Annual*, 6: 91–109.

Carroll, L. (1871) *Through the Looking-Glass, and what Alice found there*, London: Macmillan.

Castle, T. (1995) *The Female Thermometer: Eighteenth-Century Culture and the Invention of the Uncanny*, Oxford University Press.

Chasseguet-Smirgel, J. (1985) *Creativity and Perversion*, London: Free Association.

Chodorow, N. (2003) 'Uncertainty and indeterminacy in psychoanalytic theory and practice', *Common Knowledge*, 9: 463–87.

——(2004) 'The American Independent tradition: Loewald, Erikson and the (possible) rise of interpersonal ego-psychology', *Psychoanalytic Dialogues*, 14: 207–32.

Churcher, J. (2005) 'Keeping the psychoanalytic setting in mind', unpublished paper presented to the Annual Conference of the Lancaster Psychotherapy Clinic, in collaboration with the Tavistock Clinic, St Martin's College, Lancaster (9th September, 2005).

Churchill, W. (1947) The Official Report, House of Commons (5th Series), 11th November, 1947, vol. 444, cc. 206–07.

Coburn, K. (ed.) (1962) *The Notebooks of Samuel Taylor Coleridge*, vol. 2, part 1 (text), part 2 (notes), London: Routledge and Kegan Paul.

Cohen, J. (2010) 'Turning to stone: creativity and silence in psychoanalysis and art', *Bulletin of the British Psychoanalytical Society*, 46, 8: 1–9.

Coltart, N. (1992) *Slouching towards Bethlehem … and Further Psychoanalytic Explorations*, London: Free Association Books.

Conway, M.A. (1996) 'Autobiographical knowledge and autobiographical memories', in Rubin, D.C. (ed.) *Remembering our Past: Studies in Autobiographical Memory*, Cambridge: Cambridge University Press, pp. 67–93.

Conway, M.A. and Pleydell-Pearce, C.W. (2000) 'The construction of autobiographical memories in the self-memory system', *Psychological Review*, 107: 261–88.

Conway, M.A. and Rubin, D.C. (1993) 'The structure of autobiographical memory', in Collins, A.F. *et al.* (eds), *Theories of Memory*, Hillsdale, NJ: Erlbaum, pp. 103–37.

Cottingham, J. (1998) *Philosophy and the Good Life: Reason and the Passions in Greek, Cartesian and Psychoanalytic Ethics*, Cambridge: Cambridge University Press.

Damasio, A.R. (1989) 'Time-locked multi-regional retroactivation: a systems-level proposal for the neural substrates of recall and recognition', *Cognition*, 33: 25–62.

Damasio, A.R. and Damasio, H. (1994) 'Cortical systems for retrieval of conrete knowledge: the convergence zone framework', in Koch, C. and Davis, J.L. (eds), *Large-scale Neuronal Theories of the Brain*. Cambridge, MA: MIT Press, pp. 61–74.

Darwin, C. (1859) *On the Origin of Species by Means of Natural Selection, or the Preservation of Favoured Races in the Struggle for Life*, London: John Murray.

——(1871) *The Descent of Man, and Selection in Relation to Sex*, London: John Murray.

Davies, L. (2011) 'Orpheus, Eurydice, Blanchot', *Poetry Wales*, 47, 1: 27–30.

De M'Uzan, M. (1978) 'If I were dead', *International Review of Psychoanalysis*, 5: 485–90.

Diamond, D. (2010) 'Acceptance remarks for the JAPA Award', *The American Psychoanalyst*, 44, 3: 17.

Dufresne, R. (1992) 'The lady with the raincoat and the little button: the turning point of an analysis—Reflections on desire, listening, resonance, and the birth of a mutative interpretation' *Psychoanalytic Inquiry*, 12: 314–67.

Eagle, M.N. (1984) *Recent Developments in Psychoanalysis: A Critical Evaluation*, Cambridge, MA: Harvard University Press.

Eigen, M. (1996) *Psychic Deadness*, Northvale, New Jersey: Aronson.

Eissler, K.R. (1953) 'The effect of the structure of the ego on psychoanalytic technique', *Journal of the American Psychoanalytic Association*, 1: 104–43.

Eitingon, M. (1923) 'Report of the Berlin Psycho-Analytical Policlinic', *Bulletin of the International Psycho-Analytical Association*, 4: 254–69.

Eliot, T.S. (1920) 'Tradition and the individual talent', in *The Sacred Wood*, London: Methuen, pp. 42–53.

——(1969a) 'Burnt Norton' [1935], in *The Complete Poems and Plays of T.S. Eliot*, London: Faber & Faber, pp. 171–76.

——(1969b) 'East Coker' [1940], in *The Complete Poems and Plays of T.S. Eliot*, London: Faber & Faber, pp. 177–83.

Eng, E. (1984) 'Coleridge's "psycho-analytical understanding" and Freud's "psychoanalysis"', *International Review of Psychoanalysis*, 11: 463–66.

Erikson, E. (1950) *Childhood and Society*, New York: Norton.

——(1956) 'The problem of ego identity', *Journal of the American Psychoanalytic Association*, 4: 56–121.

——(1958) *Young Man Luther*, New York: Norton.

——(1968) *Identity: Youth and Crisis*, New York: Norton.

Eyre, S. and Page, R. (eds) (2008) *The New Uncanny: Tales of Unease*, UK: Comma.

Fairbairn, W.R.D. (1952) *Psychoanalytic Studies of the Personality*, London: Routledge and Kegan Paul.

Falzeder, E. and Brabant, E. (eds) (2000) *The Correspondence of Sigmund Freud and Sándor Ferenczi, vol. 3, 1920–1933*, Cambridge, MA: Harvard.

Faulkner, W. (1953) *Requiem for a Nun*, London: Chatto and Windus.

Fenichel, O. (1941) *Problems of Psychoanalytic Technique*, New York: Psychoanalytic Quarterly Inc.

——(1946) *The Psychoanalytic Theory of Neurosis*, London: Routledge & Kegan Paul.

Ferenczi, S. [1919] 'On the technique of psychoanalysis', in *Further Contributions*, pp. 177–89.

——[1928] 'The elasticity of psychoanalytic technique', in *Final Contributions*, pp. 87–101.

——(1950) *Further Contributions to the Theory and Technique of PsychoAnalysis*, 2nd edition, London: Hogarth.

——(1955) Balint, M. (ed.), *Final Contributions to the Problems and Methods of PsychoAnalysis*, London: Hogarth.

——(1988) *The Clinical Diary of Sándor Ferenczi*, Dupont, J. (ed.), Cambridge, MA: Harvard University Press.

Fonagy, P. (1999) 'Memory and therapeutic action', *International Journal of Psychoanalysis*, 80: 215–23.

Ford, J.C., Addis, D.R. and Giovanello, K.S. (2011) 'Differential neural activity during search of specific and general autobiographical memories elicited by musical cues', *Neuropsychologia*, 49: 2514–26. doi: 10.1016/j.neuropsychologia. 2011.04.032

François-Poncet, C.-M. (2009) 'The French model of psychoanalytic training: ethical conflicts', *International Journal of Psychoanalysis*, 90: 1419–33.

Freud, S. (1950–1974) in Strachey, J. (ed.), *The Standard Edition of the Complete Psychological Works of Sigmund Freud*, Volumes 1–24, London: Hogarth.

——[1896a] 'Further remarks on the neuro-psychoses of defence', *Standard Edition*, vol. 3, pp. 162–85.

——[1896b] 'The aetiology of hysteria', *Standard Edition*, vol. 3, pp. 191–221.

——[1899] 'On screen memories', *Standard Edition*, vol. 3, pp. 303–22.

——[1900] *The Interpretation of Dreams, Standard Edition*, vols. 4–5.

——[1901a] *The Psychopathology of Everyday Life, Standard Edition*, vol. 6.

——[1901b] *Fragment of an Analysis of a Case of Hysteria, Standard Edition*, vol. 7, pp. 7–122.

——[1905] *Three Essays on the Theory of Sexuality, Standard Edition*, vol. 7, pp. 130–243.

——[1909] *Notes upon a Case of Obsessional Neurosis, Standard Edition*, vol. 10, pp. 155–318.

——[1910a] 'Five Lectures on psycho-analysis', *Standard Edition*, vol. 11, pp. 9–55.

——[1910b] 'The future prospects of psycho-analytic therapy', *Standard Edition*, vol. 11, pp. 141–51.

——[1911] 'Formulations on the two principles of mental functioning', *Standard Edition*, vol. 12, pp. 218–26.

——[1912a] 'The dynamics of transference', *Standard Edition*, vol. 12, pp. 99–108.

——[1912b] 'Recommendations to physicians practising psychoanalysis', *Standard Edition*, vol. 12, pp. 111–20.

——[1913] 'On beginning the treatment (further recommendations on the technique of psychoanalysis I)', *Standard Edition*, vol. 12, pp. 123–44.

——[1914a] 'Remembering, repeating and working through (further recommendations on the technique of psychoanalysis II)', *Standard Edition*, vol. 12, pp. 147–56.

——[1914b] 'The *Moses* of Michelangelo', *Standard Edition*, vol. 13, pp. 211–38.

——[1914c] 'On narcissism: an introduction', *Standard Edition*, vol. 14, pp. 73–102.

——[1915a] 'Instincts and their vicissitudes', *Standard Edition*, vol. 14, pp. 117–40.

——[1915b] 'The unconscious', *Standard Edition*, vol. 14, pp. 166–204.

——[1916–17] *Introductory Lectures on Psycho-Analysis*, Standard Edition, vols. 15–16.

——[1918] *From the History of an Infantile Neurosis*, Standard Edition, vol. 17, pp. 7–122.

——[1919a] "'A child is being beaten": a contribution to the study of the origin of sexual perversions', Standard Edition, vol. 17, pp. 179–204.

——[1919b] 'The uncanny', Standard Edition, vol. 17, pp. 219–56.

——[1920] *Beyond the Pleasure Principle*, Standard Edition, vol. 18, pp. 7–64.

——[1923a] 'Two encyclopaedia articles', Standard Edition, vol. 18, pp. 235–59.

——[1923b] *The Ego and the Id*, Standard Edition, vol. 19, pp. 12–59.

——[1923c] 'Remarks on the theory and practice of dream-interpretation', Standard Edition, vol. 19, pp. 109–21.

——[1924] 'The dissolution of the Oedipus complex', Standard Edition, vol. 19, pp. 173–9.

——[1925a] 'A Note upon the "Mystic Writing Pad"', Standard Edition, vol. 19, pp. 227–32.

——[1925b] 'An autobiographical study', Standard Edition, vol. 20, pp. 7–74.

——[1926a] 'The question of lay analysis', Standard Edition, vol. 20, pp. 183–250.

——[1926b] 'Address to the Society of B'nai Brith', Standard Edition, vol. 20, pp. 273f.

——[1927] 'The future of an illusion', Standard Edition, vol. 21, pp. 5–56.

——[1928] 'Dostoevsky and parricide', Standard Edition, vol. 21, pp. 177–94.

——[1930] *Civilisation and its Discontents*, Standard Edition, vol. 21, pp. 64–145.

——[1933] *New Introductory Lectures on Psychoanalysis*, Standard Edition, vol. 22: pp. 5–182.

——[1937a] 'Constructions in analysis', Standard Edition, vol. 23, pp. 257–69.

——(1937b) 'Analysis terminable and interminable', *International Journal of Psychoanalysis*, 18: 373–405.

——(1954) Bonaparte, M., Freud, A. and Kris, E. (eds) *The Origins of Psychoanalysis: Letters to Wilhem Fliess, Drafts and Notes, 1887–1902*, London: Imago.

——(1998) *Bemerkungen zur Theorie und Praxis der Traumdeutung* [1922], *Gesammelte Werke, Chronologisch Geordnet*, London: Imago, vol. 13, pp. 301–14.

Fromm, E. (1941) *The Fear of Freedom*, New York: Farrar and Rinehart.

Gardner, M. (ed.) (1972) *The Wolf-Man and Sigmund Freud*, London: Hogarth.

Gillespie, W.H. [1956] 'The general theory of sexual perversion', reprinted in *Life, Sex and Death*, pp. 81–92.

——[1964] 'The psychoanalytic theory of sexual deviation with special reference to fetishism', in *Life, Sex and Death*, pp. 101–18.

——(1995) Sinason, M. (ed.), *Life, Sex and Death: Selected Writings of William Gilliespie*, London: Routledge.

Glasser, M. (1986) 'Identification and its vicissitudes as observed in the perversions', *International Journal of Psychoanalysis*, 67: 9–16.

Glover, E. (1933) 'The relation of perversion-formation to the development of reality-sense' *International Journal of Psychoanalysis*, 14: 486–504.

——(1937) 'Contribution to symposium on the theory of the therapeutic results of psycho-analysis', *International Journal of Psychoanalysis*, 18: 125–32.

Goldsworthy, A. (1989) *Touching North*, Edinburgh: Graeme Murray.

——(1990) *A Collaboration with Nature*, New York: Abrams.

Green, A. (1986) *On Private Madness*, London: Hogarth.

——(1999) *The Work of the Negative*, Weller, A. (trans.), London: Free Association.

——(2000) 'The central phobic position: A new formulation of the free association method', *International Journal of Psychoanalysis*, 81: 429–51.

Greenson, R. (1965) 'The working alliance and the transference neurosis', *Psychoanalytic Quarterly*, 34: 155–81.

——(1967) *The Technique and Practice of PsychoAnalysis*, London: Hogarth.

——(1968) 'Dis-identifying from mother: Its special importance for the boy', *International Journal of Psychoanalysis*, 49: 370–74.

Grimm, J. and W. (1877) *Deutsches Wörterbuch*, Leipzig.

Grossman, D. (1990) *See under: Love*, Rosenberg, B., (trans.), London: Jonathan Cape.

Grotstein, J. (2007) *A Beam of Intense Darkness: Wilfred Bion's Legacy to Psychoanalysis*, London: Karnac.

Gunn, T. (1993) *Collected Poems*, London: Faber and Faber.

Gurdjieff, G.I. (1963) *Meetings with Remarkable Men*, London: Routledge & Kegan Paul.

Hacking, I. (1999) *The Social Construction of What?* Cambridge, MA: Harvard University Press.

Hart, M. (2007) 'Visualising the mind: looking at Titian's *The Flaying of Marsyas*', *British Journal of Psychotherapy*, 23: 267–80.

Hartmann, H. (1964) 'Psychoanalysis and developmental psychology' [1950], in *Essays on Ego Psychology*, New York: International Universities Press, pp. 99–112.

Hass, R. (1987) 'Looking for Rilke', in Mitchell, S. (ed. and trans.), *The Selected Poetry of Rainer Maria Rilke*, London: Picador, pp. xi–xliv.

Heaney, S. (1996) *The Spirit Level*, London: Faber.

——(2002) *Finders Keepers: Selected Prose 1971–2001*, London: Faber.

Hertz, N. (1985) 'Freud and the Sandman', in *The End of the Line*, New York: Columbia University Press, pp. 97–121.

Hildebrand, P. (1988) 'The other side of the wall: a psychoanalytic study of creativity in later life', *International Review of Psychoanalysis*, 15: 353–63.

Hinshelwood, R.D. (1997) 'The elusive concept of "internal objects" (1934–1943): its role in the formation of the Klein group', *International Journal of Psychoanalysis*, 78: 877–97.

Hockey, J. and James, A. (1993) *Growing Up and Growing Old*, London: Sage.

Hoffmann, E.T.A. (1817) '*Der Sandmann*', in *Nachtstücke: Herausgegeben von dem Verfasser der Fantasiestücke in Callots Manier*, Vol. I, Berlin: Realschulbuchhandlung.

Holland, A.C. and Kensinger, E.A. (2010) 'Emotion and autobiographical memory', *Physics of Life Reviews*, 7: 88–131. doi: 10.1016/j.plrev.2010.01.006

Holt, R.R. (1972) 'Freud's mechanistic and humanistic images of man', *Psychoanalysis and Contemporary Science*, 1: 3–24.

Hopkins, B. (1997) 'Winnicott and the capacity to believe', *International Journal of Psychoanalysis*, 78: 485–97.

Ickis, M. (1959) *The Standard Book of Quiltmaking and Collecting*, New York: Dover.

Jacobs, T.J. (1999) 'Countertransference past and present: a review of the concept', *International Journal of Psychoanalysis*, 80: 575–94.

James, A., Jenks, C. and Prout, A. (1998) *Theorizing Childhood*, Cambridge: Polity.

James, A. and Prout, A. (eds) (1990) *Constructing and Reconstructing Childhood: Contemporary Issues in the Sociological Study of Childhood*, London: Falmer.

James, M. (1980) 'Are there concepts essential to the Independent Group?', *Bulletin of the British Psychoanalytical Society*, 6: 13–30.

James, W. (1920) *The Letters of William James*, James, H. (ed.), Boston, USA: Atlantic Monthly Press.

Jaques, E. (1965) 'Death and the mid-life crisis', *International Journal of Psychoanalysis*, 46: 502–14.

Johns, J. (2009) 'How do you get where you want to be when you don't know where you want to be?', *Psychoanalytic Inquiry*, 29: 223–35.

Johns, M. (2002) 'Identification and dis-identification in the development of sexual identity', in Trowell, J. and Etchegoyen, A. (eds), *The Importance of Fathers: A Psychoanalytic Re-evaluation*, London: Routledge, pp. 186–202.

Jones, E. (1954) *Sigmund Freud: Life and Work*, vol. 1, London: Hogarth.

Joseph, E. (1983) 'Identity of a psychoanalyst', in Joseph, E. and Widlöcher, D. (eds) *The Identity of the Psychoanalyst*, New York: International Universities Press, pp. 1–21.

Joseph, E. and Widlöcher, D. (eds) (1983) *The Identity of the Psychoanalyst*, New York: International Universities Press.

Kahn, L. (2012) '*Présentation du dossier*', in *Le Fil d'Œdipe, et Recherches sur l'Histoire de la Formation et de l'Enseignement: Annuel de l'APF 2012*, Paris: Presses Universitaires de France, pp. 115–118.

Kalvar, R. (2011) Instruction #48, 26th August, 2011, Street Photography Now Project, www.streetphotographynowproject.wordpress.com [accessed 24 March 2014].

Kennedy, R. (2013), *The Psychic Home: Psychoanalysis and the Human Soul*, London: Routledge.

Kermode, F. (2010) 'Eliot and the shudder', *London Review of Books*, 32, 9: 13–16.

Kernberg, O. (1995) *Love Relations*. New Haven, CT: Yale University Press.

——(1996) 'Thirty methods to destroy the creativity of psychoanalytic candidates', *International Journal of Psychoanalysis*, 77: 1031–40.

Khan, M. (1979) *Alienation in Perversions*, London: Hogarth.

King, P. (1978) 'Affective response of the analyst to the patient's communications', *International Journal of Psychoanalysis*, 59: 329–34.

——(1983) 'Identity crises: splits or compromises—adaptive or maladaptive', in Joseph, E. and Widlöcher, D. (eds) *The Identity of the Psychoanalyst*, New York: International Universities Press, pp. 181–94.

King, P. and Steiner, R. (1991) *The Freud-Klein Controversies 1941–45*, London: Routledge.

Kitto, H.D.F. (1960) *Form and Meaning in Drama*, London: Methuen, University Paperbacks.

Klauber, J. (1981) *Difficulties in the Analytic Encounter*, New York: Aronson.

——(1983) 'The identity of the psychoanalyst', in Joseph, E. and Widlöcher, D. (eds), *The Identity of the Psychoanalyst*, New York: International Universities Press, pp. 41–50.

Klein, M. (1975) *Envy and Gratitude* [1957], in *The Writings of Melanie Klein*, vol. 3, London: Hogarth, pp. 176–235.

——(1992) 'Early stages of the Oedipus conflict' [1928], in *Love, Guilt, Reparation and Other Works, 1921–1945*, London: Hogarth, pp.186–198.

——(1992) 'A contribution to the psychogenesis of manic-depressive states' [1935], in *Love, Guilt, Reparation and Other Works, 1921–1945*, London: Hogarth, pp. 262–89.

Klinger, F.M. (1878–80) *Theater*, vols. 1–8, Stuttgart: Cotta.

Kohon, G. (ed.) (1986) *The British School of Psychoanalysis: The Independent Tradition*, London: Free Association.

——(2011) 'Kafka at the borders', *Bulletin of the British Psychoanalytical Society*, 47, 1: 50–60.

Kohut, H. (1971) *The Analysis of the Self*, London: Hogarth.

Lacan, J. (1977) *The Four Fundamental Concepts of Psychoanalysis*, London: Hogarth.

——(2006) 'The function and field of speech and language in psychoanalysis' [lecture delivered in 1953], reprinted in Fink, B. (trans.), *Ecrits*, New York: Norton, pp. 197–268.

Lang, A. (1897) *The Book of Dreams and Ghosts*, London: Longmans, Green & Co.

Latour, B. (2005) *Reassembling the Social: An Introduction to Actor-Network Theory*, Oxford University Press.

Latour, B. and Woolgar, S. (1979) *Laboratory Life: the Social Construction of Scientific Facts*, Beverley Hills: Sage.

Laufer, E. (2009) 'Now and then', *Psychoanalytic Inquiry*, 29: 277–87.

Lear, J. (2003) *Therapeutic Action: An Earnest Plea for Irony*, New York: Other Press.

Lehrer, J. (2007) *Proust was a Neuroscientist*, Boston and New York: Houghton Mifflin.

Levine, H. (1994) 'The analyst's participation in the analytic process', *International Journal of Psychoanalysis*, 75: 665–76.

Lewin, B. (1955) 'Dream psychology and the analytic situation', *Psychoanalytic Quarterly*, 24: 169–99.

Lichtenstein, H. [1961] 'Identity and Sexuality', reprinted in *The Dilemma of Human Identity*, pp. 49–122.

——[1964] 'Narcissism and primary identity', reprinted in *The Dilemma of Human Identity*, pp. 207–21.

——(1983) *The Dilemma of Human Identity*, New York: Aronson

Limentani, A. (1995) 'Creativity and the third age', *International Journal of Psychoanalysis*, 76: 825–33.

Little, M. (1985) 'Winnicott working in areas where psychotic anxieties predominate: a personal record', *Free Associations*, 3: 9–42.

Locke, J. (1690) *An Essay Concerning Human Understanding*, London.

Loewald, H. [1960] 'On the therapeutic action of psychoanalysis', in *Papers on Psychoanalysis*, pp. 221–56.

——[1962] 'Superego and time', in *Papers on Psychoanalysis*, pp. 43–52.

——[1971] 'Discussion of "The regulatory principles of mental functioning" by Max Schur', in *Papers on Psychoanalysis*, pp. 58–68.

——[1975] 'Psychoanalysis as an art and the fantasy character of the psychoanalytic situation', in *Papers on Psychoanalysis*, pp. 352–71.

——[1979] 'The waning of the Oedipus complex', in *Papers on Psychoanalysis*, pp. 384–404.

——(1980) *Papers on Psychoanalysis*, New Haven: Yale University Press.

——(1985) 'Oedipus complex and development of self', *Psychoanalytic Quarterly*, 54: 435–43.

Loftus, E.F. and Loftus, G.R. (1980) 'On the permanence of stored information in the human brain', *American Psychologist*, 35: 409–20.

Mannoni, O. (1988) '*La désidentification*', in *Un si vif étonnement*, Paris: Editions du Seuil, pp. 119–136

McDougall, J. (1986) 'Identifications, neoneeds and neosexualities', *International Journal of Psychoanalysis*, 67: 19–30.

McGilchrist, I. (2009) *The Master and his Emissary: The Divided Brain and the Making of the Western World*, New Haven and London: Yale University Press.

McLaughlin, J. (1981) 'Transference, psychic reality, and countertransference', *Psychoanalytic Quarterly*, 50: 639–64, reprinted in *The Healer's Bent*, pp. 55–72.

——(2005) *The Healer's Bent: Solitude and Dialogue in the Clinical Encounter*, Hillsdale: Analytic Press.

Mellers, W. (1983) *Beethoven and the Voice of God*, London: Faber and Faber.

Milner, M. [1952] 'The role of illusion in symbol formation', in *The Suppressed Madness of Sane Men*, pp. 83–113.

——(1957) *On Not Being Able to Paint*, 2nd ed. London: Heinemann.

——(1969) *The Hands of the Living God: An Account of a Psychoanalytic Treatment*, London: Hogarth.

——(1986) *An Experiment in Leisure*, London: Virago [published originally by Milner in 1937, under the pseudonym Joanna Field].

——(1987) *The Suppressed Madness of Sane Men: Forty-Four Years of Exploring Psychoanalysis*, London: Tavistock.

Modell, A.H. (1992) 'The private self and private space', *Annual of Psychoanalysis*, 20: 1–14.

Nacht, S. (1962) 'Contribution to symposium on the curative factors in psychoanalysis', *International Journal of Psychoanalysis*, 43: 206–211.

——(1963) 'The non-verbal relationship in psycho-analytic treatment', *International Journal of Psychoanalysis*, 44: 334–9.

Neisser, U. (1967) *Cognitive Psychology*, New York: Appleton-Century-Crofts.

Nigro, G. and Neisser, U. (1983) 'Point of view in personal memories', *Cognitive Psychology*, 15: 467–82.

Nunberg, H. (1962) 'Introduction' in Nunberg, H. and Federn, E. (eds), *The minutes of the Vienna Psychoanalytic Society, Vol. 1, 1906–1908*, New York: International Universities Press.

Obama, B. (2005) 'What I see in Lincoln's eyes', *Time Magazine*, Sunday, 26th June.

Oberhuber, K. (1999) *Raphael: The Paintings*, Munich: Prestel.

Ogden, T. (1994) 'The analytic third: working with intersubjective clinical facts', *International Journal of Psychoanalysis*, 75: 3–19.

——(1995) 'Analysing forms of aliveness and deadness of the transference-countertransference', *International Journal of Psychoanalysis*, 76: 695–709.

——(2001) *Conversations at the Frontier of Dreaming*, Northvale: Aronson.

——(2003) 'On not being able to dream', *International Journal of Psychoanalysis*, 84: 17–30.

——(2005) 'On psychoanalytic supervision', *International Journal of Psychoanalysis*, 86: 1265–80.

Ohi, T. (1997) *History of Ohi Ware*, Kanazawa: Ohi Museum.

Orgel, S. (1983) 'The impact of the training analysis', in Joseph, E. and Widlöcher, D. (eds) *The Identity of the Psychoanalyst*, New York: International Universities Press: pp. 225–39.

Ornstein, P.H. (2004) 'The elusive concept of the psychoanalytic process', *Journal of the American Psychoanalytic Association*, 52: 15–41.

Parat, C.J. (1976) 'A propos du contre-transfert', *Revue Française de Psychanalyse*, 40: 545–60.

Parsons, M. (2000) *The Dove that Returns, The Dove that Vanishes: Paradox and Creativity in Psychoanalysis*. London: Routledge.

——(2002) 'Le cadre: utilisation et invention', in André, J. (ed.), *Transfert et Etats Limites*, Paris: PUF, pp. 69–84.

——(2005) 'Mankind's attempt to understand itself: Psychoanalysis and its relation to science and religion', *Fort-Da*, 11 (2): 18–33.

——(2006) 'Ways of transformation', in Black, D. (ed.) *Psychoanalysis and Religion in the 21st Century: Competitors or Collaborators?*, London: Routledge, pp. 117–31.

——(2007) 'Raiding the inarticulate: The internal analytic setting and listening beyond countertransference', *International Journal of Psychoanalysis*, 88: 1441–56.

——(2009) 'Becoming and being an analyst in the British Psychoanalytical Society', *Psychoanalytic Inquiry*, 29: 236–46.

Penfield, W. (1969) 'Consciousness, memory and man's conditioned reflexes', in Pribram, K. (ed.) *On the Biology of Learning*, New York: Harcourt, Brace and World, 1969, pp. 127–68.

Penfield, W. and Perot, P. (1963) 'The brain's record of auditory and visual experience', *Brain*, 86: 595–696.

Perelberg, R. (2006) 'The Controversial Discussions and *après-coup*', *International Journal of Psychoanalysis*, 87: 1199–1220.

——(2009) 'On becoming a psychoanalyst', *Psychoanalytic Inquiry*, 29: 247–63.

Perlow, M. (1995) *Understanding Mental Objects*, London: Routledge.

Pickering, A. (1984) *Constructing Quarks*, Edinburgh University Press.

——(1992) *Science as Practice and Culture*, Chicago: Chicago University Press.

Pillemer, D.B. (2003) 'Directive functions of autobiographical memory: the guiding power of the specific episode', *Memory*, 11: 193–202.

Plath, S. (1965) *Ariel*, London: Faber.

Pollock, G. (1982) 'On ageing and psychopathology—discussion of Dr. Norman A. Cohen's paper "On loneliness and the ageing process"', *International Journal of Psychoanalysis*, 63: 275–81.

Pontalis, J.-B. (1983) 'Reflections', in Joseph, E. and Widlöcher, D. (eds) *The Identity of the Psychoanalyst*, New York: International Universities Press, pp. 277–87.

Proust, M. (1992) *In Search of Lost Time* [1913–1927], Enright, D.J. (trans.), New York: Modern Library.

Rayner, E. (1991) *The Independent Mind in British Psychoanalysis*, London: Free Association.

——(2009) 'From Hiroshima to the present', *Psychoanalytic Inquiry*, 29: 288–300.

Reich, A. (1951) 'On counter-transference', *International Journal of Psychoanalysis*, 32: 25–31.

Renik, O. (1993) 'Analytic interaction: conceptualizing technique in light of the analyst's irreducible subjectivity', *Psychoanalytic Quarterly*, 62: 553–71.

Rilke, R.M. (1923) *Sonnets to Orpheus*, Leipzig: Im Insel.

Rivière, J. (1927) 'Contribution to symposium on child analysis', *International Journal of Psychoanalysis*, 8: 370–77.

Roazen, P. (1969) *Brother Animal: The Story of Freud and Tausk*, New York: Knopf.

Robinson, J.A. and Swanson, K.L. (1993) 'Field and observer modes of remembering', *Memory*, 1: 169–84.

Rosenfeld, H. (1987) *Impasse and Interpretation*, London: Tavistock.

Rycroft, C. (1968) 'The nature and function of the analyst's communication to the patient' [1956], *International Journal of Psychoanalysis*, 37: 469–72, reprinted in Rycroft, C., *Imagination and Reality*, New York: International Universities Press, pp. 61–8.

Sanders, D. (1860) *Wörterbuch der Deutschen Sprache*, Leipzig.

Sandler, J. (1990a) 'On internal object relations', *Journal of the American Psychoanalytic Association*, 38: 859–79.

——(1990b) 'On the structure of internal objects and internal object relationships', *Psychoanalytic Inquiry*, 10: 163–81.

Sandler, J. and Sandler, A.-M. (1998) *Internal Objects Revisited*, London: Karnac.

Schacter, D.L. (1996) *Searching for Memory: The Brain, the Mind and the Past*, New York: Basic Books.

Schacter, D.L. and Addis, D.R. (2007) 'Constructive memory: the ghosts of past and future', *Nature*, 445: 27. doi:10.1038/445027a

Schwarz-Bart, A. (1961) Becker, S. (trans.), *The Last of the Just*, London: Secker and Warburg.

Searle, J.R. (1996) *The Construction of Social Reality*, London: Penguin.

Searles, H. (1979) *Countertransference*, New York: International Universities Press.

Segal, H. (1962) 'The curative factors in psychoanalysis', *International Journal of Psychoanalysis*, 43: 212–17.

——(1990) 'Some comments on the Alexander technique', *Psychoanalytic Inquiry*, 10: 409–14.

Segal, H. and Steiner, R. (1987) 'H.A. Rosenfeld (1910–1986)', *International Journal of Psychoanalysis*, 68: 415–19.

Shengold, L. (1985) 'Review of Spence, D. (1982) *Narrative Truth and Historical Truth: Meaning and Interpretation in Psychoanalysis*, New York and London: Norton', *Journal of the American Psychoanalytic Association*, 33 (supplement): 239–44.

——(1988) *Halo in the Sky: Observations on Anality and Defense*, New York: Guilford.

Simons, D.J. and Chabris, C.F. (2011) 'What people believe about how memory works: A representative survey of the U.S. population', PLoS ONE 6, (8): e22757.

Sklar, J. and Parsons, M. (2011) 'The life cycle of the psychoanalyst', in Sklar, J., *Landscapes of the Dark: History, Trauma, Psychoanalysis*, London: Karnac, pp. 143–60.

Snell, R. (2012) *Uncertainties, Mysteries, Doubts: Romanticism and the Analytic Attitude*, London: Routledge.

Socarides, C. (1976) 'Psychodynamics and sexual object choice II: A reply to Dr Richard C. Friedman's paper', *Contemporary Psychoanalysis*, 12: 370–8.

——(1977) 'Review of Stoller, R. (1975) *Perversion: The Erotic Form of Hatred*, New York: Pantheon', *Psychoanalytic Quarterly*, 46: 330–3.

Spence, D. (1982) *Narrative Truth and Historical Truth: Meaning and Interpretation in Psychoanalysis*, New York and London: Norton.

Spillius, E. (1988) *Melanie Klein Today: Developments in Theory and Practice, Vol. 2, Mainly Practice*, London: Routledge.

——(2009) 'On becoming a British psychoanalyst', *Psychoanalytic Inquiry*, 29: 204–22.

Steiner, J. (1989) 'The psychoanalytic contribution of Herbert Rosenfeld', *International Journal of Psychoanalysis*, 70: 611–16.

——(1993) *Psychic Retreats: Pathological Organisations in Psychotic, Neurotic and Borderline Patients*, London: Routledge.

Sterne, L. (1759–1767) *The Life and Opinions of Tristram Shandy, Gentleman*. Vols. 1–9, London.

Stewart, H. (1992) *Psychic Experience and Problems of Technique*, Routledge: London.

Stoller, R. (1975) *Perversion: The Erotic Form of Hatred*, New York: Pantheon.

——(1985) *Observing the Erotic Imagination*, New Haven: Yale University Press.

Stone, L. (1957) 'Review of Alexander, F. (1956) *Psychoanalysis and Psychotherapy: Developments in Theory, Technique and Training*, New York: Norton,' *Psychoanalytic Quarterly*, 26: 397–405.

Strachey, J. (1934) 'The nature of the therapeutic action of psycho-analysis', *International Journal of Psychoanalysis*, 15: 127–59.

——(ed.)(1950–1974) *The Standard Edition of the Complete Psychological Works of Sigmund Freud*, Volumes 1–24, London: Hogarth.

——[1955] 'Appendix A: The chronology of the case of Frau Emmy von N', *Standard Edition*, vol. 2, pp. 307–9.

——[1961] Editorial footnote to S. Freud (1924) 'The dissolution of the Oedipus complex', *Standard Edition*, vol. 19, p. 173.

Symington, N. (1983) 'The analyst's act of freedom as agent of therapeutic change', *International Review of Psychoanalysis*, 10: 283–91.

Thomä, H. (1983) 'Conceptual dimensions of the psychoanalyst's identity', in Joseph, E. and Widlöcher, D. (eds), *The Identity of the Psychoanalyst*, New York: International Universities Press, pp. 93–134.

Thomä, H. and Cheshire, N. (1991) 'Freud's *Nachträglichkeit* and Strachey's "Deferred Action": trauma, constructions and the direction of causality', *International Review of Psychoanalysis*, 18: 407–27.

Thomas, D. (1952) *Collected Poems 1934–1952*, London: Dent.

Tulving, E. (1985) 'Memory and consciousness', *Canadian Psychologist*, 26: 1–12.

Van Gogh, V. (1958) *The Complete Letters of Vincent van Gogh, vols. 1–3*, London: Thames and Hudson.

Vaughan, S. and Roose, S. (1995) 'The analytic process: Clinical and research definitions', *International Journal of Psychoanalysis*, 76: 343–56.

Vermorel, M. and Vermorel, H. (1986) 'Was Freud a Romantic?', *International Review of Psychoanalysis*, 13: 15–37.

Vidler, A. (1992) *The Architectural Uncanny: Essays in the Modern Unhomely*, Cambridge, MA, and London: MIT.

Wallerstein, R. (1982) Foreword to Spence, D., *Narrative Truth and Historical Truth: Meaning and Interpretation in Psychoanalysis*, New York and London: Norton, pp. 9–14.

——(1990) 'The corrective emotional experience: is reconsideration due?', *Psychoanalytic Inquiry*, 10: 288–324.

Weinshel, E. (1984) 'Some observations on the psychoanalytic process', *Psychoanalytic Quarterly*, 53: 63–92.

——(1990) 'Further observations on the psychoanalytic process', *Psychoanalytic Quarterly*, 59: 629–49.

Wheelock, A.K., Jr. (1995) *Johannes Vermeer*, Washington: National Gallery of Art and The Hague: Mauritshuis.

Widlöcher, D. (1983) 'Psychoanalysis today: a problem of identity', in Joseph, E. and Widlöcher, D. (eds) *The Identity of the Psychoanalyst*, New York: International Universities Press, pp. 23–39.

Williams, P., Keene, J. and Dermen, S. (eds) (2012) *Independent Psychoanalysis Today*, London: Karnac.

Winnicott, C. (1989) 'D.W.W.: A reflection', in Winnicott, C., Shepherd, R. and Davis, M. (eds), Winnicott, D.W., *Psychoanalytic Explorations*, London: Karnac, pp. 1–18.

Winnicott, D.W. [1954] 'Metapsychological and clinical aspects of regression within the psychoanalytical setup', in *Through Paediatrics to Psychoanalysis*, London: Tavistock, pp. 278–94.

——[1960] 'The theory of the parent–infant relationship', in *The Maturational Processes and the Facilitating Environment*, pp. 37–55.

——[1963] 'Communicating and not communicating leading to a study of certain opposites', in *The Maturational Processes and the Facilitating Environment*, pp. 179–92.

——(1964) *The Child, the Family and the Outside World*, London: Penguin.

——(1965) *The Maturational Processes and the Facilitating Environment: Studies in the Theory of Emotional Development*, London: Hogarth.

——(1971a) *Playing and Reality*. London: Tavistock.

——(1971b) 'The use of an object and relating through identifications', in *Playing and Reality*, pp. 86–94.

——[1974] 'Fear of breakdown', *International Review of Psychoanalysis*, 1: 103–7, reprinted in *Psychoanalytic Explorations*, pp. 87–95.

——(1975) *Through Paediatrics to Psychoanalysis*, London: Hogarth.

——(1986) *Holding and Interpretation*, London: Hogarth.

——(1989) *Psychoanalytic Explorations*, London: Karnac.

Wittgenstein, L. (1980) *Culture and Value*, Von Wright G.H. (ed.), Oxford: Blackwell.

Wollheim, R. (1984) *The Thread of Life*, Cambridge University Press.

Wordsworth, W. (1822) 'Mutability', in *Ecclesiastical Sketches*, London: Longman, Hurst, Rees, Orme and Brown.

Wright, K. (2006) 'A tune beyond us', unpublished paper presented to the Annual Convention of the Independent Group, British Psychoanalytical Society, Cambridge.

——(2007) 'The suppressed madness of sane analysts', in Caldwell, L. (ed.), *Winnicott and the Psychoanalytic Tradition*, London: Karnac, pp. 165–73.

Yeats, W.B. (1950) *Collected Poems*. London: MacMillan.

Zetzel, E. (1970) 'The concept of transference' [1956], in Zetzel, E. *The Capacity for Emotional Growth*, London: Hogarth, pp. 168–81.

——[1958] 'Therapeutic Alliance in the analysis of hysteria', in *The Capacity for Emotional Growth*, pp. 182–96.

NAME INDEX

Abraham, K. 71, 79, 234
Abrams, Samuel 137, 234
Achilles 101, 103f, 108
Addis, D.R. 42, 44f, 239, 247
Agamemnon 101, 107–9
Ahlskog, G. 45, 234
Ajax 101–4, 106–110
Albano, Caterina 48, 234
Albertine 43
Alea, N. 235
Alexander, Franz 172–4, 195, 234, 247f
Alizade, Mariam 168, 234
Allende, Isabel 22, 234
Allende, Paula 22
Allison, Elizabeth xvi
Anderson, R. 184, 234
André, J. 246
Andreas-Sslome, Lou 50
Anna O. 113f
Anzieu, Didier 145f, 234
Apollo 119
Archer, J. 70, 234
Ariès, Philippe 69, 234
Aristophanes 81
Arlow, Jacob 76f, 82, 137f, 234
Athene 101–3, 106–8
Augustine of Hippo xviii, xxi, 37f, 44, 47, 223
Aunt Léonie 43

Bacal, H. 121, 234f
Bach, Sheldon 78, 235
Bacon, Francis (artist) xiii, xviii, 123
Bacon, Francis (philosopher) 63, 235
Baker, Ronald 175, 235

Baldwin, J. 68, 235
Balint, Enid 157, 192–6, 200, 220, 235f
Balint, Michael 174f, 183, 186, 188, 194f, 235
Barrett, Mark 54, 235
Becker, S. 247
Bede 22
Beethoven, L. van 84f, 93, 244
Berger, P.L. 69, 235
Berlin, Isaiah 157, 235
Bernardi, R. 71, 229, 235
Bernfeld, Siegfried 227f, 235
Bettelheim, Bruno 176f, 235
Bion, W. 4, 59, 166, 190, 198, 235
   dreaming and reverie 25, 29, 157f
   memory and desire 192f
Black, D. 246
Blanchot, Maurice 32, 235, 237
Bluck, S. 41, 235
Boghossian, P. 71, 235
Bollas, Christopher 139f, 143, 151, 189, 197–9, 236
Bonaparte, M. 240
Botella, César xvi, 13f, 57, 122, 124f, 232, 236
Botella, Sára 13f, 122, 124f, 236
Bowie, Malcolm 89f, 236
Boyden, J. 70, 236
Brabant, E. 188, 222, 238
Braque, Georges 125
Brenman, E. 198, 200, 236
Brenman Pick, Irma 142, 236
Brenner, C. 137f, 234
Brentano, F. xxii
Breuer, J. 36, 56, 113–15, 236

251

SUBJECT INDEX

Wo sonst Worte waren, fließen Funde.

Rainer Maria Rilke, *Sonnets to Orpheus*
(1923: I, 13, 7)

Made in the USA
Middletown, DE
01 July 2019